Foreign Investment Promotion

Paweł Capik

Foreign Investment Promotion

Governance and Implementation in Central-Eastern European Regions

palgrave
macmillan

Paweł Capik
Keele Management School
Keele University
Keele, UK

ISBN 978-3-030-13657-4 ISBN 978-3-030-13658-1 (eBook)
https://doi.org/10.1007/978-3-030-13658-1

Library of Congress Control Number: 2019934110

This Palgrave Macmillan imprint is published by the registered company Springer Nature Switzerland AG
The registered company address is: Gewerbestrasse 11, 6330 Cham, Switzerland

Dla Mamy i Taty

Acknowledgements

This book took much longer to complete than anticipated, or indeed wanted. Probably, it still would have been in the process of writing, or worse would have never been started in the first place, if not for a number of individuals who helped me and supported me throughout its completion.

I owe a debt of gratitude to a great number of people. Naming them all here possibly would have made up a word count close to that of the book itself, so while I do acknowledge the various kinds of contributions they offered, there are certain persons to whom I owe especially and would like to thank them.

I would like to thank my editors at Palgrave Macmillan for their help with the production of the manuscript. Thank you to Liz Barlow for helping me shape my initial ideas about the book. Great thanks to Lucy Kidwell whose endurance I tested many a time with requests for deadline extension, and whose patience and guidance were instrumental in bringing the manuscript to completion.

Several people have helped me during the research, which lays at the foundation of this book. It was the tolerance and stamina of my former PhD supervisors, which allowed me repeatedly to steer my mind back on the right track after its multiple ventures astray. I would like to offer my special thanks to Professor Martin Myant for the exceptional lessons in critical thinking, Professor Mike Danson for his continuous guidance on detailed thinking, and Dr Kathryn Burnett for assistance in my choice of the methods enabling the two.

The completion of the research would have not been possible without the data, and more importantly the providers of it. I would like to thank the many questionnaire respondents and interviewees across the Czech, Polish and Slovak regions who dedicated their time to share their knowledge of the investment promotion process with me.

A number of thoughtful readers and listeners provided their valuable feedback at various stages of my work. I thank them for helping me shape my ideas more clearly.

I thank my parents, Barbara and Marek, for their unshaken belief in me and unconditional support not only during my PhD studies but also throughout my education. I dedicate this book to them. I thank my sister Agata for paving the many paths I tread on.

I thank Monika for opening up different perspectives to me, for her continuing support and encouragement! And thanks for the help with references too!

I thank Lorna Dixon for letting me know about the newspaper advert, which brought me to what was the University of Paisley at the time. I have been lucky to enjoy support and friendship of many people while there. The often dricht evenings were so much more bearable, thanks to the cross-faculty 'footie group'. The extended discussions on the misery of the research student's existence and the discoveries of ways of improving it were possible during the long walks with the 'hiking group'.

I thank my officemates at, what became, the University of the West of Scotland, for intellectually stimulating and academically challenging debates within and outside office hours. I thank Mrs Ewa Helinska-Hughes for her warm welcome and kindness during my time in Scotland, Dr Igor Skowron for his long-standing friendship and support in crucial moments, Dr Marcin Dąbrowski for eternal readiness to engage in a discussion and Dr Paul Lassalle for stating the obvious, when the obvious was not clear.

Also, I would like to thank my colleagues at Keele Management School for their encouragement and patience with me while I worked on the book.

To all those, and to all those whom for the space limitations I could not name, but who all know who they are—Thank You!

About the Author

Paweł Capik lectures in international business at Keele Business School, Keele University, UK. Previously, he has worked at Grenoble Ecole de Management in France, as well as the University of Glasgow, Sheffield Hallam University and the University of the West of Scotland in the UK. His research interests include investment attraction and place marketing, sourcing and shoring strategies, large and small firms' internationalisation and location behaviours and their impact on regional economies. Paweł is a fellow of the Regional Studies Association, a member of the Academy of International Business (AIB) and a fellow of the Higher Education Academy. He is an alumni of The Ryoichi Sasakawa Young Leaders Fellowship Fund (SYLFF).

Contents

List of Abbreviations

CEE	Central-Eastern Europe
CEEC	Central-Eastern European Countries
EDC	Economic Development Centre
EU	European Union
FDI	Foreign Direct Investments
GDP	Gross Domestic Product
GVA	Gross Value Added
IPA	Investment Promotion Agency
IPB	The Institute for Polish Brand
ISC	Investor Service Centre
MIGA	Multilateral Investment Guarantee Agency
MNE	Multinational Enterprise
M&A	Mergers and Acquisitions
NIPA	National Investment Promotion Agency
OECD	Organisation of Economic Cooperation and Development
PAIiIZ	Państwowa Agencja Informacji i Inwestycji Zagranicznych
RAIS	Regional Authorities Investment Section
RDA	Regional Development Agency
RDS	Regional Development Strategy
R&D	Research and Development
SARIO	Slovenská agentúra pre rozvoj investícií a obchodu
SFDI	Service Foreign Direct Investments
UDC	Urban Development Corporation

UNCTAD	United Nations Conference on Trade and Development
WAIPA	World Association of Investment Promotion Agencies

List of Figures

List of Tables

1

Firm Internationalisation and Investment Attraction: An Introduction to Foreign Direct Investment in Central-Eastern European Countries

1.1 Introduction

The old maxim that "location, location, location" are the three most important factors determining company's success rings true particularly for international business (Daniels, Radebaugh, & Sullivan, 2019). Yet, business decision-makers are rarely able to have complete knowledge and understanding of the opportunities within the foreign environments to which they plan to expand (Sitkin & Bowen, 2010). Equally, the success of places within globalised economy is progressively more dependent on their participation in the international value chains facilitated by incoming foreign investors (Dogaru et al., 2015; Crescenzi & Iammarino, 2017).

The mobility of multinational enterprises (MNEs) and its integral part, the imperfect knowledge of available locations, and a growing interest from countries, regions and cities in attracting operations of foreign companies in the hope of benefiting from their expertise, technology and capital explain the growing interest in various forms of place promotion aimed at investment attraction shown by public

P. Capik, *Foreign Investment Promotion*, https://doi.org/10.1007/978-3-030-13658-1_1

authorities across the world, including Central-Eastern European Countries[1] (CEEC).

It is widely believed that, being under the constant scrutiny of shareholders, MNEs are calculating, mercenary and almost predictable. Yet usually the investment process is long and complex and the decision-makers are not immune to external pressures and persuasion, particularly if supported by hard evidence (Aharoni, 2010; Schotter & Beamish, 2013). Aware of this fact, governments and other public institutions at various levels promote their areas as prime locations to attract inward investment and profit from the advantages this brings in order to achieve their development goals (Cleave, Godwin, Sadler, & Gilliland, 2016; Harding & Javorcik, 2012; Monaghan, Gunnigle, & Lavelle, 2014).

Regions in the Czech Republic, Poland and Slovakia, the key geographical focus of this study, began emerging on the global map of foreign direct investment (FDI) destinations only since the beginning of 1990s. As relative newcomers, they have to compete with established Western European destinations and other emerging locations in the neighbouring countries, Asia and Latin America. Their accession to the European Union (EU) in May 2004 and the implementation of its *acquis communautaire* reinforced the competition between them, simultaneously burdening them with increased responsibilities for their own development (Blokker & Dallago, 2009; Swianiewicz, 2014). Consequently, an increasing number of regional authorities across Central-Eastern Europe (CEE) became involved in some form of promotion activity in order to secure the inflow of foreign investments.

The discussion presented in this book focuses on the years soon after CEEC joined the EU allowing controlling for the 'EU effect' in FDI flows, which appeared in the subsequent years (Ascani, Crescenzi, & Iammarino, 2017). Despite the passage of time, the analysis remains relevant for several reasons. There has been no major reform of the regional

[1] For the purpose of the discussion presented in this book, unless otherwise stated, Central-Eastern Europe is understood as the Czech Republic, Poland and Slovakia. A justification for the choice of the countries is offered later in the chapter. For wider discussion of the delimitations of "Eastern Europe" see, for example, Dingsdale (1999) or Smith (2002). The book focuses on the period of time before formal change of country's name from Czech Republic to Czechia, and the former name is used throughout for consistency.

governance system in any of the studied countries since the study explored in this book took place. The scope of regional authorities' responsibilities directly related to FDI promotion established in the reforms pre-EU accession remained the same, and by 2005[2] (the census year for the book), the relevant systems have been in place and continue largely unchanged since. More significantly, from the perspective of the book's theoretical contribution, the problem it addresses remains unexplored as evidenced by recently published research (e.g. Almond, Ferner, & Tregasis, 2015; Cleave et al., 2016; Monaghan et al., 2014). In this context, the lessons from a decade ago remain relevant and exhibit potential to influence the future, if discussed in the public domain. Finally, by offering a detailed account of regional investment promotion in CEE in its initial years, the book will serve as a point of reference for any future studies investigating evolution of investment promotion approaches.

Driven by a set of interlinked research questions, the book explores regional promotion aimed at investment attraction across CEEC. It proposes a novel approach to regional promotion, and identifies concepts which can be translated into actions and strategies. Subsequently it examines how far this has been achieved in Central-Eastern Europe. By so doing, the book achieves two objectives. Firstly, on the conceptual level, it develops a theoretical debate of regional promotion rooted in place marketing and regional studies literature. Key issues addressed include applicability of place marketing concepts to policies and activities aimed at investment attraction, the scope and focus of regional promotion process, the nature of the regional offer, the prescribed role of the public authorities and other actors involved in promotion and factors determining its success.

Secondly, in its empirical dimension, the book presents analysis of the purposefully collected interview and survey data in the conceptual context outlined above. The discussion offers insights into how far regions in CEEC have been successful in developing and implementing coherent strategies for their promotion to potential inward investors.

The chapter sets the stage and provides context for the discussion presented in this book. Its remaining parts proceed as follows. First, the

[2] Unless otherwise indicated, the majority of the data, facts and developments reviewed and considered in this book relate to the time around the year 2005.

review of CEEC participation in global FDI flows highlights the potential to be captured. Next, the discussion of MNEs' contribution to the transition process explains why they remain to be so keenly courted by public authorities. The subsequent parts explain the rationale behind the geographical focus of the book. Next, the overview of the MNEs' location decision process identifies the stages at which place promoters can exert influence on firms, while the discussion of the key aspects of the regional promotion process reveals how this can be achieved.

1.2 CEE Foreign Investment Inflows in the Global Context

Since late 1980s the growing interdependencies within the global economy and interconnectedness of international business operations, coupled with systematic liberalisation of the global trade and investment regime, have contributed to an increase in the mobility of capital and progressive growth of foreign investment flows. While between 1989 and 1991, the global FDI inflows reached just over 186 million USD, and in the year 2000, it peaked at 1.4 billion USD. A subsequent decline at the turn of the century soon has been followed by a steady increase and peaked at almost 2 billion USD in 2007. After the global economic crisis of 2008, these levels were only recovered in 2015 (UNCTAD, 2003, 2018).

This fluctuation has been partially attributed to the varying numbers and values of cross-border mergers and acquisitions (M&A). While in 1995 the total value of M&A reached 186 million USD, in 2000 it exceeded 1.1 billion USD. After a few years of decline the upward trend started to re-emerge, and in 2005 the global value of M&A totalled 716 million USD. The recovery from the crisis period lasted until 2016, when the global value of M&S totalled at 887 million USD.

The second component, more relevant to this discussion of inward investment flows, greenfield projects, followed a somewhat different trajectory (Table 1.1). The number of projects almost doubled between 2002 and 2003 but subsequently the growth dynamics subsided, and in 2015 there were over a thousand less FDI projects completed than in 2010 (UNCTAD, 2007, 2016).

The inward investment flows to Central-Eastern Europe have mirrored the global trends, with the region gaining an increasing share during the 1990s and early 2000s. However, despite considerable and consistent reforms and improvements in the business environment since the beginning of the systemic transformation in 1989, CEEC involvement in global capital flows remained limited throughout the 1990s and early 2000s. In 1990 the total inflow of foreign investments to (then) Czechoslovakia and Poland equalled a mere 0.15% of flows received by developed economies. Ten years later the share received by the Czech Republic, Slovakia and Poland increased to 1.45% and, in 2005, the first full year of their EU membership, reached 4%. Despite the positive trend and the fact that the three countries attracted almost 65% of all inward investments into the ten new EU Member States, this result placed the Czech Republic, Poland and Slovakia considerably behind other European nations.[3] For example, in 2005, the considerably smaller countries of the Netherlands and Belgium attracted 4.4% and 3.6% of global FDI inflows, respectively. Also, other countries in the region and beyond became increasingly appealing for investors and began attracting considerable amount of global flows. For instance, in 2005 Romania and Bulgaria, then EU-candidate countries and Ukraine received almost 2% of global investment flows, a significant increase from 0.4% in 2002 (Turnock, 1997; UNCTAD, 2004b, 2007). Consequently, while in the first half of the 2000s the three countries studied recorded a significant increase in the value of inward investments, they still lagged behind other developed economies and faced new competition from upcoming rivals.

An analysis of the number of greenfield projects further confirms this. An overall significant growth in the number of projects incoming to the Czech Republic, Poland and Slovakia does not follow the global dynamics (Table 1.1). CEEC recorded an increase (157%) in the number of projects between 2002 and 2003 which exceeded the growth within the EU (147%) but was less significant than the change globally (166%). The following years saw a temporary reversal as the CEE increase in incoming

[3] Additionally, one of the driving forces of FDI in the 1990s, the privatisation process, has come to an end. To sustain the high levels of FDI inflow, CEE economies faced the challenge of developing attractive private firms worthy of acquisition, or attract more greenfield investments (Meyer et al., 2005).

Table 1.1 Number of greenfield investment projects

	2002	2003	2004	2005	2010	2015
Czech Republic	95	144	144	149	190	113
Poland	91	154	234	270	323	234
Slovakia	44	65	87	117	103	38
World	5703	9443	10,145	10,442	15,425	14,381
EU (25)[a]	1802	2647	3057	3527	5141	4774

Source: UNCTAD (2007, p. 207, 2016, p. 213)
[a]2010 figures for EU27; 2015 figures for EU28

greenfield projects exceeded global growth by up to 20 percentage points. However, after the global crisis these proportions were reversed and appeared stable between 2010 and 2015.

Overall then, the role of CEEC in global investment inflows has grown considerably since the beginning of systemic transformation and has been reinforced by accession to the EU. On the one hand, this has been caused by increasing liberalisation of business environments and reforms aimed at attracting foreign capital, and growing mobility of global capital and its increased familiarity with this part of Europe on the other (Ascani et al., 2017; Bradshaw, 2005). However, despite considerable advances, the Czech Republic, Poland and Slovakia still attract a mere fraction of investments as compared to other European and global economies. The volumes and numbers of world investment flows indicate the scale of the phenomenon globally and the potential for CEE to benefit from it. With the increasing investment flows, the number of countries interested in attracting a share grows. A UNCTAD (2007) survey indicates that, in 2004 alone, 270 policy changes in 103 countries were introduced that made the host country environment more favourable to inward investors.[4] The majority of these changes have been adopted in developing countries, with South-East Europe and the Commonwealth of Independent States introducing 38 of them. The rising number of competitors interested in attracting FDI puts additional pressures on the public authorities in CEE who, as will be explained next, traditionally have seen inward investments as an important vehicle bringing about modernisation and structural

[4]The survey also identified 41 policy amendments in the opposite direction, most of which were concerned with extractive industries in a relatively small number of countries (UNCTAD, 2007).

change (Bradshaw, 2005; Chidlow, Salciuviene, & Young, 2009; Dogaru et al., 2015).

1.3 Political Economy of FDI in Transition

Ever since the beginning of systemic transition, the countries of Central-Eastern Europe perceived foreign direct investment as an important tool fostering structural change supporting economic development (Dogaru et al., 2015; Lipton & Sachs, 1990). The enthusiasm of public authorities and policy-makers hailing the benefits brought about by inward investments is countered by voices of scepticism from some academics who emphasise the problems they create. Whichever the viewpoint, foreign investors, along with European Structural Funds,[5] have been assigned an important role in regional policies aimed at tackling economic and social disparities across the CEEC[6] (Artisen-Maksimenko, 2000; Bradshaw, 2005; Dogaru et al., 2015).

The criticism and concerns raised revolve around the main deficiencies of the inward investment debate which assumes FDI positively contributes to growth and the development of places but offers little evidence to prove it. In other words, as argued by Pavlínek (2004), the relationship between FDI inflows and economic growth remains unclear. The critics list a number of problems and question the contribution of MNEs to the development of regions in Central-Eastern Europe and the well-being of local communities and businesses (see Table 1.2). The most important amongst them is the concentration of FDI in particular areas, notably those more developed and industrialised, thus escalating, instead of reducing, regional disparities. Across CEE in mid-2000s, inward investment has been focused in capital city regions, around large cities, and generally in the western parts of the countries, closer to the European markets (Ascani et al., 2017; Dawson, 2005; Domański, 2001). Due to

[5] While FDI has been perceived as an important driver of transition from its early beginnings, the role of Structural Funds became more prominent only as the CEE countries were approaching full membership of the European Union in May 2004.

[6] As will be demonstrated in the subsequent chapters, this has been manifested, amongst others, in the design of the investment incentives schemes and designation of special economic zones.

Table 1.2 Potential positive and negative effects of FDI in host economies

Potential POSITIVE effects of FDI	Potential NEGATIVE effects of FDI
For regional economy	*For regional economy*
Sustaining employment and creation of new jobs	Dependency on foreign capital
Labour training	External control of regional economies
Increased wages	Drainage of skilled and semi-skilled workforce from endogenous companies
Real income growth	Crowding out, suppression or destruction of endogenous firms
Increased tax base	Limiting emergence and growth of local firms
Increased exports	Regional specialisation in low-skill, labour Intensive production
Provision of some services to local communities	Branch plant syndrome
Spillovers and multiplier effects	
Opportunity for local businesses to supply to MNEs	
For regional enterprises	*For regional enterprises*
Continued and expanded production	Labour shedding
Increased labour productivity	Disinvestment and downsizing of production
	Transfer of R&D abroad
Access to investment capital	
Access to global sale and distribution networks	
Transfer of technology and managerial know-how	
Increased R&D	
Improved competitiveness	

Source: Compilation based on Navaretti and Venables (2004), Pavlínek (2004), Dunning and Lundan (2008)

the costs of land and rent, suburban areas have been preferred by manufacturing industries, and city centres (particular capital cities) have received considerable amounts of service FDI (SFDI). For example, only two cities in the Czech Republic, Praha and Brno, have attracted over 60% of SFDI, while outside Bratislavský kraj, the capital region in Slovakia, the remaining areas only managed to secure between 2.2% and 4% of Slovak's total FDI inflow. The exception is the Košický kraj, one of the regions studied during this project, which has accounted for 8.6% of total FDI stock in Slovakia in 2005 (Pavlínek, 2004). Similarly, in Poland and the Czech Republic, FDI has arguably contributed to the deepening of the regional disparities between the east and west of the country, and metropolitan and peripheral areas (Chidlow et al., 2009; Stawicka, 2006).

Another point of critique is MNEs' impact on local and regional economies. Some authors argue the long-term effects to be detrimental as FDI can create forms of local dependency on foreign capital and external control of the regional economy. Additionally, MNEs may negatively impact local businesses by attracting their skilled and semi-skilled workforce and taking over their markets. This can suppress the development of and, in some cases, destroy existing firms, and prevent the emergence of new endogenous enterprises. Such negative, crowding-out effects on local business are further amplified by a limited number and quality of local connections developed by the multinationals which restrict the multiplier effects of FDI (Capik & Drahokoupil, 2011; Hardy, 1998).

The potential and observed disadvantages of FDI in CEE, however, seem to be outweighed by the benefits they bring to regional economies, particularly when the endemic problems of those are considered. While the extent of the problems varied between, and to an extent within, the countries, a number of critical structural difficulties were shared by many Central-Eastern European states throughout the 1990s and early 2000s (Domański, Guzik, & Micek, 2003; Ezcurra, Pascual, & Rapůn, 2007). The economic heritage left by state socialism had some common features across the three studied countries, several of which persist to the current day. The economy has been traditionally dominated by heavy industry, with large shares of employment within primary sectors, profoundly underdeveloped services, overgrown state bureaucracy and an underdeveloped market institutional environment. National economies were characterised by a lack of competitiveness caused by inflexible production, hardly existent product and process innovation, low levels of capitalisation, and poorly qualified, disincentivised and demoralised management. On a sectoral level, overemployment and poor productivity have been the key features of agriculture. Industry has been dominated by heavy branches, most of which relied on outdated technology and where research and development (R&D) spending was largely a privilege of military-oriented production. Apart from selected public services, the tertiary sector has been almost absent. Insufficient and dilapidated transport and communication infrastructures, coupled with environmental damage of many areas, particularly industrial regions, complete the portrait of the post-socialist business climate in Central-Eastern Europe (Ezcurra et al., 2007; Gorzelak, 2003; Tondl & Vuksic, 2003). Considering the breadth and depth of the structural problems, it was hardly surprising that many Western economists and multilateral institutions advocated foreign investments as a vital staple of the successful transition from centrally planned to a market economy (Pavlínek, 2004).

Over the years considerable evidence emerged to suggest that foreign investors indeed offered a significant contribution to the transition process and the development of regions across Central-Eastern Europe (Dogaru et al., 2015; Domański, 2001; European Commission, 2006; Turnock, 1997). On a macro-level inward investors contributed significantly to gross fixed capital formation and output. For example, in the Czech Republic in 2005, MNEs added 34% to overall gross fixed capital formation (almost 26 points increase from 2003 levels). Similar contribution has been recorded in Poland and Slovakia, 15% and 16%, respectively, which reflected an increase of 3.8 and 7 points from 2003 levels (UNCTAD, 2005). The escalation of MNEs' contribution to national gross domestic product has been even more substantial. In 1990 foreign affiliates added 0.2%, 0.5% and 3.7% to the GDP of Poland, Slovakia and the Czech Republic, respectively, while in 2005 these contributions increased to 48.1% in the Czech Republic, 32.8% in Slovakia and 31.1% in Poland (UNCTAD, 2005). FDI also contributed to the expansion of the innovative capacity of the CEE economies. In 1993 R&D spending of MNEs in the Czech Republic and Slovakia amounted to 18% and 3.5% of the respective national totals. By comparison, in 2004 these contributions increased to almost half in the case of the Czech, and a fifth in the case of the Slovak economy (Dunning & Lundan, 2008).

Another set of advantages, as shown in Table 1.2, have been identified at the regional and local level. Regional economies benefited from expanded (in the case of greenfield projects) or maintained levels of production contributing to sustained or increasing employment levels. Regional and local government budgets benefited from an increased tax base, while local communities enjoyed improved levels of a range of the social services previously provided by the state-owned enterprises, such as sponsorship of cultural and sporting events.

In the case of brownfield investments, particularly those associated with privatisation of large, formerly state-owned enterprises, typically FDI resulted in rapid and extensive restructuring of the acquired company, including reorganisation, technology transfers, employee training and development, introduction of Western management know-how and practices, and improvements in production organisation and growth strategies.[7] Such influxes of capital, technology and business knowledge resulted in increased competitiveness of local enterprises by improving the quality of product and service offerings, productivity gains and increased sales on both domestic and international markets (Dogaru et al., 2015; Pavlínek, 2004; Rutkowski, 2006).

While the impacts of FDI vary sectorally and geographically, overall its effects are deemed helpful in addressing at least some of the structural problems of the CEE regional economies. The critical role assigned to FDI by many commentators and policy-makers in CEE evolved over the years as the developmental and transition processes started to take shape. As exemplified by the various contemporary policy measures, including investment incentives regimes and investment attraction activities performed by a range of institutions discussed later, foreign direct investments continue to be perceived as a panacea and an attractive solution for a range of regional problems, including development disparities, unemployment, industrial restructuring and the creation of the knowledge economy. It is these reasons which contribute to the sustained competition between CEE regions and their increasing involvement in promotion and investment attraction activities.

1.4 Regional Context

The interest in a 'region' as a scale of analysis presented in this book is stipulated by a number of interlinked factors. Firstly, the assertion that globalisation processes contribute to the renewed role of a region; sec-

[7]Typically but not exclusively, as there have been instances of 'buy to die' strategies employed by some MNEs. For examples and details of those, see Hardy (2009).

ondly, the importance of regional level of administration and governance within the European Union; and thirdly, by the practicality of data availability.

As stressed by Scott and Storper (2003, p. 581), the often repeated fundamental misconception of globalisation is to equate it with simple spreading of economic activity or "transformation of the economic order into liquefied space of flows", while the contrary is actually the case. Flexible specialisation and the expansion of innovative centres and industrial parks give renewed importance to localities indicated also in the political sphere by decentralisation and transfer of competencies from central to regional and local authorities (Blokker & Dallago, 2009; Dunford & Kafkalas, 1992; Pike, Andrés Rodríguez-Pose, & Tomaney, 2017). Globalisation goes along with the reassertion of concentration processes, where regional agglomerations of economic activity are the main source of growth across economies at various level of development (e.g. 40% of American employment is concentrated in 1.5% of the country's land area) (Scott & Storper, 2003). Considering such developments, some argued that governments should abandon policies supporting individual collapsing industries and devolve their powers to the regions (Malizia & Feser, 1999). Consequently, the global structural changes in international business and public policy provide regions with an increased importance and call for renewed interests in sub-national levels of analysis (Herrschel & Tallberg, 2011).

The European Union is one of the examples where some of these ideas have been implemented to a considerable degree, and for some time already. As part of public administration structures, regional authorities have gained more significance and power within the European context. With the reduced importance of the national borders as economic barriers, the old and new regional borders within the EU become more apparent, since individual regions are more exposed to competition and regional variations become more obvious (Herrschel & Tallberg, 2011; Nordström, 1996). As a remedy, firstly stated in Maastricht and then in consequent treaties, one of the main objectives of the EU is the economic and social cohesion, and levelling of income and development disparities between its regions (Alden, 1996; Blokker & Dallago, 2009). Structural funds are the financial tools supporting the EU-influenced regional development policy. On the more generic level, supported by the theoretical concepts of new regionalism, the key, long-term objective of EU-driven regional policy is to provide the regions with more autonomy and make them responsible for their own development trajectories (Bachtler & Downes, 2000; Herodes, 2011; Pike et al., 2017). In line with this aim, prior to their full membership in the European Union, the candidate countries of Central-Eastern Europe were obliged to undergo an administrative reform resulting in the decentralisation of power and the creation of regional administrations capable of facing the challenges of the globalising world (Ezcurra et al., 2007; Swianiewicz, 2014). While the extent of success of the reform in bringing about self-reliant, efficient regional administrations is often disputed (e.g. Ferry & McMaster, 2013; Guglielmetti, 2009; Miszczuk, 2003), as is the actual autonomy of the regions, for the most part, the newly created regional authorities in the Czech Republic, Poland and Slovakia have been equipped with powers allowing them to determine the strategy for their development and influence its delivery tools. These include a broad set of prerogatives and activities related to the various aspects of place promotion aimed at investment attraction.

Accordingly, from the perspective of regional policy and its measures, the administrative understanding of a region is the most appropriate one and thus was adopted in this study.[8]

In the case of Central-Eastern European Countries, *region* constitutes the level below the national, central government. There are several advantages of this. Most importantly, administrative regions have a range of autonomous, self-governance prerogatives allowing them to exercise various degrees of powers and vesting in them responsibility for the management of their areas. Additionally, in the context of academic research, administrative regions offer a wide range of statistical materials and policy documents. This is further aided by the NUTS classification (Nomenclature des Unités Territoriales pour des besoins Statiques; Nomenclature of Territorial Units for Statistics).[9] For practical reasons of

[8] For a discussion of different classifications of regions, including cultural and functional definitions, see, for example, Terlouw (2001).

[9] In the European Union the creation of NUTS areas is aimed at overcoming some of the statistical difficulties associated with changing regional borders and varying geographical and population sizes

data availability and regional policy implementation, NUTS classification is based primarily on the institutional divisions currently in force in the EU Member States. Furthermore, and as emphasised by the principles guiding the NUTS classification, the administrative regions reflect cultural and socio-economic areas within their respective countries,[10] a relevant issue from the perspective of regional promotion activities, particularly those centred on image and linkages to wider regional development strategies.

Additionally *region* as the scale of analysis of investment promotion is linked to the MNEs' location decision-making process, which as discussed next, emphasises the importance of familiarity with detailed location options during shortlisting. While MNEs usually longlist countries, it is at the sub-national level that they draw up a shortlist of investment locations for further, in-depth evaluation.

1.4.1 Regional Development and Governance in CEE

The choice of regional scale of analysis and administrative delimitation of a region is particularly relevant in Central-Eastern European Countries, where in early 2000s regionalism has been only (re-)emerging after prolonged period of sector-driven development policies (Bachtler & Downes, 2000). The EU-stipulated focus on a 'regional' rather than a 'sectoral' approach to policy-making led to the changes in academic discourse and policy design and implementation, making 'region' the focal unit of problem identification and design of strategies and solutions.

In this regard, a range of regional development challenges and characteristics, relevant to the investment promotion context, common to the countries studied can be identified. These comprise considerable regional socio-economic disparities, metropolisation, especially the dominance of a capital city region, old industrial areas with outdated or limited

of the self-governing regions. The key principles guiding the classification are: (1) institutional breakdowns, (2) favouring of regional units of general character (normative regions), (3) three-tier hierarchical classification.

[10] For a discussion of appropriateness of some of the regional boundaries in CEEC see for example Zarycki and Tucholska (2004).

economic structure undergoing rationalisation, underdeveloped rural territories with weak demographic structure and lack of alternative employment options, areas of serious environmental degradation, decentralisation and creation of new administrative regional and local governance structures (Bachtler & Downes, 2000; Domański et al., 2003; Gorzelak, 2009; Hardy, 2004).

Due to the opportunities resulting from transborder cooperation and proximity to Western markets, the "modernisation from the west" pattern, as identified by Gorzelak (2009), is the most visible fault-line of regional development dividing the countries into the relatively better off west and the poorer, underdeveloped east. Disparities are evident in the level of wealth, and other factors conditioning development. For example, GDP per capita (PPS, current prices) in 2005 in Plzeňský kraj in the west of the Czech Republic equalled 96% of the country's average and 80% in the eastern Zlinský kraj. Wielkopolskie voivodeship[11] in the west of Poland reached 107% of national average, but Podlaskie voivodeship, in the east, only 74%. Western Slovakia Trnavský kraj reached 103% of the country's average, but in the east of the country, Presovský kraj only 61%. Such disparities have been underpinned by discrepancies in developmental conditions with western parts of the countries endowed with better transport and communication infrastructure and better access to schooling and higher education (Blokker & Dallago, 2009; Domański et al., 2003). The capital cities and the regions around them have been, and in 2005 remained, the wealthiest areas in the Czech Republic, Poland and Slovakia. Praha GDP per capita equalled 209%, Mazowieckie voivodeship 151% and Bratislavský kraj 229% of respective national average values. The capital city regions have attained levels of GDP comparable to the EU average, while other regions with major urban centres perform better than primarily rural areas (Domański et al., 2003; Eurostat, 2015; Gorzelak, 2009). Additionally, while between 1998 and 2003 in the majority of countries in Western Europe the gap in development between regions converged, in all post-socialist countries, except the Czech Republic, it has widened (Gorzelak, 2009). Therefore, most regions, notably those outside capital cities (region), remain to require

[11] See the map in Fig. 1.1.

some sort of assistance, typically upgrading of infrastructure and/or business development (Bachtler & Downes, 2000; Guglielmetti, 2009).

The industrial regions, which during the initial stages of transformation in the 1990s experienced a significant decrease in employment levels, in the early 2000s remained characterised by outdated branch structure and limited efficiency. However, both the continuing privatisation processes, coupled with location of new greenfield projects, have been expected to facilitate further restructuring. And soon attracting both of these became the focus of regional policy. Equal results have been expected from foreign investors locating in rural regions and localities dominated by agricultural activity (Hardy, 2004; Pavlínek, 2004; Smith & Ferenčiková, 1998).

New regional governance structures established as a result of EU-stipulated administrative reforms were to provide a framework for tackling regional problems with new, bottom-up regional policies (Blazyca, Heffner, & Helińska-Hughes, 2002). In reality, in the initial years the administrative reforms proved to be another common challenge among the CEE countries. At the point of departure, the structures of regional (and local) government and governance were considerably underdeveloped and participatory decision-making non-existent, with policies imposed by the central government pursuing its own political agenda (Hardy, 2004; O'Dwyer, 2006). The initial, partial reforms introduced throughout the 1990s brought about only marginal change in this respect but resulted in better understanding of the nature and extent of regional problems and identification of geographical-assisted areas[12] (Bachtler & Downes, 2000; Illner, 2002). The more substantial reforms introduced in Poland in 1999, and in the Czech Republic and Slovakia in 2001, resulted in the redesign of regional boundaries, varying but overall increased decentralisation and the creation of regional governance structures where the new self-governing authorities have been equipped with policy design and implementation privileges (Illner, 2002; Swianiewicz, 2014). The reforms were soon criticised on two grounds. Firstly, the accuracy and

[12] For a comprehensive discussion of the politics and directions of early administrative reforms in the Czech Republic, Poland and Slovakia see, for example, Bachtler and Downes (2000), Illner (2002) and O'Dwyer (2006).

adequacy of the shapes of the new regions have been questioned. In fact, as Zarycki and Tucholska (2004) argue, very rarely the outline and character of a region matches the historical, cultural or economic characteristics and boundaries. More often the outlook of the regions corresponds with short-term, often unofficial, political arrangements, so the regions lack clear, common identity, thus limiting the developments in capacity-building (Blazyca et al., 2002). In this respect the CEEC regionalism compares to practices in other European countries, for instance, the UK where regionalisation in England for a couple of decades now has been moving between all-out localism and different notions of devolutions, depending on prevailing political discourse (Herrschel & Tallberg, 2011). Secondly, the actual extent of the administrative reforms has been described as incomplete as the level of, especially, finance centralisation remained high (Bachtler & Downes, 2000; Guglielmetti, 2009; Illner, 2002; O'Dwyer, 2006). Such shortcomings lead Blazyca et al. (2002) to assert that the reforms of spatial reorganisation have shifted administrative boundaries but have not been able to change the economic realities.

Despite the shortcomings, as a result of the reforms and subsequent adjustments by 2005, the regional and local governance structures have been firmly in place in the three countries studied. In the Czech Republic a three-tier organisation of public administration included 14 self-governing regions (*kraj*) (including Praha capital city region), 77 second-tier districts (*okres*) and 6249 municipalities (*obce*; basic territorial unit). A similar set up in Poland includes 16 regions (*województwo*), 379 districts (*powiat*) and 2478 communes (*gmina*). In Slovakia 8 regions (*kraj*) are further divided into 79 districts (*okres*) and 2928 municipalities (*obce*) (Eurostat, 2007; Illner, 2002). Additionally, in Poland and Slovakia, a duality of regional governance exists whereby next to the elected governance structures offices of central government are present—in Poland on a regional level, in Slovakia on regional and district levels (Swianiewicz, 2014). Similarly, three-tier frameworks operate in other European countries, for example, in Denmark and France. However, in countries with longer histories of regional governance and decentralisation, two-tier systems are often in operation (e.g. Belgium, Austria, Spain).

From the perspective of regional promotion aimed at investment attraction, a set of key relevant prerogatives and responsibilities placed on the newly created regional authorities can be distinguished. As units of self-governance, the regions (regional authorities) are legal entities acting on their own behalf. They manage their own property and finances. Self-government is executed through the regional assemblies elected in direct elections with several law-making powers. Unlike in, for example, Austria, where provincial authorities prescribe tasks for communes, regional authorities in CEEC have no supervisory powers over the lower tiers of governance. The detailed set of their core responsibilities related to regional development and investment attraction in particular vary between the three countries. For example, while the Czech regional authorities are responsible for transport infrastructure management, the Slovak ones deal with transport and communication infrastructure planning (Brusis, 2003). However, generally the regional authorities in the three countries are tasked with regional strategy design and execution, physical planning, public transportation, regional road infrastructure, selected functions in education development and management, and social and health care services (Brusis, 2003; Gorzelak, 2009; Swianiewicz, 2014). Such portfolio of duties offers scope for multidirectional development of the region (later called 'place product') and allows for involvement in a range of investment promotion activities, both of which are important focal points of the forthcoming chapters.

1.5 Firm Internationalisation Motives and Location Decisions

Having reviewed the motives behind CEE regions' interest in FDI and the rationale behind their potential involvement with promotion, it is now time to explore the motives driving firms' expansions.

The classical view of firm internationalisation (e.g. Behrman, 1972) indicates four broad sets of reasons motivating engagement in international activity:

- resources seeking motives;
- markets seeking motives;
- efficiencies seeking motives;
- strategic assets and capabilities seeking motives.

While a number of subcategories and precise reasons exist behind every internationalisation, many of the MNEs' international activities are driven by a selection of these motives, and their foreign investments are often motivated by two or more of them. Additionally, the motives change with the development of a firm and the evolution to its strategy. In general, most companies initially invest in foreign countries to acquire resources or gain access to new markets. As they grow and get established internationally, they often reassess and amend the strategy and use foreign operations as the means by which to improve their global competitive position by increasing efficiency or accessing new sources of competitive advantage (Daniels et al., 2019; Dunning & Lundan, 2008). Similarly, with progressing development, locations evolve from suppliers of (natural) resources, to markets, to efficiency and strategic assets providers, often leading to further MNEs international relocations (Capik, 2017).

Central-Eastern European Countries underwent such an evolution at varying pace, depending on their internal differentiation and industrial structure inherited from their communist past. However, overall the investors locating in CEE in the early 1990s were driven by different factors than those choosing the Czech Republic, Poland or Slovakia at the turn of the century and more recently. Initially they were seeking to expand their markets into the previously closed countries (Artisen-Maksimenko, 2000; Helinska-Hughes & Hughes, 2003), and subsequently became driven by the quest for efficiency (Chidlow et al., 2009; Stawicka, 2006). More recent evidence suggests the current inward investment projects in CEE, particularly in the service sector, are driven by the search for strategic assets and capabilities, mainly skill and knowledge-base (Capik & Drahokoupil, 2011; Dogaru et al., 2015; Fifeková & Hardy, 2010).

1.5.1 Factors Affecting Decision-Making

Whatever the driving forces behind a company's decision to invest in a particular country, the actual choice is preceded by an in-depth and usually lengthy location selection process (Daniels et al., 2019). Location decisions vary but in general involve the opening of a new facility, relocation of current operations to a new locale as well as expansion of an existing facility. Investment promotion may influence each of these, however in reality, it focuses primarily on the ways of influencing location and relocation choices rather than reinvestment and facility extension. Invariably, due to the complexity of the task and its costs, as compared to other operational and strategic choices, companies make these kinds of decisions rather infrequently. Additionally, the location process is affected by a number of factors including the personality of the decision-maker(s), relationships between the decision-makers, organisational power relationships and political behaviour, organisation strategy, information quality and availability, and conditions in the external environment (Kelly, 2009; Schotter & Beamish, 2013).

As with other strategic decisions, the choice of an appropriate location can bring success or failure to the company. It is imperative, however, to recognise that it is not the companies that make the investment decision, but people (Aharoni, 2010; Loewendahl, 2001). The decisions are usually made by a group of relevant decision-makers, and thus it is important to understand the motivation, capacities and the mechanisms guiding the individuals within such groups.

Classical decision-making theory assumes that the decision-makers are objective, fully informed and consider all available alternatives and consequences of the choices before selecting the most advantageous option. Alongside, the rational economic model assumes that decision-making is (and should be) a logical process comprising a series of steps enhancing the probability of achieving a desired outcome (Buchanan & Huczynski, 2004). In such a perspective, decision-makers use value maximising estimates and follow the alternative that best satisfies the goals of the organisation. However, the model is burdened with a number of weaknesses, particularly relevant in the case of location decision-making. Firstly, decision-makers usually face time and cost pressures, and rarely are able to equally review and consider all alternatives, of which there will be too many, and thus some of which will remain undisclosed to them. Secondly, it may not be possible to consider all consequences due to incomplete or biased information. Thirdly, the decision-makers' ability is another influencing factor. They may lack the mental capacity to store and process the relevant information, and the skills to perform the mental calculations required (Aharoni, 2010; Kelly, 2009).

Furthermore, it is now accepted within economics, management and geography that economic actions and transactions of individuals and firms are shaped by social values and contexts (Bickl, 2004; Schotter & Beamish, 2013). Hence, another point of criticism towards the rational model can be identified. The rationality (and freedom) of action of the decision-makers is constrained by three overlapping factors: (1) social norms and values, (2) expectations, demands and requests by superiors and colleagues within the company and (3) the commitments and obligations the decision-makers have imposed on themselves by earlier conduct, actions and decisions (Buchanan & Huczynski, 2004).

An alternative perspective on decision-making argues the bounded rationality within the behavioural theory of decision-making. The approach refers to individuals making decisions based on self-constructed, simplified models which extract the essential features from the problems without capturing all of their intricacies, and hence identifies a number of imperfections embedded within the decision-making process. It recognises that the definition of the circumstances might be incomplete, and that it is impossible to view all available alternatives and predict all of their consequences. Further, it argues that the final decision is often influenced by personal and political factors (Aharoni, 2010; Cyert & March, 1963). Consequently then, corporate decisions, including location choices, are prone to bias caused by a range of factors internal and external to individual decision-makers and the organisation as a whole (Kelly, 2009). The significance of the different limitations is that the decisions made are the result of individuals looking to satisfy rather than maximise the outcome, that is, they make the decisions which are "good enough" rather than "ideal" (Buchanan & Huczynski, 2004; Schotter & Beamish, 2013).

In this context, as will be argued throughout the book, investment promotion needs to be understood as a process extending beyond mere image-oriented activities to include measures and procedures creating, sustaining and developing relationships with the key decision-makers of the potential (and current) investors.

1.5.2 Location Selection Processes and Tools

On the strategic-level investment location decisions are affected by a range of factors of cultural, political and legal, economic, social and technological nature, all widely discussed in literature (e.g. Daniels et al., 2019). Amongst key political variables influencing the investment decision, political risk is probably the most important one. This includes issues related to the political system, its stability and legislation predictability but also other vital aspects of the business environment, such as the levels of bureaucracy and corruption and formal and informal institutions. From an economic perspective, the companies looking to locate in the foreign country will first identify the economic system and next scrutinise the stability and potential of the economy by assessing macro factors including unemployment levels, inflation, economic growth, public debt and expenditure and exchange rate regime. Within social environments, the incoming firms seek to recognise and understand the host country demographic dynamics and various aspects of culture. Considering the technological environment, companies will examine features that affect the technologies they use, and which have the potential of presenting them with new opportunities by creating new products and opening up new markets (Cavusgil, Knight, & Riesenberger, 2008; Daniels et al., 2019).

On the operational level, the location selection process comprises a set of complex procedures of weighing the opportunities against the risks associated with a number of pre-selected choices. The significance of each of the personal, company-level and environmental factors influencing the location decisions varies, as reflected in the weight assigned to them by companies using analytical techniques and tools supporting their decision. The weight depends on a company's unique circumstances, including internationalisation motives and timing, company size, sector(s) of operations, global strategy and mode of foreign expansion, amongst others.

Since the key aspect of the location decision is timely access to relevant information, arguably at every stage of the process there exists scope for an influence from a place promoter. However, in order to arrive at this stage of the selection process, first the companies apply scanning techniques to compare the multiplicity of potential locations. Scanning allows the location decision-makers to examine large number of alternative locations (countries) and then narrow down their number to the most promising ones. During the initial scanning, the location managers compare publicly available general information and data which leads them to the identification of a shortlist of locations to be examined more closely. Such process opens up the potential for the place promoters to be involved in the location selection process from an early stage by utilising relevant communication channels.

The second step of the scanning procedure involves the company dedicating much more time and resources to acquiring in-depth and tailored information on issues deemed significant from the company's perspective and leads to identification of potential location sites. It often involves site visits and initial negotiations with relevant partners, including public authorities, contractors and suppliers (Daniels et al., 2019). This stage of the location selection process presents the place promoters with an opportunity to employ more targeted and personalised promotion channels in order to influence the corporate decision-makers and develop a lasting relationship with them.

Once the companies have gathered the data on potential locations through the successive stages of scanning, they use grids and matrices, the two common tools, to conduct analysis of the data. In their preparation a multidisciplinary team of analysts comprising representatives from marketing, production, finance and human resources departments is often assembled. It allows avoiding internal, functional bias and assures company-wide backing of the decision. It is up to the team to devise the grid comprising variables and their weighting in line with company's specificity, objectives and strategy. While generally useful as an analytical and scoring tool, the grids tend to become vague and perplexing as the number of variables increases. Although they are useful in the ranking of the locations, they may obscure the interrelationships between their characteristics.

To demonstrate the relationship between the risks and opportunities more clearly, the companies often use another analytical tool which allows them to plot the values of selected variables, the matrices. As in the case of the grid, the risk and opportunity variables are selected based on the company's characteristics and objectives, and subsequently, they are assigned adequate weight allowing calculating scores for a selection of locations. Once this is completed, an average risk and opportunity score for all alternatives can be calculated, which subsequently permit the matrix to be divided into quadrants. The final step entails plotting the graphic representation of the studied locations onto the matrix. The outcome occasionally leads to the situation where the selection has to be made between locations offering high opportunities and high risks and low opportunities and low risks. In such situations the choice is often influenced by the decision-makers' tolerance for risk and the company's earlier experiences (Daniels et al., 2019).

The scanning process as well as analysis of grids and matrices relies heavily on reliable and current information. It is this aspect of the decision-making process, coupled with the market failure of asymmetry of information, which bounds the rationality of the MNEs and justifies the need for place promotion (Harding & Javorcik, 2012; Schotter & Beamish, 2013). Since MNEs do not have full information about all the countries, and investment opportunities in all of their regions, they are prone to making a biased decision with regard to where they invest. They tend to fill in their knowledge by making assumptions, extrapolating based on some pieces of information and relying on opinions of consultants, competitors and media (Kulchina, 2014; MIGA, 2006; Monaghan et al., 2014).

Place promoters can rarely influence the final selection of variables or outcome of the grid and matrix analysis, hence it is important for them to be involved in the scanning and analysis processes as information providers and relationship managers. Such a role, as will be explained next and subsequently argued throughout this book, expands the meaning of regional promotion aimed at investment attraction beyond the classic definition of promotion as used for product and service marketing purposes.

1.6 Regional Promotion Aimed at Investment Attraction: An Introduction

In various guises, place promotion has a long and eventful history ranging from the endorsements of ancient pilgrimage destinations (Beinart, 2001), through the promotion of settlements during Viking conquests

(Ashworth & Voogd, 1990), to the luring of industrial companies to locales undergoing industrial revolution (Ward, 1998). The practices evolved over time, becoming gradually more systematic and, arguably, increasingly more sophisticated. The latest developments include emergence of specialised activities aimed at attracting specific target groups performed by an ever-rising number of place stakeholders. Despite the growing popularity of the practice, conceptual debates about the nature, subjects and objects of promotion of places have been going on for almost half a century. Theoretical underpinnings stem from the concept of marketing and its subsequent developments and applications in spheres of public and non-profit environments. As will be proposed in Chap. 3, regional promotion aimed at investment attraction links the intellectual heritage of marketing with exogenously oriented regional development theories and related policies, to communicate the relevant information about places in a timely fashion, and facilitate and service investments.

The marketing approach offers the nearest thing to a practical expertise for those undertaking place promotion. It offers a framework for the activity and provides promotional bodies with a methodology enabling them to distinguish themselves from their competitors in a coherent way by unique and targeted advertising, successful public relations activities, negotiations with investors and a designed set of investment incentives and post-investment services (Gold & Ward, 1994; Loewendahl, 2001; Wells & Wint, 2000; World Bank, 2012). The complexity of approaches and activities, coupled with their delayed effects, makes regional promotion a long-term process comprising events, campaigns, policies and their delivery tools in a usually extended timeframe.

Young and Lever (1997, p. 332) recognise that "as the European and American cities suffer the effects of declining manufacturing bases place promotion strategies have become increasingly important to attract new investment", and this coupled with the increasing mobility of capital investment resulted in promotion activities gaining considerable momentum over the past decades. The growing importance attached to attracting FDI is evidenced by a continuous rise of the number of investment promotion agencies (IPAs) worldwide. For example, since its inception in 1995 the membership of World Association of Investment Promotion Agencies (WAIPA) has been steadily increasing to 112 in 2002, and 170 from 130 countries in 2018. Its members represent a myriad of organisations including cities, regions, national government ministries, special economic zones and export zones from all over the world, with National Investment Promotion Agencies (NIPA) of the Czech Republic, Poland and Slovakia amongst them.

FDI promotion habitually rests with specialised investment promotion agencies which enjoy diverse levels of autonomy and are supervised directly by the policy-makers on a relevant administrative level. However, given the multidimensionality of the process, the diversity of promotional activities and the complexity of some of the administrative systems, as will be discussed later, usually a range of other organisations, are involved in the process and the IPAs often play advisory and intermediary roles (Almond et al., 2015; Monaghan et al., 2014; OECD, 2003; Zanatta, Costa, & Filippov, 2006).

The growing popularity of place promotion globally, thanks to town and regional twinning initiatives, as well as the activities of international consultants looking for new contracts, has been increasingly adopted by places in Central-Eastern Europe (Capik & Drahokoupil, 2011; Florek, 2004; Young, 2005). However, unlike the flows of inward investment, the ways in which they are attracted have so far received little attention from academic audiences.

Equally, the growing popularity of investment promotion has, so far, not been matched by studies assessing its effectiveness leading its critics to question the value of the practice altogether. Admittedly, many academics and practitioners argue for the need of promotion, advocating its vital role in the development of places, but few (e.g. Charlton et al., 2004; Lim, 2005; Harding and Javorcik, 2011) offer rational, evidence-based explanations of how exactly and to what extent it is effective. The data attesting to the effectiveness of promotion activities and its direct contribution to regional development is sparse and only emerging (e.g. Cleave et al., 2016; Zimmerbauer, 2011). However, equally rare are the studies revealing the futility or wastefulness of the promotional effort.

Consequently, while it could be argued that the popularity of investment promotion as reflected by quickly spreading trend results from the fear of being left behind or, worse, accused of passiveness, rather than any documented efficiency of such activities.

1.7 Research Rationale, Focus and Contribution

The stimulus underlying this research is threefold. Firstly, it is motivated by the existing gaps in knowledge resulting from the thematical, geographical and scalar focus of the existing studies. The majority of existing studies explore the general or at most tourism-oriented promotional practices of predominantly developed countries and their (post-industrial) cities. Secondly, in line with the increase of global capital flows, Central-Eastern European Countries in recent years have witnessed growing volumes of FDI inflows, yet the distribution of foreign capital and location of FDI projects vary considerably within and between the countries and remain biased towards the capital city region. Thirdly, the popularity of investment promotion practices across the globe, as evidenced, for example, by the growing number of investment promotion agencies and consulting firms, calls for systematic international research and a switch of emphasis from the image-making activities to a comprehensive investment promotion process, which in turn will allow exploring the link between marketing practice and regional development theories, especially the exogenous ones.

Consequently, the rationale for the research presented in the book stems from several broad areas, namely the increased mobility of investments, the sustained interest of Central-Eastern European regions in attracting them and the notion of regional promotion as a complex process within broader regional developmental policies. Correspondingly, the investigation and the debate presented in this book are rooted primarily in three relevant bodies of literature including international business, regional development studies and place marketing.

Additionally, several reasons lead to the decision to present this research in a book format. CEE investment promotion remains understudied and often misunderstood for political tokenism or extravagant marketeering. It is hoped the book, presenting a comprehensive research of regional promotion in wider national, and local contexts, in an accessible manner, will publicise it amongst wider audiences, beyond academia.

Over the recent decades, MNEs have become increasingly more mobile. Globalisation and competitive pressures require them to expand into new markets, seeking efficiencies or resources and strategic assets not available in their current locations. Globally, the growing inflows of capital remain concentrated in developed Western economies. Other world regions, including Central-Eastern Europe, receive relatively small pieces of the 'investment cake'. This encourages public authorities on different levels to become more proactive in securing inward investment projects.

Regions are important areas of globalised processes. Across Central-Eastern Europe, regional authorities established in result of pre-EU accession administrative reforms have gained powers and responsibilities for the development of their areas. Traditionally, they have treated foreign direct investment as one of the key engines driving the regional restructuring and helping to deal with a range of endemic problems including unemployment, structural adjustment and social disparities. The flows of FDI into the CEE countries tend to be unevenly distributed, with disproportionate concentration in capital city regions. This indicates the failure of the National Investment Promotion Agencies (NIPAs) to ensure an adequate spread of FDI across their respective countries, and points to the need for deeper involvement of regional actors in the investment attraction process.

Regional policies, including those which help to attract foreign investments, devised on a national level take time to develop, implement and bear fruit. This period is even further extended if the relevant target groups, that is, the investors, are not made aware of them. Regional promotion, as a process embedded in place marketing and regional development theories, can offer a range of tools and methods to the authorities on how to effectively lure target audiences. However, due to the little analytical and conceptual attention dedicated to it so far, the notion itself exhibits some potential weaknesses and calls for further systematisation.

This book attempts to remedy some of these limitations by offering analysis guided by the following sets of research questions:

1. *What is the nature of place promotion in the context of foreign investment attraction?*

How to conceptualise promotion within foreign investment attraction setting? What kind of policy and operational tools does it offer to public authorities governing the region and organisations managing the investment attraction process?

2. *What is the relationship between regional promotion and wider development of a region?*

Is a 'region' an adequate scale of place to be promoted? Are there any developmental preconditions for promotion to be employed? Is promotion a universal developmental tool, or is it a privilege of certain types of regions?

3. *What is the importance of promotion in the Central-Eastern European regions' development agenda?*

How systematic is Central-Eastern European regional promotion? What are the factors determining regions' involvement in and the extent of promotion activities?

4. *What are the consequences of the different approaches to promotion governance on the strategy setting and implementation level, across the CEEC?*

How is the promotional effort organised and governed? Who are the participants of regional promotion and how do they influence the process? How is the multi-agent nature of the promotion process reflected in the actions undertaken and strategic choices? What are the links between the governance model and implementation of promotion? How diverse are the outcomes brought about by different approaches?

Elaborating answers to these questions allows the book to make contribution in several areas. The theoretical underpinnings of the place marketing concept have been largely uncritically adopted from marketing. While the direct translation of market-based practices into the public policy sphere raises a range of issues and questions, thus far few of the conceptual debates have been substantiated by relevant and sound empirical evidence. Existing studies tend to focus on issues related to image, and more recently brand building and its perception by general audiences, and tourist target groups at best. Equally, as will be demonstrated in Chaps. 2 and 3, the scalar dimension of research is biased towards nations and cities, predominantly in the post-industrial context of the Western economies. Additionally, the ephemeral studies of investment attraction practices are limited to the analysis of strategies pursued by National Investment Promotion Agencies, and case studies of company–government bargaining. Little has been said about how these processes occur on the sub-national level, in the circumstances of increased institutional thickness, intra-national competition between locales within a country or a trading bloc, and in the context of purposeful policies aimed at levelling out persistent disparities between those areas.

By offering answers to the above research questions and adopting a 'multi' approach, the book aims to offer a comprehensive account of regional promotion aimed at investment attraction in Central-Eastern European regions. The theoretical debate builds on multidisciplinary ideas rooted in place marketing, regional development studies and, where relevant, international business literature. It shows how contribution from place marketing can be translated into policies and activities of regional promotion aimed at investment attraction. Next, on empirical level, based on primary qualitative and quantitative data collected from all relevant institutions involved with the process offers comprehensive insights with regard to how coherently this has been done in the countries and regions across Central-Eastern Europe.

The empirical approach adopted in this research project builds on earlier studies and has been developed to match research objectives and provides responses to research questions. It utilises survey and interview data collected from relevant institutions in the Czech Republic, Poland and Slovakia. Postal questionnaires were used as the main research technique in collecting quantitative data from earlier identified departments of CEE regional authorities. Analysis of these, presented in Chap. 4, allowed identification of broad patterns of authority involvement in investment promotion and relate those to regions' development levels. A complementary qualitative dataset was gathered during a series of interviews with representatives of organisations actively engaged with the promotion of purposefully selected regions in each of the countries studied. The data allowed the regional promotion process to be examined in a multi-scalar and multi-agent context and provide greater detail to some of the issues detected by the survey method (Chap. 5).

Making *promotion* the focal point of the study and predefining the target group as foreign investors has allowed the focus of the research to be maintained and enabled the exploration of issues omitted earlier. The study offers a more holistic examination of the promotion process, including, amongst others, institutional arrangements of promotion on the regional level and its implications for coherence of strategies adopted and actions performed. Further, it provides an exploration of budgetary commitments, long-term plans and the popularity of the different promotional tools across Central-Eastern European regions—an area so far largely overlooked by academic research.

The survey-based part of the research explores investment promotion activities of regional authorities in the context of their developmental responsibilities. It reveals that on the regional level, investment promotion in CEE remains the responsibility of often poorly equipped individuals and is a largely inconsistent and under-budgeted practice dominated by often ad-hoc actions disconnected from wider development objectives. However, several exceptions in the Czech Republic, Poland and Slovakia prove that promotion is gaining popularity and becoming better understood. The analysis offers inconclusive perspectives on the relationship between regional promotion and development, as both wealthy and underdeveloped regions engage in comprehensive promotion, and equally there are instances of both types implementing it only in a restricted fashion.

The qualitative data gathered during the course of interviews confirms these findings and adds new facts and perspectives. Promotion of the regions is conducted within a characteristic governance framework, where the varying levels of regional authority engagement are related to the powers and activities of the National Investment Promotion Agency and intensity of efforts of other organisations involved in promotion. The examination of the actions executed by individual agents reveals the political dimension of investment promotion process and discloses the diverse extent of internal coherence conversely proportional to the degree of power centralisation. The dominant role of the NIPA does not seem to ensure coordination of actions, or a desired flow of information amongst the participants of the process, which further compromises the inter-institutional synergy.

Finally, by mapping the involvement of CEE regions in promotion, the study sheds further light on the only emerging understanding of the relationship between promotion, FDI distribution and regional development.

1.8 Research Design and Approach

Regional promotion aimed at investment attraction is a complex process, interconnecting regional governance and policy with practices originating in marketing. Consequently, its investigation calls for a selection of corresponding methods and techniques. In the course of the study discussed here, multiple secondary data sources were consulted while the primary data were collected with the use of two techniques—survey and interviews.

The secondary data was principally used to put the study in broader context and guide the selection of national and regional study areas. Next, linking it with the analysis of the survey and interview data allowed to develop answers to the research questions. The principal aim of the multiplicity of data sources and research techniques was to assure a comprehensive and wholesome exploration of the regional promotion process in Central-Eastern Europe.

The general approach developed in this study builds on works of Burgess (1982), Ward (1998), Wells and Wint (2000), Loewendahl (2001), Lever (2001), Florek (2004), Bickl (2004), Young 2005), Monaghan et al. (2014) and Almond et al. (2015). The predominantly individual case and single method studies have been adapted and used to inform the hybrid methodology pursued here.

Due to the undocumented nature of CEE regional promotion parts of this research were inevitably exploratory in nature. However, the aim of the study was not merely to map the state of regional promotion aimed at investment attraction in CEE, but also to investigate the factors influencing it. For this reason, this research also has an apparent explanatory dimension.

The choice of the methodology, and the data gathering and analysis techniques characteristic of it, has been driven by the research objectives and the very nature of the researched phenomenon, regional promotion aimed at investment attraction (Bauer & Gaskell, 2000; Silverman, 2018). Qualitative study has been developed for two main reasons. Firstly, qualitative methods offer useful strategies for discovery and exploration of new domains. Secondly, qualitative data are valuable in explaining, supplementing and validating the quantitative data gathered in the same context (Miles & Huberman, 1994). Analysis of the survey data allows exploring the extent of CEE regional authorities' involvement in promotion in the context of the level of regional development. However, the various levels of CEE regions' engagement in promotion are not satisfactorily explained solely by the survey data gathered, or by the data derived from secondary sources. The analysis points to other matters, namely the relationships between the regional authorities and other participants of the promotion process, which by their nature are better investigated with the use of qualitative techniques. Consequently, the qualitative method enabled examining regional promotion process in a multi-scalar and multi-agent context, therefore, allowed exploring selected themes in greater detail and unveiled realities undetectable by the survey method (Gaskell, 2000; Patton, 1990).

The initial empirical parts of the discussion examine the involvement and practices of regional authorities as main players in regional governance. The consideration of the survey data with socio-economic variables, particularly those related to regional development, including the unemployment rate, the size of the regional economy (regional gross domestic product [GDP]) and wealth (regional GDP/per capita and regional authorities' budgets), amongst others, provides insights into the regional authorities' commitment and indicates the links between the process of promotion and regional development policies and strategies.

The results of such analysis however do not provide full answers to the research questions, therefore the second empirical section examines activities of other organisations engaged in promotion of selected regions. The results of both parts of the study provided comprehensive answers to the research questions and informed drawing of the final conclusions.

1.9 Selection of Study Areas

The choice of the studied countries and regions within them was guided by a systematic rationale underpinned by the research questions and resulted from relating the existing literature and theoretical considerations to the contexts of the secondary data provided by the national statistical offices and other relevant agencies.

Before the final decision regarding the selection of the countries to be studied was made, a number of options were considered. In addition to those which have been selected, Hungary and Ukraine were taken into consideration. However, after consulting relevant data, it was decided to concentrate on the Czech Republic, Poland and Slovakia.

In early 2000s, The Czech Republic, Poland and Slovakia were the three countries usually in stark and direct competition for FDI projects in this part of Europe (Helinska-Hughes & Hughes, 2003). They regularly occupied positions in close proximity to one another on the UNCTAD Inward FDI Potential Index. For example, in 2002 the Czech Republic was ranked 40, Poland 43 and Slovakia 45. The following year brought only minor changes and the countries were ranked 39, 43 and 46, respectively. Additionally, all three countries have been receiving high inflows of the foreign capital, large parts of which were greenfield in nature (UNCTAD, 2004b, 2005, 2006). Simultaneously, they shared several institutional commonalities, which allowed controlling for divergent approach to regional governance. At the beginning of the study, all three countries were preparing to join the European Union, an event which was preceded by often lengthy negotiations in some 21 different subject areas, including regional policy and governance. In effect of the negotiations, and one of the conditions for accession, the previously heavily centralised administrations devolved powers to the newly formed regional structures. Within the broad framework of decentralisation, the particular reforms took different directions and pace; however, by 2003 all three countries implemented the changes and created self-managing regions (Blokker & Dallago, 2009; Hughes, Sasse, & Gordon, 2004; Swianiewicz, 2014).

The forthcoming EU membership also had a considerable impact on the FDI inflows to all the candidate countries, including the Czech Republic, Poland and Slovakia. The years immediately before the accession to the EU marked renewed interests of multinational companies in Central-Eastern Europe. After 1 May 2004, this interest was further strengthened. In 2005 $11.7 million marked the highest ever inflow of foreign capital to the Czech Republic, while in 2006 both Poland and Slovakia received their record levels of FDI, $13.9 and $4.1 million, respectively (UNCTAD, 2005, 2007).

The choice of the countries is further supported by the timing of this research. As noted, the accession to the EU required the countries to design and implement regional governance structures and processes. By the time this research was initiated and the primary data collection had taken place (May 2005–January 2006), the regional authorities of the three countries selected for the study had at least five years to stabilise, establish effective self-governance mechanisms and design development strategies, including those related to investment promotion.

It is the set of such a rationale which favoured the selection of the Czech Republic, Poland and Slovakia for this study exploring regional promotion aimed at investment attraction.

1.9.1 Regions

A 'region' became the focus of this study for a number of interconnected reasons emerging from both theoretical debates to date and the deficiency of empirical evidence. Firstly, on the generic theoretical level, there are strong claims that regions are the most important spatio-economic units (Herrschel & Tallberg, 2011). For example, Storper (1997) perceives the region as the nexus of untraded interdependencies, where the local scale is too small to allow for a meaningful exchange of synergies, and the national scale too large to enable effective functioning of institutions requiring spatial proximity. Additionally, a region is perceived as the adequate entity for governance of political and social processes (Illner, 2002; Lidström, 2011; Pike, Rodríguez-Pose, & Tomaney, 2016; Taylor, 1993).

These different arguments are reflected in the European Union approach to governance and redistribution of resources, where the fading influence of the nation-state is paralleled with the transfer of sovereignty to the European level, and increased importance of governance at the regional level (Blokker & Dallago, 2009; Ferry & McMaster, 2013; Herodes, 2011). The latter process is particularly important in the Central-Eastern European context, where the accession to the EU, amongst other factors, was conditioned by the establishment of credible regional (self-)governance structures.

While the self-governing regions in the Czech Republic, Poland and Slovakia vary in size of population, and hence are categorised differently under NUTS classification ('kraj' in the Czech Republic and Slovakia for statistical purposes is classified as a NUTS III area, and 'voivodeship' in Poland is classed as NUTS II [Eurostat, 2007]), their authorities have a similar range of powers related to regional governance. Consequently, the size of the region has implications for its potential offer (i.e. place product), but is less relevant in the context of authorities' relative engagement in promotion, its planning, organisation and delivery. Therefore, it is the responsibility and privilege of self-governance, as defined by the Assembly of European Regions, and not peculiar characteristics that makes the 'administrative region' most appropriate in CEE for the purpose of this study.[13]

Secondly, as explained in Chap. 1, while the MNEs' location decision-making process focuses on countries in the initial stages, closer to the final decision it has a strong regional emphasis.

Thirdly, from an empirical perspective, as shown in the next chapter, regions remain significantly underexplored in the context of generic promotion and particularly investment attraction. The study of promotion practices of the regions in countries in stark competition for inward investment offered a unique opportunity to gather and reflect upon empirical evidence shedding light on the role of (regional) scale in place promotion and links between the process and aspects of regional development. Subsequently, the analysis of the data collected allowed to provide

[13] Where the size of the region can potentially matter, for example, in promotion spending levels, this has been taken into consideration.

answers to the research questions and contributed new knowledge by filling in the persistent empirical gap in the broader theoretical context.

The choice of particular regions for an in-depth study of regional promotion aimed at investment attraction—Jihomoravský kraj in the Czech Republic, Wielkopolskie voivodeship in Poland and Košický kraj in Slovakia—was guided by specific selection criteria informed by the literature and a desk-based research supplemented with secondary statistical data.

The regions are not case studies per se as described by Denscombe (2003), but rather studied examples, that is, the regions studied are not objects in themselves but are used to explore the phenomenon in focus (regional promotion). Consequently, the approach adopted here, to some extent, builds upon the case study method in, for example, taking advantage of a natural, pre-existing setting and occurrence of the phenomenon, and using various data sources and related data collection techniques. The regions are, to some extent, used for both theory-building and theory-testing (Yin, 2003).

The reasons for choosing a specific region were twofold: (1) the examples contained crucial elements significant for the study (e.g. relevant levels of national FDI stock), and (2) allow to predict certain outcomes if the theory holds true. Furthermore, as other research has identified that national western border proximity is one of localisation factors for the FDI (Ascani et al., 2017; Domański, 2001), the selection of regions allowed controlling for the geographical location (see Fig. 1.1).

For the purpose of the qualitative part of the research, it was decided to focus on regions of second-tier importance and avoid the capital city regions. Foreign capital tends to concentrate around the latter areas, which could have influenced the findings of the study. In order to explore the role of promotion in regional development, it is therefore justified to study the approaches adopted by areas which perceive FDI as a significant factor contributing to their development by solving the structural problems of unemployment, outdated technology and peripherality, and those which need to make an effort to secure the inflow of such investments. Consequently, the main rationale for the selection of the regions studied was their approximated socio-economic position within the respective countries.

Fig. 1.1 Map of the study area. *Source*: Own work map to be included here

Table 1.3 presents selected regional characteristics of the regions in their national contexts.

The number of population indicates the size of the local market as well as labour resources. The purchasing capacity of the market is reflected in the value of GDP per capita, while the volume of GDP reflects the size of the regional economy indicating, amongst other things, robustness of potential cooperation and supplier networks. All of which are regularly mentioned amongst the main localisation factors for MNEs (Daniels et al., 2019; Dunning & Lundan, 2008; Hoover, 1975) also within the CEE context (Dogaru et al., 2015; Domański, 2001; Meyer et al., 2005).

Table 1.3 Regions within their respective countries (selected statistics for 2003)

	Population			GDP (current prices)			GDP per capita (current prices)			FDI stock-
	Country (mln)	Region (% of country)	Region's position within country	Country (mln, national currency)	Region (% of country)	Region's position within country	Country (national currency)	Region (% of country)	Region's position within country	region's position within country
Jihomoravský kraj (Czech Republic)	10.2	11.0	3	2,414,669 (CZK)	10.3	3	236,714 (CZK)	93.6	2	4
Województwo Wielkopolskie (Poland)	38.2	8.8	3	842,120 (PLN)	9.2	3	22,048 (PLN)	104.9	3	3
Košický kraj (Slovakia)	5.4	14.3	2	1,202,687 (SKK)	12.7	2	223,564 (SKK)	89.0	4	2

Source: Own compilation of data sourced from national statistical offices and NIPAs

Undoubtedly, previous FDI projects act as an inducement for supplier industries and a guarantee of attractiveness of the place. Current FDI stock therefore can be treated as a proxy for overall regional investment climate and indicates the attitudes of the regional authorities to the investors. On the other hand, the successful ventures present the regional authorities with the potential to enhance their promotional efforts by using them as flagship projects and the region's ambassadors (Crescenzi & Iammarino, 2017; Loewendahl, 2001; OECD, 2015). These issues are explored further in the empirical chapters.

1.10 Research Process and Data Sources

A comprehensive desk-based research preceded the undertaking of this study and informed the successive analysis. Secondary data sources informed the selection of the study areas and provided preliminary information about the institutions involved in the regional promotion process. Subsequently, it also supported the analysis of the primary data collected with questionnaires, and the qualitative data gathered in the course of the interviews.

The study utilises the data obtained from multiple sources, including the Czech, Polish and Slovak statistical offices, national banks, National Investment Promotion Agencies, regional development agencies and the United Nations Conference on Trade and Development.

To allow accurate international comparisons on the country and regional levels, especially of the figures concerned with monetary values, two main provisions have been introduced. Firstly, where appropriate, the monetary data obtained from the national sources (e.g. regional GDP, regional authorities' budgets) were converted into US dollars[14] using the annual average exchange rate between the Czech and Slovak koronas, the Polish złoty and the USD, as provided by the respective national banks. In instances where national statistics were provided in Euro, these were

[14] The choice of USD was dictated by two premises: (1) USD remains the main currency used by the majority of the international organisations providing macroeconomic and FDI figures (including OECD and UNCTAD), and (2) to allow the results of this study to be easily comparable not only in the European but wider context.

converted into dollars using the rate provided by the European Central Bank, so as to avoid multiple conversions compromising the accuracy of the data. The same procedure has been applied to convert relevant questionnaire data (e.g. figures on promotion spending). Secondly, while national sources were preferred to control for the different methodologies applied by the various national institutions engaged with measuring the flows of foreign capital, as well as to obtain verified information, the United Nations Conference on Trade and Development data were used, particularly those published in the World Investment Reports series.

The questionnaire and semi-structured interviews were used to collect primary data. Survey data was collected from all Czech, Polish and Slovak regional authorities, while organisations involved with investment promotion in selected regions were the source of qualitative interview data. However, before the main data gathering methods could have been employed, the individual and collective (organisational) respondents had to be identified.

Regional authorities in many respects are the primary shapers of the development trajectories of their areas (Blokker & Dallago, 2009; Miszczuk, 2003; Pike et al., 2016). A desk-based research enabled the identification of regional development and regional promotion units within the structures of each of the Czech, Polish and Slovak regional authorities. Next, the hard copy of the questionnaire with accompanying covering letter was sent to the senior officers in charge. The letter and the questionnaire introduction encouraged collective completion of the survey, which was to ensure the accuracy and reliability of the information provided.

Regional promotion aimed at investment attraction is a multi-scalar process involving directly a multiplicity of organisations (Almond et al., 2015; Young, 2005)—a set of which is further expanded when the indirect involvement is concerned. It is, however, virtually impossible to pinpoint all of the latter type, whose role is often very intangible and varies from one case of investment project to another (Bickl, 2004). Therefore, this study focused on those agencies and organisations which are either legally bound or voluntarily remain actively engaged in the investment promotion process. The identification of these, from amongst the plethora of institutions, and initial review of their contribution, was one of the focuses of the desk-based research. Next, the key informants within the organisations identified were approached and subsequently an interview meeting was scheduled.

The organisations studied, as shown in Table 1.4, included local and regional authorities, National Investment Promotion Agencies and their

Table 1.4 List of organisations involved in the study

Region (country)	Organisation
Jihomoravský kraj (Czech Republic)	Jihomoravský kraj Regional Authorities (Department of Regional Development)
	Regionálni rozvojová agentura jižni Moravy (Regional Development Agency South Moravia)
	Jihomoravskě inovačni centrum (South Moravian Innovation Centre)
	CTP Invest
	Magistrát města Brna, Kanceláře strategie města (Brno City Authorities; City Strategy Department)
	Sdružení pro zahraniční investice (Association for Foreign Investment)
	CzechInvest
Wielkopolskie voivodeship (Poland)	Urząd Marszałkowski Województwa Wielkopolskiego, Departament Rozwoju Regionalnego (Wielkopolskie Regional Authorities; Department of Regional Development)
	Wielkopolska Agencja Rozwoju Przedsiębiorczości (Wielkopolska Agency for Enterprise Development)
	Cetrum Obsługi Inwestora (Investor Assistance Centre)
	Urząd Miasta Poznania; Biuro Obsługi Inwestorów i Promocji Inwestycji (Poznań City Authorities; Investors Assistance and Investment Promotion Office)
	Instytut Marki Polskiej (The Institute of the Polish Brand)
	PAIiIZ (Economic Promotion Department)
	PAIiIZ (Regional Cooperation Department)
Košický kraj (Slovakia)	Košickýsamoprávny kraj, Odbor regionálneho rozvoja (Košický kraj Regional Authorities, Department of Regional Development)
	US Steel Kosice Economic Development Centre
	Spišská regionálna rozvojová agentúra (Spiš Regional Development Agency)
	Magistrát mesta Košice, oddelenia strategického rozvoja (Kosice City Authorities, Department of Strategic Development)
	SARIO Regional Office in Košice
	SARIO

Source: Own work

regional offices, regional development agencies, other relevant public agencies and private organisations, including industry groupings and individual companies.

1.11 Book Structure

The remainder of the book proceeds as follows. Chapters 2 and 3 contextualise the issue of place promotion by offering a critical discussion of the concept of place marketing. They introduce the notion of place promotion aimed at investment attraction as a process and elaborate its key aspects in the context of promotional tools and regional development instruments. In the subsequent parts of the book, the constructed proposition will serve as a framework for analysis.

Chapters 4 and 5 constitute the main empirical parts of the book. The former offers an overview of the promotional activities of Central-Eastern European regional authorities and examines the extent of their involvement with the process as well as factors conditioning it. Next, Chap. 5 explores regional promotion in a multi-scalar context in selected regions, identifies distinct organisational arrangements and investigates how those are reflected in actions performed by participating promotion actors. Chapter 6 brings the discussion to a close by summarising the key empirical observations and drawing conclusions significant for the furthering of the theoretical debate.

References

Aharoni, Y. (2010). Behavioural elements in foreign direct investment decisions. *Advances in International Management, 23*, 72–112.

Alden, J. (1996). Regional development strategies in the European Union; Europe 2000+. In J. Alden & P. Boland (Eds.), *Regional development strategies; A European perspective*. London: Jessica Kingsley.

Almond, P., Ferner, A., & Tregasis, O. (2015). The changing context of regional governance of FDI in England. *European Urban and Regional Studies, 22*(1), 61–76.

Artisen-Maksimenko, P. (Ed.). (2000). *Multinationals in eastern Europe*. Houndmills: Macmillan Press.
Ascani, A., Crescenzi, R., & Iammarino, S. (2017). The geography of foreign investments in the EU neighbourhood. *Tijdschrift voor economische en socialte geografie, 108*(1), 76–91.
Ashworth, G. J., & Voogd, H. (1990). *Selling the city: Marketing approaches in public sector urban planning*. London: Belhaven Press.
Bachtler, J., & Downes, R. (2000). The spatial coverage of regional policy in central and eastern Europe. *European Urban and Regional Studies, 7*(2), 159–174.
Bauer, M. W., & Gaskell, G. (Eds.). (2000). *Qualitative researching with text, image and sound*. London: Sage Publications.
Behrman, J. N. (1972). *The role of international companies in Latin America: Autos and petrochemicals*. Lexington, MA: Lexington Book.
Beinart, J. (2001). Image construction in premodern cities. In L. J. Vale & S. B. Warner Jr. (Eds.), *Imagining the city—Continuing struggles and new directions*. New Brunswick, NJ: CUPR.
Bickl, M. (2004). *Image management in old-industrial regions: Policy learning, governance and leadership in North East England and the Ruhr*. PhD Thesis, University of Durham, Durham.
Blazyca, G., Heffner, K., & Helińska-Hughes, E. (2002). Poland—Can regional policy meet the challenge of regional problems? *European Urban and Regional Studies, 9*(3), 263–276.
Blokker, P., & Dallago, B. (2009). Introduction: Regional diversity and local development in new Member states. In *Regional diversity and local development in the new member states*. Basingstoke: Palgrave Macmillan.
Bradshaw, M. (2005). Foreign direct investment and economic transformation in Central and Eastern Europe. In D. Turnock (Ed.), *Foreign direct investment and regional development in east central Europe and former soviet union*. Aldershot: Ashgate.
Brusis, M. (2003). Regionalisation in the Czech and Slovak Republics: Comparing the influence of the European Union. In M. Keating & J. Hughes (Eds.), *The regional challenge in central and eastern Europe, territorial restructuring and European integration*. Paris: Presses interuniversitaires européennes/Peter Lang.
Buchanan, D., & Huczynski, A. (2004). *Organizational behaviour: An introductory text*. Harlow: Prentice Hall.
Burgess, J. (1982). Selling places: Environmental images for the executive. *Regional Studies, 16*(1), 1–17.

Capik, P. (2017). Backshoring: Towards international business and economic geography research agenda. *Advances in International Management, 30*, 141–155.

Capik, P., & Drahokoupil, J. (2011). Foreign direct investments in business services: Transforming the Visegrád Four region into a knowledge-based economy? *European Planning Studies, 19*(9), 1611–1631.

Cavusgil, S. T., Knight, G., & Riesenberger, J. R. (2008). *International business: Strategy, management, and the new realities*. Upper Saddle River, NJ: Pearson.

Charlton, A., Davis, N., Faye, M., Haddock, J., & Lamb, C. (2004). *Industry targeting within foreign investment promotion*. Oxford Investment Research Working Paper, Oxford.

Chidlow, A., Salciuviene, L., & Young, S. (2009). Regional determinants of inward FDI distribution in Poland. *International Business Review, 18*(2), 119–133.

Cleave, E., Godwin, A., Sadler, R., & Gilliland, J. (2016). The role of place branding in local and regional economic development: Bridging the gap between policy and practicality. *Regional Studies, Regional Science, 3*(1), 207–228.

Crescenzi, R., & Iammarino, S. (2017). Global investments and regional development trajectories: The missing links. *Regional Studies, 51*(1), 97–115.

Cyert, R. M., & March, J. G. (1963). *A behavioural theory of the firm*. Englewood Cliffs, NJ: Prentice-Hall.

Daniels, J. D., Radebaugh, L. H., & Sullivan, D. P. (2019). *International business: Environment and operations* (16th ed.). London: Pearson.

Dawson, A. (2005). Foreign direct investment: A sectoral and spatial review. In D. Turnock (Ed.), *Foreign direct investment and regional development in east central Europe and former Soviet Union*. Aldershot: Ashgate.

Denscombe, M. (2003). *The good research guide*. Maidenhead: Open University Press.

Dingsdale, A. (1999). Redefining 'Eastern Europe': A new regional geography of post-socialist Europe? *Geography, 84*(3), 204–221.

Dogaru, T., Burger, M., Karreman, B., & Van Oort, F. (2015). Functional and sectoral division of labour within central and eastern European countries: Evidence from greenfield FDI. *Tijdschrift voor economische en socialte geografie, 106*(1), 120–129.

Domański, B. (2001). *Kapitał zagraniczny w przemyśle Polski*. Kraków: IGiGP Uniwersytetu Jagiellońskiego.

Domański, B., Guzik, R., & Micek, G. (2003). Zróżnicowanie regionalne krajów Europy Środkowowschodniej i jego zmiany w latach 1995–2000. *Biuletyn Komitetu Przestrzennego Zagospodarowania Kraju PAN, 204*, 125–142.

Dunford, M., & Kafkalas, G. (1992). Global local interplay; corporate geographies and spatial development strategies in Europe. In M. Dunford & G. Kafkalas (Eds.), *Cities and regions in the new Europe*. Belhaven Press, London.

Dunning, J. H., & Lundan, S. M. (2008). *Multinational enterprises and the global economy*. Cheltenham: Edward Elgar.

European Commission. (2006). *Study on FDI and regional development*. Copenhagen: Copenhagen Economics.

Eurostat. (2007). *Regions in the European union: Nomenclature of territorial units for statistics*. Luxembourg: European Communities.

Eurostat. (2015). *Eurostat regional yearbook 2015*. Luxembourg: Eurostat.

Ezcurra, R., Pascual, P., & Rapûn, M. (2007). The dynamics of regional disparities in central and eastern Europe during transition. *European Planning Studies, 15*(11), 1397–1421.

Ferry, M., & McMaster, I. (2013). Cohesion policy and the evolution of regional policy in central and eastern Europe. *Europe-Asia Studies, 65*(8), 1502–1528.

Fifeková, M., & Hardy, J. (2010). *Business service foreign direct investment in central and eastern Europe: Trends, motives and impacts*. Brno: Economy and Society Trust.

Florek, M. (2004). Możliwości zastosowania narzędzi marketingu w gminie (w kontekście wyników badań w gminach regionu wielkopolskiego). In H. Szulce (Ed.), *Obszary i możliwości wykorzystania marketingu*. Poznań: Zeszyty Naukowe AE.

Gaskell, G. (2000). Individual and group interviewing. In M. W. Bauer & G. Gaskell (Eds.), *Qualitative researching with text, image and sound*. London: Sage Publications.

Gold, J. R., & Ward, S. V. (1994). Forward. In *Place promotion; the use of publicity and marketing to sell towns and regions*. Chichester: John Wiley & Sons.

Gorzelak, G. (2003). *Economic and social cohesion in an enlarged EU: Comments on the post-socialist transformation*. Glasgow: EPRC Symposium materials.

Gorzelak, G. (2009). Regional development and Central and Eastern Europe. In P. Blokker & B. Dallago (Eds.), *Regional diversity and local development in the new member states*. Basingstoke: Palgrave Macmillan.

Guglielmetti, C. (2009). Local development in a European Union perspective: Cohesion and regional policies in central and eastern Europe. In P. Blokker

& B. Dallago (Eds.), *Regional diversity and local development in the new member states*. Basingstoke: Palgrave Macmillan.
Harding, T., & Javorcik, B. (2011). Roll out the red carpet and they will come: Investment promotion and FDI inflows. *The Economic Journal, 121*(557), 1445–1476.
Harding, T., & Javorcik, B. (2012). *Investment promotion and FDI inflows: Quality matters*. University of Oxford Department of Economics Discussion Paper Series, No. 612.
Hardy, J. (1998). Cathedrals in the desert? Transnationals, corporate strategy and locality in Wrocław. *Regional Studies, 32*, 639–652.
Hardy, J. (2004). Rebuilding local governance in post-communist economies: The case of Wrocław. *Poland, European Urban and Regional Studies, 11*(4), 303–320.
Hardy, J. (2009). *Poland's new capitalism*. London: Pluto Press.
Helinska-Hughes, E., & Hughes, M. (2003). Joining the competition: Central and eastern European challenge to established FDI destinations? In N. Phelps & P. Raines (Eds.), *The new competition for inward investment*. Cheltenham: Edward Elgar.
Herodes, F. (2011). The regional institution's dilemma—How regional organisations adapt to EU membership. In T. Herrschel & P. Tallberg (Eds.), *The role of regions? Networks, scale, territory*. Kristianstad: Kristianstads Boktryckeri.
Herrschel, T., & Tallberg, P. (2011). Introduction—Regions, 'fuzziness' as opportunity?. In *The role of regions? Networks, scale, territory*. Kristianstad: Kristianstads Boktryckeri.
Hoover, E. M. (1975). *An introduction to regional economics* (2nd ed.). New York: Alfred A. Knopf.
Hughes, J., Sasse, G., & Gordon, C. (2004). *Europeanization and regionalization in the EU's enlargement to central and eastern Europe*. Basingstoke: Palgrave Macmillan.
Illner, M. (2002). *Multilevel government in three central eastern European countries and its reforms since 1989*. EUI Working Papers, No 2002/07.
Kelly, P. (2009). *International business and management*. Andover: Cengage Learning.
Kulchina, E. (2014). Media coverage and location choice. *Strategic Management Journal, 35*(4), 596–605.
Lever, J. (2001). *The effectiveness of place imagery in English local authority inward investment promotion—An evaluation*. MPhil Thesis, Manchester Metropolitan University, Manchester.

Lidström, A. (2011). Regional self-government and democracy. In T. Herrschel & P. Tallberg (Eds.), *The role of regions? Networks, scale, territory*. Kristianstad: Kristianstads Boktryckeri.

Lim, S. H. (2005). Foreign investment impact and incentive: A strategic approach to the relationship between the objectives of foreign investment policy and their promotion. *International Business Review, 14*, 61–76.

Lipton, D., & Sachs, J. (1990). Creating a market economy in Poland. *Brooking Papers on Economic Activity, 1*, 75–147.

Loewendahl, H. (2001). A framework for FDI promotion. *Transnational Corporations, 10*(1), 1–42.

Malizia, E. E., & Feser, E. J. (1999). *Understanding local economic development.* Rutgers, NJ: CUPR.

Meyer, K. E., Ionascu, D., Kulawczuk, P., Szczesniak, A., Antal-Makos, Z., Tȯth, K., & Darskuvenie, V. (2005). *The changing patterns of foreign direct investment in EU accession countries: Insights from a new survey*. CEES Working Papers, No. 57.

Miles, M. B., & Huberman, A. M. (1994). *Qualitative data analysis*. London: SAGE Publications.

Miszczuk, A. (2003). *Regionalizacja administracyjna III Rzeczypospolitej: Koncepcje teoretyczne a rzeczywistość*. Lublin: Wydawnictwo UMCS.

Monaghan, S., Gunnigle, P., & Lavelle, J. (2014). 'Courting the multinational': Subnational institutional capacity and foreign market insidership. *Journal of International Business Studies, 45*(2), 131–150.

Multilateral Investment Guarantee Agency (MIGA). (2006). *FDI promotion*. Retrieved November 29, 2006, from www.fdipromotion.com/toolkit/user/content_page.cfm

Navaretti, G. B., & Venables, A. J. (2004). *Multinational firms in the world economy*. Princeton, NJ: Princeton University Press.

Nordström, L. (1996). European developing regions—Reality or chimera? In J. Alden & P. Boland (Eds.), *Regional development strategies; A European perspective*. London: Jessica Kingsley.

O'Dwyer, C. (2006). Reforming regional governance in east central Europe: Europeanization or domestic politics as usual? *East European Politics and Societies, 20*(2), 219–253.

OECD. (2003). *Checklist for foreign direct investment incentives policies*. Paris: OECD Publications.

OECD. (2015). *Policy framework for investment 2015 edition*. Paris: OECD Publishing. Retrieved from https://doi.org/10.1787/9789264208667-en

Patton, M. Q. (1990). *Qualitative evaluation and research methods*. Newbury Park, CA: Sage.
Pavlínek, P. (2004). Regional development implications of foreign direct investment in central Europe. *European Urban and Regional Studies, 11*(1), 47–70.
Pike, A., Rodríguez-Pose, A., & Tomaney, J. (2017). Shifting horizons in local and regional development. *Regional Studies, 51*(1), 46–57.
Pike, A., Rodríguez-Pose, A., & Tomaney, J. (2016). *Local and regional development* (2nd ed.). London: Routledge.
Rutkowski, A. (2006). Inward FDI, concentration and profitability in the CEECs: Were the domestic firms crowded out or strengthened? *Transnational Corporations, 15*(3), 105–139.
Schotter, A., & Beamish, P. W. (2013). The hassle factor: An explanation for managerial location shunning. *Journal of International Business Studies, 44*(5), 521–544.
Scott, A. J., & Storper, M. (2003). Regions, globalization, development. *Regional Studies, 37*(6/7), 579–593.
Silverman, D. (2018). *Doing qualitative research* (5th ed.). London: Sage Publishing.
Sitkin, A., & Bowen, N. (2010). *International business: Challenges and choices*. Oxford: OUP.
Smith, A., & Ferenčiková, S. (1998). Inward investment, regional transformations and uneven development in eastern and central Europe. *European Urban and Regional Studies, 5*(2), 155–173.
Smith, D. J. (2002). Framing the national question in central and eastern Europe: A quadratic nexus? *Global Review of Ethnopolitics, 2*(1), 3–16.
Stawicka, M. (2006). *Atrakcyjność Inwestycyjna Polski*. Warszawa: CeDeWu.PL.
Storper, M. (1997). *The regional world. Territorial development in a global economy*. New York: The Guilford Press.
Swianiewicz, P. (2014). An empirical typology of local government systems in Eastern Europe. *Local Government Studies, 40*(2), 292–311.
Taylor, P. J. (1993). *Political geography*. Harlow: Longman.
Terlouw, K. (2001). Regions in geography and the regional geography of semi-peripheral development. *Tijdschrift voor Economische en Sociale Geografie, 92*(1), 76–87.
Tondl, G., & Vuksic, G. (2003). *What makes regions in Eastern Europe catching up? The role of foreign investment, human resources and geography*. ZEI Working Papers, vol. B12.
Turnock, D. (1997). Urban and regional restructuring in eastern Europe: The role of foreign investment. *GeoJournal, 42*(4), 457–464.

UNCTAD. (2003). *World investment report 2003: FDI policies for development: National and international perspective*. Geneva: United Nations.
UNCTAD. (2004a). *What services do IPAs target?* UNCTAD Investment Brief, no.1/2004.
UNCTAD. (2004b). *World investment report 2004: The shift towards services*. Geneva: United Nations.
UNCTAD. (2005). *World investment report 2005: Transnational corporations and the internationalisation of R&D*. Geneva: United Nations.
UNCTAD. (2006). *World investment report 2006: FDI from developing and transition economies: Implications for development*. Geneva: United Nations.
UNCTAD. (2007). *World investment report 2007: Transnational corporations, extractive industries and development*. Geneva: United Nations.
UNCTAD. (2016). *World investment report: Investor nationality—Policy challenges*. Geneva: United Nations.
UNCTAD. (2018). *Word investment report: Investment and new industrial policies*. Geneva: United Nations.
Ward, S. V. (1998). *Selling places, the marketing and promotion of towns and cities 1850–2000*. London: E&FN Spon.
Wells, T. L. Jr., & Wint, A. G., 2000, *Marketing a country—Promotion as a tool for attracting foreign direct investment*. FIAS Occasional Paper 13, IFC-MIGA, Washington.
World Bank. (2012). *Investment climate: Global investment promotions best practices*. Washington: The World Bank Group.
Yin, R. (2003). *Case study research: Design and methods*. London: Sage.
Young, C. (2005). Place marketing for foreign direct investment in central and eastern Europe. In D. Turnock (Ed.), *Foreign direct investment and regional development in East-Central Europe and the former Soviet Union*. Kent: Ashgate.
Young, C., & Lever, J. (1997). Place promotion, economic location and the consumption of city image. *Tijdshrift voor Economische en Sociale Geografie, 88*(4), 332–341.
Zanatta, M., Costa, I., & Filippov, S. (2006). *Foreign direct investment: Key issues for promotion agencies*. UNU Policy Brief, No.10, UNU-MERIT, Maastricht.
Zarycki, T., & Tucholska, A. (2004). Region, którego miało nie być; Paradoksy tożsamości województwa świętokrzyskiego świętokrzyskiego kontekście krajowym i europejskim. In W. Łukowski (Ed.), *Tożsamości regionów w Polsce w przestrzeni europejskiej*. Katowice: Wolny Sojusz Europejski.
Zimmerbauer, K. (2011). From image to identity: Building regions by place promotion. *European Planning Studies, 19*(2), 243–260.

2

Place Marketing, Promotion and Investment Attraction

2.1 Introduction

According to Ward (1998) every town, city and region, sure of its competitive place advantages, is selling itself. Traditional tourist resorts are facing new competitors—old industrial towns whose factories and docks are transformed into heritage sites and leisure centres. The attractiveness of established national, regional and urban economies is continuously threatened by the growing competitiveness of new investment destinations. Comparably, with the intensifying mobility of the rising creative class, urban and suburban areas strive to create pleasant living environments contributing to a high quality of life. While the claim that all countries, cities and regions are engaged in promotion activities is surely an overgeneralisation, growing research evidence demonstrates that a rising number of places across the world undertaking some form of promotion is hard to deny. And nearly three decades ago, the collapse of communism has triggered the entry of a new set of places into the "place marketing game" (Ward, 1998, p. 1), while the 2004 and 2007 enlargements of the European Union secured common set of rules of that game across Europe.

P. Capik, *Foreign Investment Promotion*, https://doi.org/10.1007/978-3-030-13658-1_2

By reviewing the literature on what became known as 'place marketing', the chapter explores its nature, relationship to promotion and usability in the context of foreign direct investment (FDI) attraction. The chapter demonstrates that place promotion has a potentially vital role to play in FDI-based regional development, but the practices and principles need to be incorporated at the different stages of policy-making and implementation. As the reviewed global examples indicate, such a comprehensive approach is rare, and investment attraction policies and actions are often characterised by fragmentation, lack of long-term perspective and overemphasis of incentive measures not accompanied by the communication processes.

2.2 Place Marketing in Context

The term *marketing* is commonly used, and regularly abused in various spheres of everyday life. Frequently (and mistakenly), it is used interchangeably with *promotion*, while referring merely to *advertising*. According to Frain (1994) marketing is vital everywhere where exchange is required, yet the opinions on what it actually encompasses and what it does not are varied and vividly discussed. Both classical and recent definitions of marketing and its scope neither clearly include the possibility of place marketing, nor deliberately eliminate it.

Denison and McDonald (1995, p. 57) define marketing as "a management process responsible for identifying, anticipating and satisfying customer requirements profitably". Their definition stresses the importance of customer and earnings, but also the role of the organisation's management. Every aspect of a firm's operations needs to be based on the vital role of the customer, who in return will provide the profit. Although vital components, neither advertising nor promotion is the only activity in the process. Marketing additionally encompasses research, product design and development, forecasting and planning as well as related financial functions (Frain, 1994). Subsequently, Kotler and Armstrong (2001, p. 6) further extended the definition and scope of marketing activities: "marketing is a social and managerial process whereby individuals and groups obtain what they need and want through creating and exchanging products and values with others". This definition takes marketing out of its traditional business domain and includes wider society in the process. It points to the variety of existing markets and target groups. Furthermore, it broadens the scope of marketing to include non-commercial activities, and indicates other than the financial dimensions of profit. The process of exchange provides profits of some value, not necessarily monetary, to both sides participating in the procedure. The authors also specify a number of diverse marketing activities including product development, research, communication, distribution, pricing and service. All of which are included in one of the fundamental concepts of marketing—the marketing mix—comprising the 7Ps: product, price, place (i.e. distribution), promotion, people, process and physical evidence. It is a set of tactical and controllable marketing tools, which the company employs to cause the awaited response in the targeted market. Thus, as Kotler and Armstrong (2001) emphasise, marketing is not only about selling, however selling makes it all worthwhile, that is, generates the satisfaction for customers, and profit for the company. Thus, in the investment promotion and regional policy sphere, the aim would be to generate satisfaction for the investor (i.e. 'customer') and profit for the 'company', that is, regional authorities and the broader regional economy and citizens. The foundation of such thinking has been laid with Kotler and Levy's (1969) remarks on the need to expand the marketing theory from the profit sector into societal organisations and groupings. The idea was then extended by Kotler (1972) into a concept of generic marketing, as a "disciplined task of creating and offering values to others for the purpose of achieving a desired response" (Kotler, 1972, p. 46).

While these early conceptual developments help, place marketing remains an elusive concept.

For several decades now planners, geographers, economists, sociologists and others dealing with issues of urban and regional development have tried to define it. Some of the initial definitions emphasise the "marketing" or "commodification" components, such as product design, exchange process, sales, generating customers' satisfaction (e.g. Kotler, Apslund, Rein, & Haider, 1999; Kotler & Gertner, 2002; Rainisto, 2003). Others stress the "urban", "region" or "country", that is, place, factor and highlight the matters of place management and development (e.g. Cleave, Godwin, Sadler, & Gilliland, 2016; Markowski, 2002; Rudolf, 1999; Sienkiewicz & Kowalik, 2004; van den Berg, Klaassen, & Meer, 1990; Zimmerbauer, 2011). Although some aspects of the two approaches overlap, it is important to note how the different issues are emphasised, reflecting the lack of common and systematic views on the subject. Moreover, not only are there various definitions but, more crucially, there is little agreement concerning 'the name of the game'. For example, Girard (1997), Szromnik (1997) and Rudolf (1999) argue that regional, urban, territorial, place and communal (German: komunales) marketing is all the same since the subject is invariably some type of space. It should be recognised, however, that those terms describe places at various scales, possessing diverse characteristics and administrative arrangements. Such differentiation bears consequences for the practical applicability of place marketing (Capik, 2007), as well as for its general theoretical considerations. Overall, the differences in the terminology used highlight a wider conceptual challenge with directly applying marketing approaches to places. Yet and paradoxically, often in existing literature, those terms are used as synonyms—and for consistency a similar approach is adopted in the forthcoming sections of the chapter introducing the different approaches to defining 'place marketing', its nature and scope, and offering its critique. However, the emphasis is placed on particular differences in theoretical approaches and practical applications resulting from the peculiar character of regional space.[1]

2.2.1 Commodification of Places

Kotler, Haider, and Rein (1993), Kotler et al. (1999) introduce the idea of strategic place marketing as the most adaptive and productive solution to the problems faced by towns, cities, regions and nations. In their view, the aim of strategic place marketing is to design the community in a way that guarantees satisfaction of the needs of its main participants. Success is attained when citizens, workers and business firms are satisfied with their community and when the expectations of visitors, new business and investors are met. In line with this proposition, place marketing includes:

[1] For a discussion of the complexity and nature of "region", see, for example, Paasi and Metzger (2017).

- designing the right mix of community features and services;
- setting attractive incentives for the current and potential buyers and users of its goods and services;
- delivering a place's products and services in an efficient, accessible way;
- promoting the place's values and images so that potential users are fully aware of its distinctive advantages (Kotler et al., 1999, p. 18).

These actions determine the place's success in attracting and satisfying its five potential target markets—producers of goods and services, corporate headquarters (and regional offices), inward investors and exports markets, tourism and new residents. Success is determined by the place authorities' ability to perform the following fundamental tasks:

- interpretation of events and actions in the broader environment;
- comprehension of the needs, wants and behaviour choices of internal and external neighbourhoods;
- constructing an achievable vision of what the place can be and the creation of an actionable plan to match it;
- building internal consensus and effective organisation;
- progress evaluation at every stage of plan completion.

Thus, in short, "place marketing means designing a place to satisfy the needs of its target markets" (Kotler & Gertner, 2002, p. 253).

Presented approach indicates the complexity of the development process and highlights some of its critical dimensions (e.g. political) and issues (e.g. long-term vision) closely associated with creation of a place. However, it falls short of providing directions related particularly to the diversity of place customers and the different aspects of the 'product' they may seek, as well as the measures for their satisfaction, hence in many respects remains simplified, if not simplistic.

Firstly, it fails to recognise the peculiar characteristics of different scales of places including towns, regions (including transnational regions, e.g. Euroregions) and countries, the diverse powers and responsibilities of their governing authorities and the specific problems they face. The attempt to apply the same set of marketing principals to the management of every type of place seems overoptimistic. Every scale of a place—

neighbourhood, city, region and country—has particular problems and objectives to address, often requiring place-tailored strategies and approaches (Pike, Rodríguez-Pose, & Tomaney, 2016). Additionally, the scope of powers and authority vested with various administrative levels vary (e.g. Swianiewicz, 2014), and places have limited influence on the design of their features (e.g. motorway access) and services (e.g. tax exemptions). Consequently while some of the marketing principles may be applicable on a country level, on the regional or local scale, they need to be considerably adjusted or abandoned altogether.

Secondly, the presented approach excludes geographical location and place characteristics (or the L-advantages, within the Dunning's Eclectic Paradigm) as co-determinants of its success. Place characteristics remain to be important in location decisions, even if weighted and analysed differently. The new sets of place attributes play vital roles (Merlevede & Schoors, 2004; Stawicka, 2006; Dogaru, Burger, Karreman, & Van Oort, 2015; UNCTAD, 2018), as do the fresh definitions of accessibility for new economic activities.

Secondly, originating from one of marketing's activities, product development, that is, the design of community in such a way that it satisfies its participants' needs, is recommended. Although this may be possible in theory, in practice is hard to achieve. Places, apart from their physical and technical outlook, encompass a cultural dimension. These are entities whose values, beliefs and identity develop at different speeds over long periods of time (Bialasiewicz, 2002; Szczepański, 2004). Also, as justly noted by Fretter (1993), the activities undertaken by place authorities in order to improve the *place product* belong to their natural duties and do not constitute a set extraordinary actions performed according to and because of marketing principles.

Thirdly, the measures of success are equally debatable. The citizens' satisfaction and well-being must be the priority of every public authority, and the presence of investors and tourists should be considered as a means of achieving it rather than the aim in itself. Yet, the local population is missing in the presented approach. It is not to say the indicated target groups are unimportant, but their 'satisfaction', however full, should be operationalised as a tool helping to achieve the aim of local (regional) community welfare.

2.2.2 Regional Policy and Governance Perspective

The parallel approach, while related, is more allied to the subject of management of places and development policy. Based on Szromnik's (1997, p. 40) view that marketing is a specific "way of thinking about the success", place marketing is a philosophy of achieving defined aims by spatial units (communities, cites, regions). The process takes place in the reality of constant competition for scarce resources and is based on the assumption that the results are primarily influenced by correct classification of the clients and partners. It is a market-oriented place management aimed at satisfying the expectations of the local inhabitants, potential guests and investors (Sienkiewicz & Kowalik, 2004) by recognising them in advance and anticipating their changes. Therefore, *place marketing* is a deliberate and systematic activity performed by (place) authority, aimed at recognising, creating and satisfying the needs of its population and wider target groups. It includes "a set of marketing activities" carried out by territorial authorities and organisations within the framework of the planning and policy processes with the objective to develop economic, social, cultural, tourist and identity aspects of local communities (Girard, 1997).

Similarly, in their classic book, Ashworth and Voogd (1990) argue that urban marketing is a process in which urban activities are as closely as possible correlated with demands of targeted customers in order to maximise the social and economic performance of the area in line "with whatever goals have been established". One needs to agree with the authors that this "certainly implies much more than a fashionable terminology and city promotion through four-colour leaflets" (Ashworth & Voogd, 1990, p. 11). However, these all-encompassing approaches seem to contribute little novelty to the discussion, and instead provide a base for Paddison's (1993) argument that place marketing is rather a new name for a set of actions that have been practised for a long time. Thus, it is yet another attempt to adopt the theory derived from the private into the public sector (Markowski, 2002). Young and Kaczmarek (1999) argue that urban marketing is a mixture of planning and marketing activities. Perhaps, it would be more appropriate to say it is an attempt to mix marketing principles and some of its practices into planning, or, from the perspective of this book, into the regional policy.

The idea of demand creation seems to be overestimated, especially when considering foreign investors. As indicated, growing competition for FDI makes it consumers' (i.e. foreign investors) rather than producers' (the authorities) market. Furthermore, what many authors have repeatedly stressed (e.g. Harding & Javorcik, 2012; Madsen, 1992; Monaghan, Gunnigle, & Lavelle, 2014; Quelch & Jocz, 2005) is the lack of adequate resources for effective place marketing activities at the disposal of the agencies. Assuming the main goal of any public authority to be the prosperity of citizens, investing in 'new products' and hoping to find customers for them may be considered risky and lack public legitimacy.

The idea of place (be it a community, region or other) marketing in the context of the proposed discussion seems superficial, and contrary to some authors' views that marketing theory cannot be easily directly applied to regional development. The use of marketing terminology while discussing established regional policy activities and measures does not change that situation. Paraphrasing what Asheim, Cooke, and Martin (2006) have said about the increasingly debated notion of clusters, it can be concluded that "mere popularity of the construct is by no means a guarantee of its profundity. As is so often in the policy sphere, the rush to apply the cluster [place marketing] concept in national and regional development policies has run ahead of many theoretical, conceptual and empirical issues".

However, a more market-oriented and research-driven approach in regional development policies and urban management is possible and indeed needed to safeguard a region's prosperity and the well-being of communities in an increasingly competitive global economy (Bonetti & Masiello, 2014). As argued by van den Berg et al. (2002, p. 5), "by adopting marketing principles the municipal organisation may become more customer-oriented, ready to give service to, and mind the interests of, the city's customer". Furthermore, Gold and Ward (1994) indicate that marketing approach offers the nearest thing to a practical expertise for those undertaking place promotion. It offers the tools for such activity, giving the promotional bodies a methodology that enables them to identify the place identity and competitive assets, and target their promotional activities at defined groups considered strategic to the development of the area. It is place promotion that is explored next.

2.3 Place Promotion

In the corporate world, promotion is a direct way in which an organisation communicates with its various target audiences with the aim of moving forward in a distribution channel a product, service or an idea. It attempts to influence the knowledge, attitudes and behaviour of its recipients (Brassington & Pettitt, 2003; Clow & Baack, 2018). Promotion mix comprises the following five elements, its main tools: (1) advertising is any paid[2] form of non-personal, mass communication. Personal selling, (2) on the other hand, involves interpersonal communication in the form of retail or door-to-door selling. Sales promotion (3) engages short-term schemes stimulating the purchase of the promoted object, while publicity and public relations (4) involve coordinated activities building good relations with many interest groups, not just the customers (Clow & Baack, 2018). Direct marketing (5) borrows from all of these elements and involves creating one-to-one relationships with individual customers in the mass markets. Additionally, Belch and Belch (2004) distinguish the sixth element of promotion—interactive/Internet marketing, which relies on the interactive media and allows the "back-and-forth flow of information whereby users can participate and modify the form and content of the information they receive in real time" (Belch & Belch, 2004, p. 20).

Essentially promotion aims to communicate the qualities of the product and persuade the target customer to purchase it (Kotler & Armstrong, 2001). More precisely individual objectives can be identified reflecting the purposes and advancement of particular promotional campaigns and the tools employed. Communication objectives include creating awareness and knowledge about the product, its attributes and benefits, image creation, development of favourable attitudes, as well as preferences and purchase intentions (Belch & Belch, 2004).

In the context of this book—the question arises how this part of marketing can be applied to various aspects of regional development and

[2] The *paid* aspect indicates that space and time for an advertising message normally must be purchased. A sporadic exception to this are the public service announcements, whose advertising space and/or time is donated by the media (Belch & Belch, 2004).

more specifically to investment attraction. How could promotion be understood within the policy context aimed specifically at FDI attraction, when a product is a socially and economically diversified multidimensional space, namely a region?

Place promotion has a long and eventful history, ranging back from ancient times when the rulers of pilgrim cities, such as Jerusalem, and later Mecca, Rome, Santiago de Compostela and others, utilised verbal and written channels of advertising hoping to attract larger numbers of pilgrims than rival destinations (Beinart, 2001). Similarly, during Viking times Leif Ericsson promoted "Vinland" to his natives hoping to encourage them to settle in the newly found lands (Ashworth & Voogd, 1990). Increasingly, more systematic practices appeared over the last one and a half centuries to include specialised activities aimed at attracting specific target groups, notably tourist and industrial investors (Ward, 1998). In yet more recent times, as recognised by Ashworth and Voogd (1994), planners turned to a set of marketing techniques, important among which is promotion. Arguably, as stressed by, despite differences that distinguish it from private sector application, promotion is the only "P" in the marketing mix that can be applied by the public authorities (Borchert, 1994). Furthermore, some authors assign promotion a critical role in the localities' attempts to manage the impact of globalisation and political change (e.g. Cleave et al., 2016; Paddison, 1993; Young & Kaczmarek, 1999).

2.3.1 The Purpose of Place Promotion

Young and Lever (1997, p. 332), considering promotion as an "an important element of entrepreneurialism of the city", assert that the promotion campaign is designed to increase the knowledge and understanding of a place. On the other hand Paddison (1993, p. 340) gives promotion a broader role "rather than advertising per se", and argues that it seeks to rebuild and reconstruct the image of the place. Similarly Wu (2000) indicates that in the case of places, promotion presents and represents a new image to raise the competitiveness of the area. The aim of image recreation is to overcome the negative perceptions of the past and to attract investment.

van den Berg et al. (2002, p. 107) argue that "image and identity are important promotion factors, but cannot by themselves change the general perception of a city or a region". Therefore, image-linked activities cannot be isolated, and should be considered as a vital addition to the broader development strategy and everyday life of a region (Borchert, 1994; Kulchina, 2014). "Every aspect of public policy from street cleaning to the provision of housing, from equal opportunities to public transport, from the award of public contracts to sewage outfalls can be made to bear the imprint of place selling ethos" (Ward, 1998, p. 3). Indeed, the publicising of places' features and advantages acts alongside other elements such as financial packages, infrastructural improvements, and land and facility provisions in an attempt to influence earlier recognised economic decision-makers (Harding & Javorcik, 2012; Lever, 2001; Monaghan et al., 2014; Young & Lever, 1997). Thus, place promotion includes all or a purpose-defined selection of the promotion mix tools, used in conjunction with place development policies fostering the activities of selected target groups—be it tourists, new settlers or investors.

2.4 The Process of Regional Promotion Aimed at Investment Attraction

The understanding of promotion specifically aimed at attracting FDI should not be limited to mere image and advertising campaigns. It needs to be more comprehensive and include a set of activities and policies oriented towards investment generation, and methods of their application. To that end, Loewendahl (2001) in his seminal work distinguishes four consecutive stages of investment promotion: (1) strategy and organisation (including setting the development policy context, structure of investment promotion, competitive positioning and sector targeting strategy), (2) lead generation (targeted promotion), (3) facilitation (project handling) and (4) investment services (aftercare, product improvement, monitoring and evaluation). While the initial stage is concerned with planning and strategy setting, the remaining three involve concrete actions and activities, and thus could be called promotion per se.

Consequently, in one of the first and most influential works on the subject, Wells and Wint (2000) set out how in general terms place promotion aimed at investment attraction strives to achieve a set of interconnected objectives:

- improve the image of the place held by the investment community;
- generate investment;
- provide investment and post-investment services.

Meeting these objectives can be supported by a number of promotional tools, which emphasises the link between investment attraction and promotion understood in its marketing context. Figure 2.1 illustrates the proposed nexus between the objectives and the promotional tools. The creation or enhancement of image is aided by all of the promotion mix tools. Investment generation benefits mostly from the use of direct marketing actions, sales promotion techniques (including the use of investment incentives) and personal selling events. Similarly, the latter are

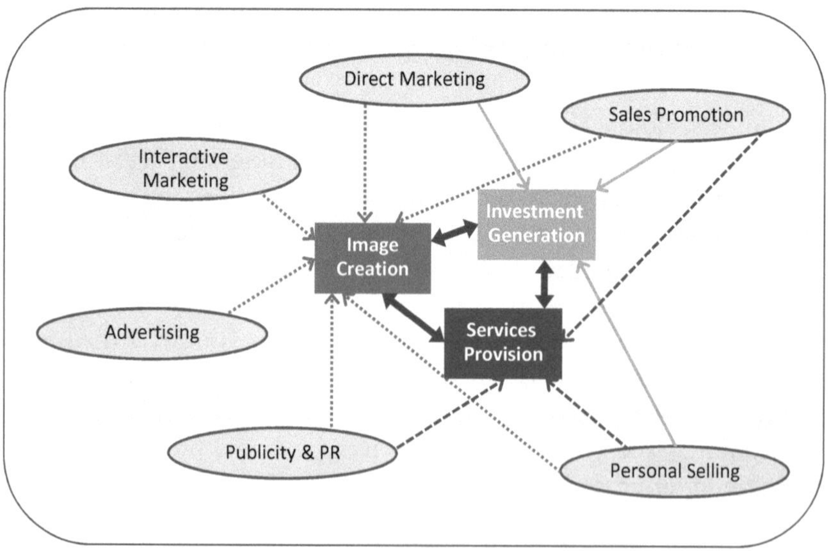

Fig. 2.1 Promotion mix–FDI attraction objectives nexus. *Source*: Own work

the basis for the provision of investment services, which additionally is supported by publicity and PR activities.

In their study Wells and Wint (2000) identify the different stages of countries' FDI promotion. Initially, National Investment Promotion Agencies (NIPAs) are more concerned with image-building activities, and gradually move towards investment generation and service provision. In recent decades we have seen multiple examples of this, reflecting the learning process of the agency, that is, initially the IPAs embark on what seems to be the easiest and most popular activity—advertising—and only later their activities become more sophisticated and complete.

However, such a gradual approach unnecessarily expands the (lengthy by nature) timespan of places' investment promotion attempts, increasing the risk of losing out on some of the projects captured 'in the mean time' by competing areas. All three objectives are interlinked and should not be considered as substitutes but complementary. The image-building process is a complex and time-consuming one. Several techniques and tools that it requires can also be used to achieve the other two objectives (Fig. 2.1). Investment-generating activities (e.g. investment and trade missions, participation in investment exhibitions, preparation and implementation of investment incentives schemes) can be utilised to create an image of a region as a place welcoming for the investors—a picture which will be further strengthened by swift provision of adequate services for both potential and current investors. Promotion thus does not stop with successful attraction of an investor. Aftercare services aim to encourage the company to expand, but also by 'word-of-mouth' communicate the positive impressions of the place and attitudes of its authorities. Often, however, this part is unjustly considered as less important and traditionally NIPAs tend to focus their efforts on either image building or investment generation (OECD, 2018).

2.4.1 Investment Incentives as a Promotion Measure

From a regional development perspective, apart from image-improvement (or indeed creation) activities, a set of investment incentives are usually included in the FDI attraction schemes. Since early 1980s, national governments have increasingly adopted a variety of measures to facilitate the entry of foreign companies. Organisation for Economic Cooperation and Development (OECD) defines foreign investment incentives as "measures designed to influence the size, location or sector of FDI investment projects by affecting their relative cost or by altering the risks attached to them through inducements that are not available to comparable domestic investors" (OECD, 2003, p. 11). Incentives exclude the broader non-discriminatory policies, such as general infrastructural improvements, the common legal regime for FDI, the universal regulatory and fiscal regime for business operations or national treatment. While these policies influence the locational decision of multinational enterprises, they are not FDI incentives per se (UNCTAD, 2018). The incentives could be directed at start-up costs or aim to reduce operational costs; however, for a potential investor the decisive factor is how the measures influence the total expected value of the investment project (Navaretti & Venables, 2004) and how that compares to costs at alternative locations, or in marketing terminology what level of satisfaction does it generate.

Since their humble beginnings in the mid-nineteenth-century USA and Canada, incentives have increasingly become an integral part of investment attraction and in the mid-1990s over 100 countries provided various FDI subsidies, while in 2018 UNCTAD reported virtually all countries running variety of investor support and enticement schemes (Blomström & Kokko, 2003; UNCTAD, 2018; Ward, 1998). Next to liberalised legal frameworks for foreign entities' operations and guarantees for repatriation of investment (regulatory incentives), tax (fiscal) incentives and investment subsidies (financial incentives) are amongst the most important ones. Additionally, as presented in Table 2.1, some authors (e.g. Navaretti & Venables, 2004) distinguish another category of incentives, which is largely a hybrid of the earlier types, and while designed to attract FDI often benefit the wider business community in the area (e.g. on-demand infrastructural improvements).

The UNCTAD (2000, 2018) and OECD (2015) studies demonstrate that most countries utilise a mix of incentives to reach their investment objectives. Advanced, developed, wealthy economies, however, more often can afford to implement financial incentives such as grants, subsidised credits and loans guarantees, as they come directly from the authorities' budget and as such, they are not frequently offered by the poorer countries. The amount of the incentives offered can reach considerable sums. For example, in the early 1990s the Portuguese government's financial incentives for Volkswagen and Ford plants totalled over 250,000 USD per employee, and Mercedes-Benz received 160,000 USD per employee from Alabama state authorities, while Newcastle upon Tyne subsidised the Siemens plant with around 50,000 USD per employee in the mid-1990s (Navaretti & Venables, 2004). Similarly, Blomström and Kokko (2003) refer to studies reporting subsidies of around 30,000 ECU per worker for investments in Belgium, France and Luxembourg.

Less-prosperous places tend to use fiscal incentives (tax reductions or exemption, Table 2.1) that do not require the upfront use of public funds. As explained in the OECD (2015) study, those countries are also more likely to offer regulatory incentives in the form of lenient environmental, social or labour market requirements. Such incentives are sometimes negotiated as a part of improvised strategies for luring significant individual FDI projects, but more commonly are granted in connection with targeted strategies.

2.4.1.1 Incentives and the Regional Scale

Incentives are commonly used as a regional policy tool. National governments designate priority regions and offer a selection of incentives (Table 2.2) for companies (and sectors) willing to invest in particular areas, or more precisely in carefully selected localities (e.g. special economic zones) (UNCTAD, 2000, 2018).

Alternatively, in more decentralised systems, national governments delegate some of the incentive-granting powers to regional jurisdictions. The main advantage of giving the lower administrative level a freer hand lies in the more intimate knowledge of the socio-economic situation, industries and individual investment projects that is available locally (OECD, 2003). As discussed in Chap. 1 there is a clear rationale for such an approach. While, when searching for a new location, multinational enterprises tend to longlist countries; it is at the regional level that the MNEs draw up a list of possible areas that they want to evaluate in depth.

Table 2.1 Types of investment incentives

	Regulatory incentives	Fiscal incentives	Financial incentives	Other
Character of the incentive (examples)	Exemption/(preferential treatment) from national/regional/local rules and regulations most often environment, social and labour market-related	Permanent or temporary Tax exemptions or reductions based on: Profit, capital investment, labour, sales, value added, import, export, particular expenditure; Examples: Tax holidays, income tax reductions, accelerated depreciation of machinery and so on.	Related to financing of new investments or operations; – Grants covering capital/production/ marketing costs (e.g. real estate, wage/training subsidies) – credits and insurance at subsidised rates – (government) equity participation	Range of measures providing advantage to foreign firms, e.g.: – subsidised infrastructure/ services, – special market preferences – preferential exchange rates
Main features	– linked with targeted strategies, – individually granted in 'negotiated strategies' – uncommon – confined to specific sectors in usually developing economies	– indirect subsidy – legislative in nature, (hence often also available for local companies) – often part of broader package	– direct subsidy – lowering the relocation costs – attempt to correct market imperfections and lower the transaction costs	– hybrid of the remaining types – could be granted on individual basis (e.g. market preference) or be generic and available to all companies willing to invest in the area (e.g. infrastructure)

Source: Own compilation, based on Navaretti and Venables (2004), OECD (2015), UNCTAD (2018)

Table 2.2 Regional and sectoral incentives

Objective	Rationale	Incentives offered
Regional incentives	Shared infrastructure, equity considerations	Exemption from import duties on capital goods, equipment or raw materials, parts and inputs related to the production process; accelerated depreciation on machinery; income tax reduction/tax holiday; investment and reinvestment allowances; allowances for staff training, loss carry forward and carry back for income tax purpose; preferential treatment of capital gains
Sectoral investment	Spillover effects, industrial strategy and policy, national security	

Source: Compilation based on UNCTAD (2000, p. 17)

In this situation the policies and facilitation on the regional level can play a critical role in securing the mobile investment project (Harding & Javorcik, 2012; Loewendahl, 2001). In reality, also in CEE, governments adopt a mixed approach reflecting general national fiscal regimes, where regional and local authorities exercise power over selected tax issues such as real estate tax, land tax and others.

In the context of proposed approach to place promotion, the flexibility of the incentive regime is also important—an issue often omitted by the current literature. Whether nationally, regionally or locally granted, the incentives can be set at fixed levels (absolute or relative) for investments meeting particular conditions such as the number of created workplaces or amount of invested capital in particular sectors. Fiscal incentives are by nature less flexible than financial ones (Lim, 2005), however, this refers to the process of their design and change and not the approach in their application. The authorities may also choose to operate more elastic incentive schemes and decide on the level of public support on an individual basis. Often a mixed approach might be adopted with set incentive ceilings allowing room for individual negotiations.

In a promotional sense, incentives should be perceived as 'sales promotion' (Table 2.3); however, in more flexible regimes, where the level of public support is negotiated individually, their role resembles 'personal selling' activities. The importance and the potential risks of investment incentives in a regional context are best exemplified by a case presented by Zanatta, Costa, and Filippov (2006, p. 4).

Table 2.3 Tools and channels in investment promotion mix

Elements of promotion mix	promotional tools and channels in the FDI context
Advertising	Range of media channels (including FDI and sector-specific media): TV, radio, press (including online), leaflets, posters, billboards, promotional literature (e.g. sectoral studies), novelty items/gadgets, logos, slogans
Sales promotion	Promotional packages including investment incentives—Tax exemptions, (in)direct subsidies, some services including supply chain development, matching prospective investors with local partners and fostering their cooperation, acquiring permits and approvals from various governmental agencies
Personal selling	Participation in trade fairs, investment fairs and exhibitions, road-shows, seminars, investment and trade missions, negotiations, some services including preparation of itineraries for visits of prospective investors, conducting feasibility studies
Publicity and PR	Media: Editorials, news stories; special events (sports, cultural, investor-oriented) organisation and sponsoring; press conferences; lobbying
Direct marketing	Establishing contact directly with selected companies: Direct mailing, calling, in-house seminar visits, sales presentations, database management
Interactive marketing	Dedicated website, electronic media (CD, interactive TV, etc.) online advertising

This is not a complete list but a selection of possible channels, tools and activities. While some of the tools can be deployed in various promotion mix elements, only the primary one was indicated

Source: own compilation based on Wells and Wint (2000), Belch and Belch (2004), MIGA (2006), World Bank (2012), OECD (2018)

In 1999, Ford had already identified a location for its new assembly plant in the Brazilian South state of Rio Grande do Sul. When the new state government decided to review the terms of the contract considering it too costly for the state Ford decided to look for a different location. Subsequently several other Brazilian states started to compete against each other, each making alluring offers to Ford. The Northwest state of Bahia won the war, by offering Ford a broad incentive package encompassing land and special incentives from the National Automotive Regime, despite the fact that the programme had been discontinued in 1998. The federal government backed Bahia's offer to Ford, reopening the Automotive Regime for one more year and throwing in credits from the National Bank for Economic and Social Development (BNDES). Thus Ford decided to move to Bahia instead of Rio Grande do Sul.

This example demonstrates the complicated relationships between various levels of public authorities and their impact on the FDI attraction process. It also reveals the political and economic complexity of investment incentives and their potential to reinforce the intra-national competition. The risk of "bidding wars" is especially high when individual projects of significant size fitting in with regional development objectives are involved (OECD, 2003). However, FDI attraction strategies based solely on grant handouts may end up being counterproductive, as the companies will be prone to leave the location after the grant has been spent in order to chase the next hot deal (Quelch & Jocz, 2005).

The competition between the different regions in Brazil illustrates how on the national level such intra-national rivalry is a zero-sum game, where one region's win can only happen at another's loss. However, as pointed out by Hoover (1975), such a situation may have some advantages—particularly for competently administered areas. Most importantly, it leads to an increase in efficiency of public authorities' spending and improvement in public services. It fosters upgrading of human capital and protection and improvement of regional amenities. On a micro level, it stimulates entrepreneurial and innovative behaviours and encourages cooperation between businesses—all of which are in the regional (and national) interest.

2.4.2 Communication Instruments and Channels of Regional Promotion

The carriers of place promotional information are largely derived from corporate practices and adjusted accordingly. However, current place marketing literature does not provide enough empirical evidence to allow a thorough analysis of usability or effectiveness of any of the promotional tools. Consequently, such an examination ought to be hypothetical and incomplete. Nevertheless, at this stage it is helpful to review the FDI promotional mix and explore the potential it offers.

As illustrated by Table 2.3, places can choose to employ a selection of various promotional tools and measures reflective of their targeting strategy and influenced by overall investment promotion approach. Different set of tools will be useful in securing call-centre investment, a pharmaceutical R&D centre or a car assembly facility. The main publicity-oriented and awareness-building elements include advertising in various media, place logos, slogans, public relations, TV programmes, songs, flagship development projects, flamboyant architectural and urban design statements, trade fairs, cultural and sporting spectacles, novelty icons, heritage, public art, discreet lobbying of decision-makers and much else besides (Fitzsimons, 1995; Kulchina, 2014; Ward, 1998). The aim of all those is invariably to create and deepen the knowledge and understanding of the place and secure positive public relations by communicating its advantages and achievements. Adequate place promotion activities (in a narrow understanding, i.e. communication: advertising, PR), on a general level, should aim to communicate the policies and actions undertaken by public authorities. They require precise definitions of interdependent variables such as target group, message content and channels of communication.

The presented set (although largely indicative and by no means complete) has not always been this varied. Initially places relied heavily on simple advertising techniques, and only with the emergence and later developments of other promotional tools have they been adopted to suit places' needs (Pasquinelli & Teräs, 2013; Rupik, 2005; Ward, 1998).

Yet, *advertising* remains the most popular tool of place promotion, and its main objective is to introduce and present a place to its potential customers (Czornik, 2000; Kotler & Armstrong, 2005). Advertising is the primary tool creating a place's image and symbolic appeals. It is fundamental in raising awareness of what a place has to offer, particularly as its products and services are difficult to differentiate on functional attributes (Belch & Belch, 2004).

Advertising is a pervasive means that allows multiple repetitions of the message and enables the place customer to receive and compare the messages of other competitors. As a highly public mode of communication, advertising provides the potential place customers with a common message ensuring they know that their motivation for choosing the location will be widely understood.

Simultaneously, it also presents the opportunity to dramatise the place and its potential via the artful use of print, sound and colour, although its success at expressiveness may distract from the message. Being impersonal and unable to engage in a dialogue with its audience, advertising is less compelling than personal presentation requiring direct and quick responses from the audience—as is the case in (for instance) direct marketing or personal selling (Kotler et al., 1999).

The choice of particular means of advertising depends not only on potential customers' characteristics and interests, but also on campaign budget and the actual message that is to be conveyed to the target groups. Promoting the place's image requires different approaches and tools than the advertising of particular place assets. Another determinant of the tools being used is the stage of the potential customer decision-making process (Ashworth & Voogd, 1990). Essentially places aim to persuade decision-makers or those who have influence over their decisions, therefore by its nature, place advertising resembles business-to-business and trade advertising practices (Belch & Belch, 2004).

An important advantage of advertising is its cost-effectiveness, which makes it a very popular tool amongst place promoters who often spend considerable amounts of money on image-creation practices. For example, in the late 1980s Cleveland and Chicago campaigns reached $1.1 million and $1 million, respectively, while in the 1990s the Forward Atlanta campaign has been running at $1–2 million annually. Within the UK, the Urban Development Corporations (UDC) by the early 1990s were spending 2.5% of their budgets on advertising. The highest spending UDC, the London Docklands Development Corporation, spent £28 million on advertising and publicity between 1981 and 1992. By 1994 its annual budget had risen to nearly £4 million and its typical advertising spending varied between 1% and 4% of total expenditure, which was more than on community programmes (Ward, 1998). Media advertising such as TV, print or radio remains popular particularly amongst NIPAs—according to OECD (2018) 61% of them use international and domestic media, despite relatively high costs and limited targeting possibilities. For smaller organisations, including regional ones, most of the promotional activities are limited to advertising, while in order to secure the expected response from the targeted groups, the remaining promotional tools and channels also need to be utilised.

Comparably to advertising, *publicity* involves non-personal communication to mass audiences, but unlike advertising, in most cases, it comes free of charge. Place authorities seek to obtain media attention and get them to cover or run a favourable story on the place and its sub-products to affect awareness, knowledge, opinions and consequently the behaviour of targeted audiences. It is important to differentiate between publicity and *public relations* (PR), which involves broader activities including systematic and planned distribution of information expected to control and manage the image and nature of publicity a place receives (Clow & Baack, 2018).

Publicity and PR entail probably the widest range of activities performed by the place authorities and other agencies somehow involved with place promotion. The most important tools of PR include press relations, event publicity and lobbying. As Kotler et al. (1999) argue, editorial copy has five times more power in influencing the audience than advertising. PR advantages stem from the level of credibility—news stories and articles authored by independent journalists are considered to be more trustworthy than pre-ordered, designer ads (Clow & Baack, 2018). Additionally it is much cheaper, therefore more and more commonly used (Kulchina, 2014; Ward, 1998). PR indirect activities have an ability to reach the prospects that stay away from salespeople (place representatives) and advertisements, yet still, comparably to advertising, PR has the potential to dramatise the place. In so doing, the campaigns usually omit negative features of the place but always accentuate the positive ones. However, the media are beyond control of individuals and agencies promoting the place; therefore, there are numerous problems and risks with uncontrolled messages being presented, which from the promotional perspective are not useful, and often could be damaging for the place image and overall promotional efforts (Papadopoulos & Heslop, 2002).

Sales promotion comprise three main components—communication, invitation and incentive. Communication relies on the various means of sales promotion (Table 2.3) to gain potential customers' attention and provide them with information that may lead to greater interest in the place. These also include a unique invitation to engage in direct transaction. While advertising gives a reason for target groups to "purchase", sales promotion presents an incentive to "purchase", hence the inclusion of investment incentives in this channel of promotion as proposed in the framework above (Clow & Baack, 2018; Kotler et al., 1999).

Two main categories of sales promotion can be distinguished: first, consumer-oriented activities are targeted directly at the final users; and second, trade-oriented sales promotion is aimed at wholesalers and intermediaries. Thus, in the investment attraction context, places' sales promotion should be based on consumer-oriented activities; however, as will be discussed later, there is a need for places to devise measures aimed at persuading organisations and individuals advising on and influencing MNEs' location selection process.

Individual confrontation, cultivation and guaranteed response are considered to be the main advantages of *personal selling* techniques. In the investment context, the main tools of this promotion mix element, starting with more general and finishing with precisely targeted ones, include participation in sectoral and general investment trade fairs and exhibitions (e.g. MIPIM in Cannes, Global City in Lyon, Expo Real in Munich, Central European Property and Investment Fair in Warszawa, Real Estate World series, URBEST in Metz); organisation of seminars, trade and investment missions, road-shows; and conducting feasibility studies and negotiations.

Personal contact offers communication flexibility, provides the opportunity of quick responses by both parties involved and allows for the adjustment of the possible offer (Belch & Belch, 2004). Frequently, the established contacts are further cultivated to often become long-term relationships between the regional authority and its customers (Kotler et al., 1999; OECD, 2018). The major disadvantages of that tool include the need for primary research and selection to be carried out before establishing the contact, and its selectiveness. However, such selectiveness offers the potential to win over the investor with the carefully tailored offer. Furthermore, as Quelch and Jocz (2005, p. 235) indicate, the tool also has some potential in place for image building, for "despite the potency of the electronic communications in the global village, it is, in the final analysis, the quality of personal one-to-one interactions that forms the most lasting perceptions of the country".

Comparably the application of *direct marketing* in place promotion, especially aimed at FDI attraction, requires precise targeting and needs to be preceded by a thorough research process. However, this promotion mix element carries several characteristics that make the effort worthwhile. It provides the agency with the control over who is getting the message and allows customisation of it depending on the target's specific features. Moreover, the person (company) receiving the message can interact and communicate directly with the agency, ask questions and offer suggestions. The agency is able to measure the response instantly and determine the improvements to be made in the promotion activities to grant its success. But perhaps, the most important characteristic of direct marketing is the ability to create a relationship, which can be a promising start to winning the investment (OECD, 2018; World Bank, 2012).

The last of the promotional elements is also the latest to be added to the mix and was brought about by the recent advancements in communication technologies. *Interactive marketing*, unlike traditional forms of promotion, allows the users to perform a variety of functions, including customisation of the information they want to receive, alterations of the information and images, making inquiries and responding to questions (Clow & Baack, 2018). The most popular medium is the Internet. Since the mid-1990s, place promotion sites have proliferated on the World Wide Web. In general, as the Internet itself, these appeared initially in the USA, but their numbers have since increased significantly worldwide. Websites provide relatively cheap and effective means of delivering the promotional message to unrestricted numbers of potential place customers. Generally, however, until recently the tourism-themed websites were usually more developed than those promoting business investments. Additionally, websites may be less effective in active promotion since inherently they rely on potential investors seeking information (Ward, 1998; World Bank, 2012).

Direct marketing and personal selling measures are more efficient, therefore more commonly used in investment generation activities. Comparably, advertising and PR instruments are normally employed in awareness-raising and image-building actions. The remaining objective of FDI promotion, investment servicing, is achieved through a mix of personal selling and sales promotion measures. The usefulness and applicability of each tool and channel of promotion are further influenced by the characteristics of the target group and the place's overall approach to investment promotion.

2.5 Conclusions

The chapter provided a discussion of the development of *place marketing* and a critical assessment of the notion itself, as well as its elements. Further, it introduced the concept of *place promotion* and explored it within the marketing framework, stressing the complexity of the process and its components in the FDI context. The critical discussion of these issues addressed the initial set of research questions about the nature of place promotion from the perspective of investment attraction. It also offered a partial response to questions about the relationship between regional promotion and the wider development of a region.

The key critique of the *place marketing* concept focuses on limited empirical testing and evidence supporting the concepts directly derived from marketing literature and applied to various place development policy areas, and overemphasis of image-related issues as determinants of places' success. Further points of critique are associated with the lack of recognition of different scales of places and the consequences of it; inconsistent terminology, conceptualisation and delimitation of the scope of *place marketing*, and vague, if existent, effectiveness measures. Finally, the novelty and originality of the concept remains unclear.

The innovative and panacea-like nature of *place marketing* has been largely exaggerated. The concept, rather than offering pioneering solutions and approaches to the development of places, either oversimplifies their nature or presents best practices in policy design and implementation that have been in use for a considerable amount of time and advances continually. Additionally, the applicability of the uniformed rules of the concept at various spatio-administrative scales is unclear. This underlines the nature of existing writing which scarcely is empirically based.

Conversely, the mere existence of the idea is proof of a need for even more 'target group' driven approaches of development policies in an era of ever-increasing competition between nations, regions and cities.

References

Asheim, B., Cooke, P., & Martin, R. (Eds.). (2006). *Clusters and regional development: Critical reflections and explorations*. London: Routledge.

Ashworth, G. J., & Voogd, H. (1990). *Selling the city: Marketing approaches in public sector urban planning*. London: Belhaven Press.

Ashworth, G. J., & Voogd, H. (1994). Marketing and place promotion. In J. R. Gold & S. V. Ward (Eds.), *Place promotion; the use of publicity and marketing to sell towns and regions*. Chichester: John Wiley & Sons.

Beinart, J. (2001). Image construction in premodern cities. In L. J. Vale & S. B. Warner Jr. (Eds.), *Imagining the city—Continuing struggles and new directions*. New Brunswick, NJ: CUPR.

Belch, G. E., & Belch, M. A. (2004). *Advertising and promotion: An integrated marketing communications perspective*. Boston: McGraw-Hill.

Bialasiewicz, L. (2002). Upper Silesia: Rebirth of a regional identity in Poland. *Regional and Federal Studies, 12*(2), 111–132.

Blomström, M., & Kokko, A. (2003). *The economics of foreign direct investment incentives*. Working Paper 168, Stockholm School of Economics, Stockholm.

Bonetti, E., & Masiello, B. (2014). Attracting R&D foreign direct investment through an evolutionary model of place marketing. The case of Ireland. *International Journal of Management Cases, 16*(4), 4–17.

Borchert, J. G. (1994). *Urban marketing: A review, Abhandlungen—Antropogeographie Insitut für Geographische Wissenschaften, Band 52*. Berlin: FU Berlin.

Brassington, F., & Pettitt, S. (2003). *Principles of marketing*. Harlow: Prentice Hall.

Capik, P. (2007). On scale and the unclear nature of place branding. *Regions, 268*(1), 22–23.

Cleave, E., Godwin, A., Sadler, R., & Gilliland, J. (2016). The role of place branding in local and regional economic development: Bridging the gap between policy and practicality. *Regional Studies, Regional Science, 3*(1), 207–228.

Clow, K. E., & Baack, D. (2018). *Integrated advertising, promotion, and marketing communications* (8th ed.). New York: Pearson.
Czornik, M. (2000). *Promocja miasta*. Katowice: AE.
Denison, T., & McDonald, M. (1995). The role of marketing past, present and future. *Journal of Marketing Practice: Applied Marketing Science, 1*(1), 54–76.
Dogaru, T., Burger, M., Karreman, B., & Van Oort, F. (2015). Functional and sectoral division of labour within central and eastern European countries: Evidence from greenfield FDI. *Tijdschrift voor economische en socialte geografie, 106*(1), 120–129.
Fitzsimons, D. S. (1995). Planning and promotion: City reimaging in the 1980s and 1990s. In W. J. V. Neill, D. S. Fitzsimons, & B. Murtagh (Eds.), *Reimaging the pariah city; urban development in Belfast and Detroit*. Aldershot: Avebury.
Frain, J. (1994). *Introduction to marketing*. London: Pitman.
Fretter, A. D. (1993). Place marketing: A local authority perspective. In G. Kearns & C. Philo (Eds.), *Selling places; the city as cultural capital, past and present*. Oxford: Pergamon Press.
Girard, V. (1997). Marketing terytorialny i planowanie strategiczne. In T. Domański (Ed.), *Marketing terytorialny—strategiczne wyzwanie dla miast i regionów*. Łódź: Uniwersytet Łódzki.
Gold, J. R., & Ward, S. V. (1994). Forward. In *Place promotion; the use of publicity and marketing to sell towns and regions*. Chichester: John Wiley & Sons.
Harding, T., & Javorcik, B. (2012). *Investment promotion and FDI inflows: Quality matters*. University of Oxford Department of Economics Discussion Paper Series, No.612.
Hoover, E. M. (1975). *An introduction to regional economics* (2nd ed.). New York: Alfred A. Knopf.
Kotler, P. (1972). A generic concept of marketing. *Journal of Marketing, 36*, 46–54.
Kotler, P., Apslund, C., Rein, I., & Haider, D. H. (1999). *Marketing places—Europe: How to attract investments, industries, residents and visitors to cities, communities, regions and nations in Europe*. London: Financial Times-Prentice Hall.
Kotler, P., & Armstrong, G. (2001). *Principles of marketing*. Upper Saddle River, NJ: Prentice Hall.
Kotler, P., & Armstrong, G. (2005). *Marketing: An introduction*. Upper Saddle River, NJ: Pearson-Prentice Hall.
Kotler, P., & Gertner, D. (2002). Country as brand, product and beyond: A place marketing and brand management perspective. *Brand Management, 9*(4–5), 249–261.

Kotler, P., Haider, D. H., & Rein, I. (1993). *Marketing places: Attracting investment, industry and tourism to cities, states and nations*. New York: The Free Press.

Kotler, P., & Levy, J. S. (1969). Broadening the concept of marketing. *Journal of Marketing, 33*, 10–15.

Kulchina, E. (2014). Media coverage and location choice. *Strategic Management Journal, 35*(4), 596–605.

Lever, J. (2001). *The effectiveness of place imagery in English local authority inward investment promotion—An evaluation*. MPhil Thesis, Manchester Metropolitan University, Manchester.

Lim, S. H. (2005). Foreign investment impact and incentive: A strategic approach to the relationship between the objectives of foreign investment policy and their promotion. *International Business Review, 14*, 61–76.

Loewendahl, H. (2001). A framework for FDI promotion. *Transnational Corporations, 10*(1), 1–42.

Madsen, H. (1992). Place marketing in Liverpool: A review. *International Journal of Urban and Regional Research, 16*, 633–640.

Markowski, T. (2002). Marketing miasta. In *Marketing terytorialny, Studia KPZK*. Warszawa: PAN.

Merlevede, B., & Schoors, K. (2004). *Determinants of FDI in transition countries*. Economic, Econometric and Cross-Disciplinary Aspects of European Union Enlargement Conference, Florence.

Monaghan, S., Gunnigle, P., & Lavelle, J. (2014). 'Courting the multinational': Subnational institutional capacity and foreign market insidership. *Journal of International Business Studies, 45*(2), 131–150.

Multilateral Investment Guarantee Agency (MIGA). (2006). *FDI promotion*. Retrieved November 29, 2006, from www.fdipromotion.com/toolkit/user/content_page.cfm

Navaretti, G. B., & Venables, A. J. (2004). *Multinational firms in the world economy*. Princeton, NJ: Princeton University Press.

OECD. (2003). *Checklist for foreign direct investment incentives policies*. Paris: OECD Publications.

OECD. (2015). *Policy framework for investment 2015 edition*. Paris: OECD Publishing. Retrieved from https://doi.org/10.1787/9789264208667-en

OECD. (2018). *Mapping of investment promotion agencies in OECD countries*. Retrieved from www.oecd.org/investment/Mapping-of-Investment-Promotion-Agencies-in-OECD-Countries.pdf

Paasi, A., & Metzger, J. (2017). Foregrounding the region. *Regional Studies, 51*(1), 19–30.

Paddison, R. (1993). City marketing, image reconstruction and urban regeneration. *Urban Studies, 30*(2), 339–350.

Papadopoulos, N., & Heslop, L. (2002). Country equity and country branding: Problems and prospects. *Brand Management, 9*(4–5), 294–314.

Pasquinelli, C., & Teräs, J. (2013). Branding knowledge-intensive regions: A comparative study of Pisa and Oulu high-tech brands. *European Planning Studies, 21*(10), 1611–1629.

Pike, A., Rodríguez-Pose, A., & Tomaney, J. (2016). *Local and regional development* (2nd ed.). London: Routledge.

Quelch, J., & Jocz, K. (2005). Positioning the nation-state. *Place Branding and Public Diplomacy, 1*(3), 229–237.

Rainisto, S. K. (2003). *Success factors of place marketing: A study of place marketing practices in northern Europe and the United States*. Espoo: Helsinki.

Rudolf, W. (1999). *Marketing terytorialny jako rynkowo zorientowana filozofia zarządzania miastem i regionem, Prace z Zakresu Ekonomii i Politologii, nr 1* (pp. 57–70). Kielce: WSEiA.

Rupik. (2005). Rozwój koncepcji marketingu terytorialnego—analiza historyczna. In H. Szulce & M. Florek (Eds.), *Marketing terytorialny; możliwości aplikacji, kierunki rozwoju*. Poznań: AE Poznań.

Sienkiewicz, P., & Kowalik, A. (2004). Zarządzanie marketingowe jako narzędzie wspierania konkurencyjności regionów. Retrieved March 1, 2004, from www.finanse.info.pl/artykuly/5146.htm

Stawicka, M. (2006). *Atrakcyjność Inwestycyjna Polski*. Warszawa: CeDeWu.PL.

Swianiewicz, P. (2014). An empirical typology of local government systems in eastern Europe. *Local Government Studies, 40*(2), 292–311.

Szczepański, M. (2004). Regional identity: Within the sphere of basic concepts and research methodology. In W. Łukowski (Ed.), *Tożsamość regionów w Polsce i przestrzeni Europejskiej*. Katowice: Ruch Autonomii Ślaska.

Szromnik, A. (1997). Marketing terytorialny—geneza, rynki docelowe i podmioty oddziaływania. In T. Domański (Ed.), *Marketing terytorialny—strategiczne wyzwania dla miast i regionów*. Łódź: Uniwersytet Łódzki.

UNCTAD. (2000). *Tax incentives and foreign direct investment—A global survey, ASIT advisory studies no.16*. Geneva: United Nations.

UNCTAD. (2018). *Word investment report: Investment and new industrial policies*. Geneva: United Nations.

van den Berg, L., Braun, E., & Otgaar, A. H. J. (2002). *Sports and city marketing in European cities*. Rotterdam: Euricur.

van den Berg, L., Klaassen, L., & Meer, J. (1990). *Marketing metropolitan regions*. Rotterdam: Euricur.

Ward, S. V. (1998). *Selling places, the marketing and promotion of towns and cities 1850–2000*. London: E&FN Spon.

Wells, T. L., Jr., & Wint, A. G. (2000). *Marketing a country—Promotion as a tool for attracting foreign direct investment*. FIAS Occasional Paper 13, IFC-MIGA, Washington.

World Bank. (2012). *Investment climate: Global investment promotions best practices*. Washington: The World Bank Group.

Wu, F. (2000). Place promotion in Shanghai, PRC. *Cities, 17*(5), 349–361.

Young, C., & Kaczmarek, S. (1999). Changing the perception of the post-socialistic city: Place promotion and imagery in Lodz, Poland. *The Geographical Journal, 165*(2), 183–189.

Young, C., & Lever, J. (1997). Place promotion, economic location and the consumption of city image. *Tijdshrift voor Economische en Sociale Geografie, 88*(4), 332–341.

Zanatta, M., Costa, I., & Filippov, S. (2006). *Foreign direct investment: Key issues for promotion agencies*. UNU Policy Brief, No.10, UNU-MERIT, Maastricht.

Zimmerbauer, K. (2011). From image to identity: Building regions by place promotion. *European Planning Studies, 19*(2), 243–260.

3

Regional Product, Its Image and the Politics of Investment Attraction

3.1 Regional Product

Before promotion can start, it is vital to know what is actually being promoted and how the consumption of it occurs (Ashworth & Voogd, 1990; Ward, 1998). It is in this respect that promotion is strongly linked to another 'P' in the marketing mix concept, namely the product.

Kotler and Armstrong (2005, p. 223) define product as "anything that can be offered to a market for attention, acquisition, use or consumption and that might satisfy a want or need". In this sense, and also from a perspective of place promotion, apart from tangible goods, *product* also includes services. For example, a car essentially provides the service of transportation, comparably to a worker providing the service of labour. The concept of *product* embraces physical objects, services, events, persons, places, organisations, ideas or combinations of these items (Clow & Baack, 2018; Jobber, 2007).

Defining or even describing place product causes many conceptual problems. There is no clear consensus and different approaches emerge from the literature. Some adopt a spatio-structural perspective, while others offer function or target market-based definitions.

P. Capik, *Foreign Investment Promotion*, https://doi.org/10.1007/978-3-030-13658-1_3

Places are locations and areas, and they are "peculiar quasi-products" (Markowski, 1997, p. 50) which influences their promotion. A region cannot be simply considered as a product in a "commercial sense" (Parkerson & Saunders, 2005; Pike, 2011; van den Berg, Braun, & Otgaar, 2002), and consequently, Borchert (1994) observes a number of contradictions while considering place product within the marketing mix framework. The diversity of places, the networks of relations between them, the complexity of problems and objectives, the varieties of institutions involved with the regional development make the idea of commodified region inapplicable in practice, unless defined more specifically, with recognition of its elements and prospective customers. It is clear that a destination differs from other products, in that it is not an individual product but rather a composition, a bundle of different material and non-material elements, some of which are often beyond the control of those promoting it (Florek, 2005b; Morgan, Pritchard, & Piggot, 2002). Place product therefore is best identified by the facilities or activities it accommodates or broadly as an entity. For example, Domański (1997) and Rainisto (2003) argue that place product is the total service and product offering of the place. Others (e.g. Ashworth & Voogd, 1990; Markowski, 2002) offer a more analytical perspective and separate the urban product into two main parts: contributory elements (e.g. specific services, isolated city characteristics, the image) and the nuclear product—the city as a whole. This city-based idea can also be applied on the regional level.

Van den Berg et al. (2002) offer a yet more detailed perspective and approach the question of place product from the perspective of sub-products' spatial concentration and their intensity. The authors distinguish three urban product levels transferable to the regional scale: facility, cluster and city (region). The facility level, that is, the tangible offer includes museums, shopping centres, infrastructure, investment incentive schemes—the individual features determining place attractiveness for the chosen target market. The cluster level refers to the spatial concentration of 'facility' and on the regional scale, this includes industrial parks, special economic zones and harbours but also cities with a dominant function. On the third level, comparably to the idea of nuclear product, a region is regarded as a 'brand' characterising a range of regional sub-products.

Ashworth and Voogd (1990) further stress the complex nature of place product in their discussion of applicability of buyer benefit analysis—a process of dividing the market into groups according to the different benefits that consumers seek from the product (Kotler & Armstrong, 2005, p. 194). The authors demonstrate that there are many products offered simultaneously to the same customer through the same service. Those products and services additionally may be valued differently by the different customer groups. For instance, museums for local inhabitants could provide a pleasant family pastime while for visitors they often constitute the main motivation to visit the place. At the same time both groups benefit from the opportunity of mixing with high culture and its educational aspect. Consequently, the urban places offer different values for the different target groups. While the tourists will be looking for cultural and entertainment attractions, the investors would rather be concerned with adequate workforce availability, transport and market capacity (Daniels, Radebaugh, & Sullivan, 2019; Navaretti & Venables, 2004).

A place is not only an arena and container of activity-based products, but also a specific product itself. It is promoted to various sets of customers, which means that the same space, its attributes and facilities are expected to simultaneously attract possibly conflicting clients—holiday-makers and industry, new settlers and financial headquarters. Such "multi-selling" is possible, because the trading in places does not involve any physical transfers and the sale of it does not affect the stock nor does the consumption by one customer limit the consumption by another (Ashworth & Voogd, 1994). However, this is often only partially true. The actual stock of place remains constant; however, the possibilities of purchase for future clients are decreasing in their quantity and quality, that is, places' capacity is being filled. An investment promotion agency (IPA) can efficiently provide services to a certain number of investors, before the service quality drops (Loewendahl, 2001; World Bank, 2012). The defined locale can accommodate only a limited number of premises or enterprises; comparably the road network is capable of accommodating a finite number of heavy goods vehicles. The availability of other sub-products, such as a competitively priced labour force, is directly affected by growing numbers of investors locating in the area. The growing Slovak automotive industry exemplifies such a situation. Due to shrinking numbers of suitable labour force, the companies not only try to headhunt employees from their direct competitors (PSA Citroen admitted approaching Volkswagen employees) but also start recruiting in other Slovak regions and the neighbouring nations (*Rzeczpospolita*, 2005). Furthermore, the located activities reciprocally influence themselves, and the success of a place sold simultaneously to variety of target groups is uncertain (Kotler, Apslund, Rein, & Haider, 1999). Different scales of places are influenced by those factors to varying degrees. Naturally, a region, given its size, is influenced to a lesser extent than a neighbourhood within a city, but more than the territory of a country.

The scale in place product promotion indeed plays a crucial role. On a national scale the country could be perceived as a product, while regions would constitute a group of sub-products, and cities and communities would be further down in such hierarchy. All these may reinforce each other, be largely indifferent or contradict and interfere with each other (Ashworth & Voogd, 1990; Mudambi et al., 2018). In practice usually all three relationships appear continuously evolving and changing. Generally, and as will be demonstrated later, the scale increases complexity and provides more risks of conflicting interests.

Therefore, product development is an additional controversial issue associated with regional promotion. The development and possible fall of regions depend on a multiplicity of factors (Pike, Rodríguez-Pose, & Tomaney, 2016). Regions are largely products of past processes, inherited from previous generations. They can sell only what they already possess—their environmental, physical, locational and functional attributes, which often are difficult and time-consuming to change (MacKinnon, Dawley, Pike, & Cumbers, 2019). While Ashworth and Voogd (1990) argue that these are only place's resources, in light of Sliepen's concept, the product character of those "contributory" elements needs to be stressed. It is further emphasised when considering the product life cycle which is better applicable on a 'sub-product' rather than 'nuclear' regional product level—the importance of particular sub-products in the location decision-making process (hence the demand for it) changes quicker than the preference for a particular location (nuclear product). Comparably it is relatively quicker to introduce innovation in a single 'contributory element' (or a group of them) such as road infrastructure, property availability or post-investment services, than to change and improve the location on the whole. Major and long-lasting product improvements are more fundamental and have the potential to reposition a place into completely new markets, as exemplified by the case of Birmingham in the UK, where the creation of a conference centre allowed the city to catch the attention of business tourists, the customers it once had no chance of attracting.

In the case of FDI product development refers to supply-side policies that improve the competitive advantage of a location and its attractiveness for the investors. In that sense the FDI product development involves activities in four main (sub-product) areas:

- infrastructure and property development;
- supply chain development;
- innovation development;
- skills development (Loewendahl, 2001; World Bank, 2012).

Thus, FDI place product development, in the case of a region, can be considered as improvements to its components—infrastructure, economic base, environment and society—with the recognition that to change some of them may be more time and resource consuming. The identification of what is easy and what is difficult to change (as indeed is the prioritisation and coordination of change) is a challenge for agencies involved with regional promotion and development (MacKinnon et al., 2019).

There are clear peculiarities in the nature of a place product and hence in the promotion of it, when compared with the tangible, corporate product. As indicated, direct commodification of places suggested by some authors (e.g. Kotler et al., 1999) is too simplistic, as places are multidimensional and complex packages of goods, services and experiences that are consumed in a variety of ways (Gold & Ward, 1994). Furthermore, they are characterised by longevity and lack of flexibility, and cannot be isolated from their environment. The fact is that places provide a "line of products" that are difficult to isolate from their environment and, additionally, are highly interdependent (van den Berg et al., 2002). Further characteristics of place product include intangibility (non-materiality), immobility limiting the possibility of real time comparison with place products elsewhere, complexity and internal variety (e.g. includes non-material services and tangible goods) and varied durability and life expectancy of the sub-products and the mega-product (Florek, 2005b).

The question arises how such compound characteristics of the place product can be portrayed in order to create its functional generalisations, the image of a place. It is the nature of place image, its importance and creation that are discussed next.

3.2 Complexity of Regional Image

The creation and use of place images are possibly the most widely researched and discussed areas within place marketing literature (e.g. Barke & Harrop, 1994; Bradley, Hall, & Harrison, 2002; Burgess, 1982; Cleave, Godwin, Sadler, & Gilliland, 2016; Gold & Ward, 1994; Pasquinelli & Teräs, 2013; Zimmerbauer, 2011). Initially, the urban-centric studies more recently also debate the national scale, while regional dimension remains largely underexplored. Additionally, there is a deficiency of studies explaining how the images are being consumed at the time when, as has been indicated earlier, place promotion is usually excessively reliant on actions aimed at image (re)creation.

Places have identities that define its essential characteristics, typical features that allow places to differentiate themselves from one another (Barke & Harrop, 1994; Pasquinelli & Teräs, 2013). Image, on contrary, is how the place is being perceived by the outside parties. It is a sum of simplified beliefs, ideas and impressions, feelings and attitudes, pieces of information and associations linked with a place held by its audiences (Anholt, 2010; Florek, 2005b). It can be influenced by 'objective' identity but also images can exist independently of it, as is the case with stereotypes, that is, judgements (positive or negative) based on belief. Stereotypes are emotionally loaded and contradictory to real facts, yet always appear to be completely truthful, and therefore are relevant to regional promotion in two ways. Firstly, promotional materials, like other forms of communicated substance, assist in upholding of the stereotypes as copywriters often use them to communicate with their audience. Secondly, stereotypes are being used to counter-balance other stereotypes

(Anholt, 2010; Gold & Ward, 1994). Stereotypes are more general while images are rather individualised perceptions of a place and its population. Also, stereotypes tend to remain unchanged over long periods of time, which highlights their detachment from people's lived experiences. Therefore, even if generally positive, stereotypes are not always helpful in creating desirable perceptions of a place (Schatz, 2013).

An image, Kotler et al. (1999) argue, is a critical feature of a place determining the way inhabitants, business and tourists respond to it. A place's image is multifaceted, includes both factual and affective information (Anholt, 2010; Papadopoulos & Heslop, 2002) and reflects individuals' experiences and relationship with the place. "The physical settings of a place encourage people to identify with the place, as long as they reflect spatial identity and urban values, as an area that provides a feeling of sense of belonging" (Saleh, 2001, p. 328).

The linking of the deeper meanings of a place with the promotional objectives is rarely done in a convincing way. All too often images exclude much that makes up the reality of a place, or they appreciate the aspects of a place that narrow its meaning (Anholt, 2010; Schatz, 2013). Images are constructed from different sources of information, ranging from companies' marketing distribution to perceptions of environmental quality, from personal experience of living in different places to prejudices stemming from stereotyped images used by the media (Kulchina, 2014). They may often be embedded in a variety of cultural milieus including literature, legends, poetic metaphor and even planning documents. Images depend on a multiplicity of factors that are difficult or indeed often impossible to control (Papadopoulos & Heslop, 2002; Supphellen & Nygaardsvik, 2002). Further, not everything that shapes a place image "is done with deliberate intention of influencing it. A lot can happen by accident and deliberate actions often have unintended consequences" (Anholt & Hildreth, 2005, p. 169). Finally, those who are responsible for place image, its creation and communication do not always know how to handle the task (Capik, 2007; Go & Govers, 2013).

Ashworth and Voogd (1990) distinguish three target group images: entrepreneurial, tourist and residential, while Madsen (1992) argues these are only the ideal types, and as his study of Liverpool's promotion campaign indicates, all three need to be incorporated in a successful place promotion. In other words a tourist can be a potential investor, who will come to the area when they know it is good for living. Yet, the attempts to create a single image of the place carry a risk of oversimplification, and different strategies may need to be developed to respond to the complexity of the targeted groups (Go & Govers, 2013). Approaching this issue from the national perspective of Iceland, Gudjonssen (2005) indicates how tourist-preferred images might collide with other sectors characteristic for the national economy including aluminium production, whaling and fishing industries.

Kotler et al. (1999) offer another classification of place images, applicable to any of the target group types, and define five possible image situations:

- overly attractive image—places do not need to promote their images anymore since their (environmental or tourist) capacity is exceeded;
- positive image—when places do not need to change their images but should actively promote it;
- weak image—dominant in most places, needs to be fostered and promoted more aggressively;
- contradictory images—as the effect of either incoherent campaigns or positive images being overwhelmed by the negative ones;
- negative image—places suffer from adverse perceptions and attitudes, hence need to make extensive efforts to overhaul them.

Considering the three latter types the primary objective of place promotion campaign is to construct a new image of a place to substitute either vague or negative images held by current or potential residents, investors and visitors. Image promotional campaigns in such cases need to be performed carefully, and avoid "over-promising and under-delivering" (Fitzsimons, 1995, p. 43). If the reality does not correspond with the image presented, the audiences attracted by the promotion may become cynical. If the image campaign is meant to produce sustainable and shareable benefits, it needs to be both credible and backed up by substance (Schatz, 2013).

On the other end of the spectrum we find examples where the image has not caught up with reality (Parkerson & Saunders, 2005). For instance, regardless of major changes in local conditions the perception of such places like Gwent in Belgium or Birmingham in England throughout 1990s and early 2000s remained negative (Go & Govers, 2013). Images are difficult and time-consuming to change (van den Berg et al., 2002), so the promotional campaigns should be designed in a way which enables the image to change at least simultaneously with the reality.

Places' images exist through their distinction from other places' images (Ashworth & Voogd, 1990). A place must be conscious of other places' images, often also at a different spatial scale, which in the case of regions in Europe seems to be of great importance. A situation of what Madsen (1992, p. 634) termed "shadow-effect" often occurs when analysing various scales. A place's (community, city) image is overshadowed by another's (usually larger units like region or country) both negative and positive images. Such a situation was present up until recently across the Central-Eastern Europe, where only a few major cities' reputations, notably Prague, Warsaw and Bratislava, were recognised and stimulated mental associations outside their countries. Other places, including regions, tend not to exist in the collective consciousness of the international community, that is, are characterised by weak image (Kotler et al., 1999). Overshadowing also happens on an international scale. Lodge (2002) describes a situation when countries experience negative perceptions originating from their relative locations. A reasonably stable country may be grouped with its unstable neighbours, or a bigger, noisier neighbour may overshadow a small, clever country. Anholt (2006) explores this issue further and in describing the "continent branding effect" argues that many poor countries and their cities have no international image at all and end up sharing their reputations, "often unfairly and inaccurately", with the most prominent and most notorious countries on their continent. "Lagos, like Nigeria, and like most cities and most countries in Africa, suffers from 'continent branding effect': none of these places have been able to create a separate, unique international reputation, and so they are obliged to share a generic continent brand called Africa" (Anholt, 2006, p. 3).

However, overshadowing can also produce positive effects. Quelch and Jocz (2005) demonstrate how local and regional promotion associated with the Olympic Games in Los Angeles, Atlanta and Salt Lake City had an impact on the national image. Such positive *image spillover* was even more significant in the case of smaller host countries, including Greece and Spain, during and after the Athens and Barcelona Olympics (Belloso, 2011).

3.2.1 "I ♥ NY": Use of Slogans, Anchors and Flagships in Image Creation

Complementary to image, a slogan (derived from the Gaelic term for battle cry; a short phrase communicating descriptive or persuasive information about the place) is another compulsory element of promotional activities. In fact many promotional campaigns over the years have been organised around slogans—"Cool Britannia", "Scotland the Brand", "Spain—Everything Under the Sun", "Glasgow's Miles Better". Some of them are more convincing and better crafted (e.g. "New Era. New Attitude. Newcastle") than others (e.g. "Make it in Livingstone", "Do It In Dundee"). Additionally some are based on already existing ones, for example, "I ♥ Cleveland", obviously imitating acclaimed "I ♥ New York". Others try to contradict them—such as Minneapolis' "Move over New York, Apple is our middle name" (Dinnie, 2011; Supphellen & Nygaardsvik, 2002; Ward, 1998).

Arguably slogans play an important role of differentiating the place, and their main purpose is to create both awareness and image of the location. Places are multidimensional and choosing a slogan often proves a difficult task, however a good slogan constitutes a base from which a place's image can be further amplified. Slogans are useful in creating enthusiasm and they help to catch the attention, but to generate significant image effects, they need to be supported by other promotional tools (Kotler et al., 1999). An effective place slogan should meet four criteria. It needs to: (1) coordinate with other place brand identity elements (logo, symbols, name, jingles, packages, etc.); (2) communicate a place's key descriptive features; (3) describe a place's benefits in a short and memorable way; and (4) cause image effects (Supphellen & Nygaardsvik, 2002).

An important instrument in the process of regional promotion, especially when the region already exists on investors' mental map, is what marketers call an "anchor" (Anholt, 2010). It is the characteristics of a place already recognised and accepted by the target group which can be used to tie down new attitudes and behaviours. Because it symbolises something that is already accepted by the potential customer, it arguably could be the starting point of image campaigns. An anchor can be an architectural feature but also an institution, development park or environmental feature, but it needs to be selected in tandem with the identification of the target group and the attempted image.

Moreover, the use of flagship projects, especially in urban regeneration, is a common feature of place promotion. Constituting proof of the change and dynamism of the promoted place, flagship projects are often the most visible elements of promotional materials (Dinnie, 2011; Go & Govers, 2013). In the context of FDI attraction flagship investment projects are often used by promoters in hope of creating demonstration effects, whereby the example of a successful (big or/and well-regarded) investor is believed to testify to the attractiveness of the area and positive attitudes of public authorities (OECD, 2018; Wells & Wint, 2000; World Bank, 2012).

The regional scale implies certain representation problems with the use of both anchors and flagships. The icons need to be chosen carefully in order to be representative for the whole region and not just for the locality they come from. Additionally they need to be consistent with the overall message of the campaign, although as evidence suggests this is not always the case and there have been many logical inconsistencies in promotional efforts of British and other local authorities simultaneously promoting dynamism and heritage, or development possibilities alongside unspoilt landscape (Ashworth & Voogd, 1990).

3.2.2 Image and Investment Attraction

For Quelch and Jocz (2005, p. 234), "It is axiomatic, that a country will benefit from possessing a favourable image". Indeed when investors have limited knowledge or unjustifiably negative perceptions of a location and its advantages, the efforts to generate investment are bound to be less effective. Therefore, as indicated by the Multilateral Investment Guarantee

Agency (MIGA)—World Bank Group organisation dealing with investment guarantees and offering advice for investment promotion agencies—image and also awareness-building activities are arguably the cornerstones of place promotion aimed at investment attraction. Early on this has been indicated by Burgess (1982, p. 2), who argued that "place images may well play an important part in location decisions". Comparably Papadopoulos and Heslop (2002) emphasised that a personal view of "the investor" is pivotal in location decision. Also Burgess and Wood (1988) and Young and Lever (1997) stressed the importance of investors' knowledge and level of familiarity with the location and highlighted that the images of the "destination" held by local and regional firms differ significantly from perceptions held by companies relocating internationally.

The creation of a particular positive image by the promotional agents may act as a location factor for companies in specific sectors, particularly the creative industries. Young and Lever's (1997, p. 338) early study of Manchester's image campaign confirms that "image was of vital importance" in the location decisions of firms working in the media and design industries. However, significantly, the study has also found that the image of Manchester city was considerably less important in the relocation decision-making than assumed by Central Manchester Development Corporation, the city's main promoter.

Investment promotion agencies commonly use various image-building techniques (OECD, 2018; World Bank, 2012), yet Wells and Wint's (2000) research results illustrate that the majority of the IPAs are under no illusion that image promotion individually will generate investment, hence they tend to focus on changing or enhancing the country's image as a place to invest. Those IPAs that expected image-building activities to generate investments directly (e.g. Jamaica National Investment Promotion, Costa Rican Investment Promotion Agency) ended up disappointed that their actions were not successful (Wells & Wint, 2000). Thus, in line with earlier discussion, image building should rather be perceived as an essential component amongst a set of wider activities developed to generate and service FDI (Loewendahl, 2001; MIGA, 2006; OECD, 2018). Promotion cannot only be focused on and limited to image-building activities. It must go beyond that to include interlinked practices ranging from awareness building to detailed offer preparation and negotiations to the provision of a wide array of quality services for the investors. Such a wide range of promotional activities requires careful and logical targeting, the involvement and participation of various agencies, and needs to be conducted with the recognition of the place's competitors. It is the various participants of place promotion process that are discussed next.

3.3 Participants of the Regional Promotion Process

The process of place promotion in broad terms directly involves two groups of participants—the 'producers' or 'sellers' of place and its 'customers', the 'buyers'. Additionally, a third group needs to be acknowledged, for its very existence encourages active promotion in the first place—the 'competitors'. The 'producer' group is internally complex and comprises diverse agencies and organisations on all levels of the administrative hierarchy. 'Customers' group complexity to a degree can be controlled through the level and precision of targeting—the more targeted the promotion activities the more elaborate they are. Targeting limits the number of potential customers, simultaneously increasing the quantity of promotional campaigns, as trying to promote a region to only one group of customers is a rather risky business. At the same time, promoting everything to everybody brings equally little effect (Kotler et al., 1999). The third group—the 'competitors'—has a less direct influence on place's promotion, however it is the understanding of competitors' advantages that allows places to increase their own attractiveness and successfully position themselves.

3.3.1 The Promoters

The organisation of promotion is an important factor determining its success and making demands on organising capacity (Klijn, Eshuis, & Braun, 2012; van den Berg et al., 2002). Promotion results depend on a vision and strategy, public–private networks, leadership, political and societal support and spatial-economic conditions. Often multiple organisations, agents and agencies are directly and indirectly involved with place promotion (Fig. 3.1). This is sometimes not adequately recognised in literature which tends to generalise the issue by personifying the place (as for shorthand, has been done here), that is, stating that "a place" does this or that (e.g. Kotler et al., 1999; Rainisto, 2003). In reality, as evidenced by the subsequent chapters, even when only the main organisation responsible for promotion is considered (e.g. regional authority), the existence and significance of a variety of departments and other smaller units needing to coordinate their activities must be acknowledged (Almond, Ferner, & Tregasis, 2015; Bickl, 2004; Monaghan, Gunnigle, & Lavelle, 2014).

However, in most cases, the pool of organisations involved is greater and, as a result, regional promotion is influenced by and needs to take account of national promotion efforts, as well as individual cities and communities' practices, the coordination of which involves numerous agents (Young, 2005). Moreover, as illustrated by Fig. 3.1, regions are often promoted not only by their authorities but also by private and public enterprises and a variety of institutions, including chambers of commerce, developers, universities and tourism and cultural organisations. The variety of promoters means that inevitably activities of some will be less coordinated and coherent than those of others, which leads Bickl (2004) to distinguish between those actively and consciously promoting the place, and those that by their mere existence contribute to the process, that is, the "image makers" and "image doers".

Comparably in the FDI context, the group of 'place promoters' is internally complex and multilayered. It can include a plethora of organisations ranging from transnational partnerships (e.g. euroregions, Centrope) to very local ones (e.g. local authorities, local chambers of commerce and other business organisations).

Thus, the inherent feature of place promotion (comparably to other issues in regional development and governance) is multiplicity of vertical and diagonal networks and connections (Almond et al., 2015; Monaghan et al., 2014; Young, 2005)—all explored in subsequent parts of the book.

There is no single structure of investment promotion, which would suit all places. The organisation of it varies between countries and reflects key

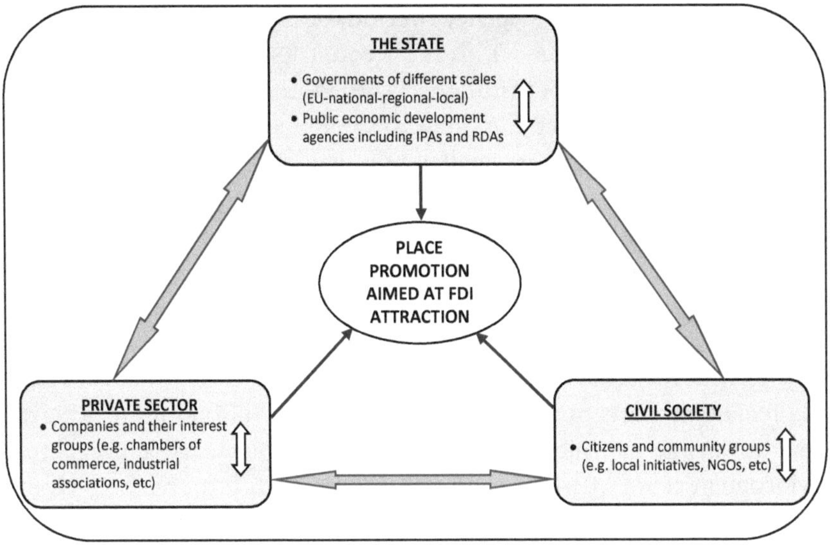

Fig. 3.1 Interactions of place promotion stakeholders in the FDI attraction context. *Source*: Adapted from Bickl (2004, p. 108)

objectives underpinning FDI attraction, size of countries, as well as their administrative governance structures, and in particular the importance and the powers of regions (Loewendahl, 2001; OECD, 2015). Invariably, the organisational structure influences the efficiency of performed actions.

FDI promotion is often executed by a purposefully designated organisation, the investment promotion agency (IPA), whose fundamental task is to facilitate the flow of information to the investors as best it can (considering the limitations of staffing, budget and data resources) (World Bank, 2012). IPAs promote locations to foreign investors by disseminating information about investment opportunities in the country (region), providing services for the investors, contributing to the improvements in the overall investment climate and creating a positive image of the country (region) externally. The powers and authority of IPAs vary, determining the scope of their activities. Some IPAs additionally are involved with export promotion, industrial development, entrepreneurship support and small and medium enterprise development. While many of these functions may be entrusted to a single agency (e.g. SARIO, CzechInvest,

Industrial Development Agency Ireland, Hungarian Investment and Trade Development Agency), in most countries those tasks are distributed across a range of institutions (OECD, 2018; Zanatta, Costa, & Filippov, 2006). Distinct IPAs have been established in large countries such as the UK, but also in smaller ones including Slovakia or Bulgaria. Conversely such large countries as the USA and China until recently did not have national IPAs and instead relied on regional ones (Loewendahl, 2001). This, as suggested by Zanatta et al. (2006), may lead to conflicts as various agencies compete between themselves, weakening the bargaining power of the country as a whole. In fact, the contrary is often true. It lays outwith the scope of responsibilities for the regional IPA to consider the remaining parts of the country over which it has no influence. The vital advantage of regional IPAs is their local knowledge and expertise (Monaghan et al., 2014; OECD, 2003), and such intra-national rivalry between regional IPAs can increase their efficiency and quality of actions, providing them with a competitive edge on the international level. Additionally national IPAs, however strong and competent, often fail to secure an even and adequate distribution of investment across the regions within a country—as is the case for example in the Czech Republic and the UK, where the majority of foreign capital is concentrated in the capital city region.

Whether operating on a regional or national level, the IPAs should be sufficiently autonomous from the authorities, providing the agency with flexibility, making it less prone to political processes and hence increasing its credibility with the investors. Further, the IPAs require links with other place stakeholders (regional, national) both public and private, to coordinate actions and assure "that an area's final offer is more than the sum of its parts" (Loewendahl, 2001, p. 8).

In reality, FDI promotion often occurs in a blurry institutional framework, where functions are divided amongst a multitude of organisations of different forms, often with overlapping jurisdictions (Almond et al., 2015; Zanatta et al., 2006). Furthermore, FDI promotion entails some activities usually attributed to private organisations, for instance advertising and others more typical of public administration, such as negotiations and some of the investment services (OECD, 2018; Wells & Wint, 2000).

In these circumstances some authors argue for an alternative framework of FDI promotion, namely a partnership. Indeed, examining Chilean FDI promotion, Quelch and Jocz (2005) argue that public–private partnership is the most successful way to secure investment. More generally, looking into overall regeneration, Ward (1998) stresses the importance of private sector involvement in public authorities' efforts in the USA and the UK. In this context the partnership is of twofold importance. It plays a role in bringing in new investments, but also it acts as "a litmus test for the reception a future investor might expect, a sign of a degree of local friendliness to external business investors" (Ward, 1998, p. 194). Additionally public–private partnership offers a broader funding base and expertise in the promotional efforts. It also may increase the coherence of actions allowing for efficient use of (usually scarce) resources. Further, partnerships by default contain feedback mechanisms and foster communication between their stakeholders, which contributes to more efficient place product improvements (OECD, 2018; Parkerson & Saunders, 2005; Ward, 1998).

In the context of the argument presented in this book, partnership is potentially relevant in one other aspect. EU-stipulated regional policy and access to structural funds are conditioned by the regional and local governance structures' ability to create and operate within broad partnerships (Guglielmetti, 2009; Herodes, 2011). While such partnerships will be usually specifically created to generate and execute regional development strategy and operational plans, they also create linkages, which potentially could be used for investment promotion purposes.

3.3.2 Customers and Target Groups

The addressees of promotion form another large and internally diversified group participating in the process and it is not satisfactory to identify them merely as mobile companies and tourists. Indigenous inhabitants and particularly local businesses are equally relevant clients, for as early argued by Fretter (1993, p. 168) "It is no use attracting new investments if you cannot keep what you already have".

Due to their heterogeneity, the segmentation of the target markets is a multilevel and complex process. The diverse target groups include decision-makers, opinion-makers within and outwith the location, consumers of local/regional/national produce and services (Ashworth & Voogd, 1990; Szromnik, 1997), corporate headquarters, as well as manufacturers and conventioneers (Kotler et al., 1999; Rainisto, 2003).

According to arguably one of the most imperative marketing principles, selling starts with the customer—the target group. To its residents a region is a place to live, work and relax in. It is also a supplier of a range of facilities (e.g. communal infrastructure) and services such as education and healthcare. To commuters a region is a workplace, to companies it is a place to locate, do business and recruit employees. To tourists and other visitors it offers a combination of culture, education and entertainment (Kotler et al., 1999). Places, thus, supply different functions to a variety of their consumers (van den Berg et al., 2002) who perceive the location in diverse ways. The multiplicity of targets (including the ones that should be avoided), products and services offered make the promotion process a particularly complex one (Florek, 2005b).

The target groups, some authors argue (e.g. Gilmore, 2002), are not explicitly mutually exclusive. However, while naturally some of the places' functions and characteristics will be appreciated simultaneously by several groups (e.g. both inhabitants and companies will welcome access to higher education; tourists, investors and inhabitants will benefit from quality transport infrastructure), in essence equating the three generic types, without recognising their peculiar requirements and internal diversification, is a first step to failure of any promotional effort. In fact, as Skinner (2005) emphasises, it is very likely that different segments may have not merely different but conflicting needs, wants and behaviours. Therefore, "the messages designed to attract each different segment may also have to be vastly different in order to ensure the place is perceived as favourable by each different segment" (Skinner, 2005, p. 301).

Consequently, targeting and proper recognition of customers' needs seem to be crucial for successful regional promotion activities. It dictates the message to be conveyed and also impacts the channels and tools to be used. First, however, it is vital to distinguish the sub-segments within the broad groups. For example, Domański (1997) divides local inhabitants into two major groups bearing distinct characteristics: highly mobile and immobile. Those immobile tend to be elderly, often economically inactive and less entrepreneurial. Growing and competitive places wanting to attract new residents should therefore target their activities at the first group. However, the other group should not be ignored as those individuals can potentially contribute to raising awareness and establishment of positive images amongst the prior cohort.

Foreign direct investors comprise a comparably varied group. Promotion activities, the choice of channels and particular tools to be used are influenced by particular type(s) of investor(s) and a particular type(s) of project(s) for investment. The most generic target groups could be determined based on investors' sector of industry (i.e. sectoral targeting), country of origin and operation (i.e. geographical targeting) and particular qualities of a class of investors (i.e. attributes targeting), such as size, growth rate, export intensity of production, labour intensity of production, level of technology (Harding & Javorcik, 2012; OECD, 2018; Wells & Wint, 2000). All these provide context for the usability and attractiveness of the individual promotional elements, tools and channels discussed above.

Wells and Wint (2000, p. 20) demonstrate how "some promotion agencies adopt a general approach to promotion and others use a mix of techniques that include targeted and general techniques". However, in their study of National Investment Promotion Agencies' targeting strategies, Charlton, Davis, Faye, Haddock, and Lamb (2004) have found that more than 70% of the agencies use industrial sector segmentation, that is, selectively try to attract some industries over others. The most commonly targeted branches are high-value sectors, in particular life sciences and healthcare services, information and communications technology (ICT) and business support services, transport and logistics, infrastructure, agri-business, bio-, green- and nanotechnologies, chemicals, engineering and other advanced manufacturing and high-tech services (OECD, 2018). Moreover, in most cases the NIPA's choice of target industries appears to be closely associated with the characteristics of the domestic economy (Charlton et al., 2004; World Bank, 2012). This indicates a much more logical and coherent approach to FDI promotion than thought earlier, and stresses the usability of place promotion concepts in territorial development (Charlton & Davis, 2006; Harding & Javorcik, 2012).

Some NIPAs focus promotion resources on industries where they could generate the highest volume of inward FDI (i.e. the most mobile sectors, industries in which a country has a comparative advantage). Other NIPAs focus their promotion on improving the quality of FDI flows (i.e. increasing the diversity of the national economic base, and bringing in new technology and skills). A small number of agencies also indicate the interlinkages within the supply chain between various sectors as target determinants.

The other approach to target group selection in a way links the aforementioned strategies and is based on two fundamental characteristics of FDI—vertical and horizontal integration—and identifies the main motivations for a firm internationalisation within each group (Young, 2005). While horizontal FDI is driven by market access and is characterised by sales to local markets, vertical FDI seeks factor costs advantages, efficiency or strategic assets. Each type involves specific decision-making issues, offering scope for place promoters to tailor their messages, choice of promotional tools and actions.

Promotion activities can also be targeted at particular types of investment projects (Wells & Wint, 2000; World Bank, 2012). Brownfield investments have different characteristics to greenfield investments, and mergers and acquisitions (including privatisation), all of which should be considered while deciding on a place's target groups. Places need to develop a deep understanding of MNC strategies to be able to provide the right conditions for foreign investors without compromising domestic development priorities (Zanatta et al., 2006).

Inclusion of geographical context into targeting strategies, by recognising the diversity of country-specific cultural contexts, may further increase the efficiency of promotional efforts, particularly when image-building and personal selling techniques are being used. Slater, Paliwoda, and Slater (2007) recognise the importance of ethnicity in the MNE internationalisation process, however in general place marketing literature lacks purposeful studies of geographical targeting.

Finally, apart from directly attracting investors there are numerous agencies, "the influencers of company moves, investments and developments" (Fretter, 1993, p. 169), which have different awareness levels, hold diverse images of a place and express various needs but which also need to be included in places' promotion strategies, for example, the estate and relocation agents, banks, financial institutions, accountancy and the consultancy firms and so on. Also, with the growth of capital flows and MNEs development the market of location services is expanding rapidly. The location consultancies become increasingly important sources of information for (hence influence on) the MNEs.

Regardless of how the target groups are defined, this requires the 'promoters' to perform their activities driven by the chosen principle. Charlton et al. (2004) found links between the NIPA's organisation structure and approach to targeting, where dedicated staff would service the priority sectors. Further, over 80% of the agencies offer special investment facilitation services and incentive packages to targeted industries, and all of the OECD NIPAs give priority to potential investors in target industries, which in practice means focusing communication activities on audiences related to those industries (OECD, 2018). The popularity of some target groups and similarity of adopted approaches emphasise the degree of competition between places. The following section explores the nature of such competition.

3.3.3 The Competitors

'Competitors' constitute a final but by no means less important group of place promotion participants. Kotler et al. (1999) recognise three types of place competitors: (1) a superior competitor is a region having an advantaged position over others, while (2) peer competitors are equally attractive, and a (3) weak competitor is in an underprivileged position.

Despite widely acknowledged ongoing competition between places for various resources, including inward investment, place promoters rarely make effort to understand their competitors (Fretter, 1993; Wells & Wint, 2000; UNCTAD, 2017). This is particularly clear when analysing images promoted by places. Over the decades several studies indicated that similar if not identical slogans and imagery is commonly used to promote diverse places declaring them to be bigger, better, centrally located and more easily accessible (e.g. Burgess, 1982; Madsen, 1992; Ward, 1998; World Bank, 2012; Young & Lever, 1997).

Competitiveness has been the buzzword in many regional policies world over, for some time now (Gardiner et al., 2004; Pike et al., 2016). Yet it is often treated as an absolute term and equated to efficiency, and it remains unorthodox to acknowledge its relative dimension. In other words places are either competitive or not, while it is rarely recognised who the competitor is and what is the competition based on.

In the FDI promotion context according to OECD (2003), apart from the awareness and image-building dimension, competition needs to be considered also from the perspective of investment incentives. In that sense competition could be defined as a situation in which place authorities are induced to introduce or modify incentives (i.e. making them more generous) as a result of the incentive strategies pursued elsewhere. Two interrelated types of competition could be identified. Targeted competition takes place when authorities aim to attract individual FDI projects by outbidding the incentives of other jurisdictions. In such cases, due to their more flexible nature, the financial incentives are used more commonly (albeit not exclusively) as a tool. However, in most cases the application of the FDI incentives does not involve targeted competition. Instead regime competition takes places in situations where the general generosity (or design) of place's FDI incentives is selected in response, or in an anticipatory manner, to the incentive practices of other areas. Importantly, regime competition has implications both for the design of rules-based FDI approaches and for the amounts spent on pursuing specific practices.

3.4 Politics of Place Promotion

Comprehensive in its nature and organisational complexity, the process of place promotion aimed at investment attraction comprises a clear political dimension stretching beyond political economy of FDI, as discussed earlier.

Place promotion and FDI attraction require involvement and cooperation of various private and public agencies (Fig. 3.1), often having divergent aims and objectives. To be successful the promotional activities need to be consistent and coherent with other segments of the place development strategy, hence the main responsibility for initiating the promotional action is usually vested with public authorities (OECD, 2015; Parkerson & Saunders, 2005).

Place promotion in practice poses some fundamental questions about the future directions to be taken by the place—how it is meant to be presented in campaigns, what groups should be targeted, what will be the sources of financing and how should the responsibilities be divided (Morgan et al., 2002)—issues that provide choices and have distributional implications, therefore, are political. 'Glasgow's Miles Better' campaign from the early 1990s offers a good example. In its aftermath, general acclaim has been mixed with strong criticism from some quarters regarding the image campaign and the direction that promotion was taking the city's economy. Similarly, the failure of the Birmingham campaign supporting the bid for European Capital of Culture has led not only to a new approach being adopted but more importantly to a change in leadership of Marketing Birmingham. The city's business community was dissatisfied with the agency's focus on tourism, contributing to change in government and city leadership at the next local elections (Parkerson & Saunders, 2005).

Political pressures, dominated by short-term views, have the power and ability to disturb the efforts that by their nature are long-term—(re) establishment of place's image, awareness of the destination and its particular location advantages, incentive regimes stability, sustained budgetary commitment, and organisation and power distribution. One of two major motives often causes political turbulence. Firstly, the resources constraint, that is, the lack of sufficient resources, effectively leads to problems with their division and distribution. Secondly, it is the process complexity, that is, the multiplicity of constituencies that need to come together and agree on a common action (Morgan et al. (2002). While centralised, fairly authoritarian administration is able to impose control and coherence over the various components of promotional campaign (e.g. image, slogan, incentives), it is rather difficult within more devolved systems to develop "a coherent brand of a myriad of products and environments" (Hall, 2002, p. 326).

While in the context of regional promotion, these ideas are put to test in Chap. 4, overall such situations, albeit for opposing reasons, have been common in the case of regional and local authorities in CEE countries. The idea of cooperation or partnership in mid-2000s remained a novelty, and the lack of contact or indeed competition often better described the relations between them (Guglielmetti, 2009; Myant & Smith, 2006). Furthermore, when other, non-public actors take part in promotion, the cooperation and agreement within one territorial unit may be an additional challenge. The allocation of power between the agents involved is often uneven from the beginning. To what degree various pressure groups (cultural, social) get their views recognised and accepted depends on local power structure and distribution, political culture and the ability of the groups to forward their cause (Almond et al., 2015; Monaghan et al., 2014).

The complementing aspect of politics within the place promotion context is concerned with countries' external relations. Foreign affairs policies pursued by national governments arguably have a threefold impact on FDI flows. Firstly, good relations with foreign countries often serve as an encouraging factor for a home country company to consider investment opportunities abroad. Secondly, what is more relevant to place promotion, the direction and stability of national politics, specifically the foreign policy, is one aspect contributing to a country's image (Kotler et al., 1999). For example, consistently pursued aims of accessing international organisations and clubs, such as WTO, NATO or the EU, or better yet, supplying the leaders of these organisations, contribute to positive external perceptions. Thirdly, such policies can impact the behaviour of the home country's multinationals worldwide, leading to strategic responses of other businesses and in some cases image effects (Quelch & Jocz, 2005).

3.5 Factors of Successful Promotion

Current literature falls short of providing a detailed recipe for success in place promotion. Reviewing one-and-a-half century of practice, Ward (1998, p. 28) quipped that "The most popular approach in city marketing simply reflects what appear to have worked somewhere else."

However, given the discussion above, it is possible to identify factors that to various extents contribute to a success of particular campaigns, and therefore argue they should be considered and included in promotional efforts of places. Despite the interlinkages and connections between these factors, there is no consensus on their importance and universality. What is clear, however, is their emphasis extending beyond the image-focused matters. In general, as shown in Table 3.1, two groups of such 'success factors' can be distinguished—those linked with the organisation of promotion and those associated with its implementation.

On an organisational level the cooperation of a wide group of place stakeholders, the organising capacity and quality of leadership dedicated to the cause are perceived determinants of successful place promotion (Lodge, 2002; OECD, 2015; Rainisto, 2003). Effective place promotion depends on stakeholders having common grounds and rallying around the chosen strategy (Cleave et al., 2016). For example, in smaller countries the nations tend to be more homogenous and "the political and business elites know each other and can more easily formulate a common policy" (Quelch & Jocz, 2005, p. 234).

Comparably such developed networks bring down the transaction costs for the potential investors. Both set of perspectives are equally valid on the regional level. Furthermore, some authors argue that a national promotional programme needs to be more than the sum of its consecutive parts. In ensuring that, strong cooperation between various agents is compulsory (Almond et al., 2015; Florek, 2005a). A national airline needs to work with tourist boards, the investment agency with export promoting organisations and the chamber of commerce, and national promotional efforts must be coordinated with regional and city scales (Quelch & Jocz, 2005; Young, 2005). Such cooperation (or partnership) is perceived to guarantee the consistency in strategy design and implementation (Klijn et al., 2012), but also secures coherence of the communicated messages.

Dedicated and committed leadership is another factor contributing to the effective place promotion (Monaghan et al., 2014; Rainisto, 2003). Strong leadership has a potential to mobilise members of the partnership and boost the activities towards a common goal (Pasquinelli, 2013). Lodge (2002), by comparing the successful branding campaign of New

Zealand with the failure of efforts in Ontario, accentuates the quality aspects of leadership and stresses the importance of decision-making powers and "a corporate mind" (p. 384) attitudes of agents chairing the campaign.

Place promotion is a lengthy exercise that "cannot be successful overnight and on an inadequate budget" (Quelch & Jocz, 2005, p. 235), therefore dedication of the place authority reflected in budgetary commitments is another important factor vital in securing positive outcomes of place promotion activities (Lodge, 2002). Additionally Quelch and Jocz (2005) underline the significance of involving a national leader in the promotional programme. The authors point to three benefits of head of state participation. Firstly, it emphasises the importance of a campaign and shows the commitment of the government. Secondly, their personal involvement in promoting the country potentially can impress the MNE executives contemplating investment. Thirdly, such high level of commitment is necessary to motivate the different groups within the country, including business, arts and sports communities. The authors further argue that continuous leadership guarantees sustained commitment and long-term coherence.

On the operational level (Table 3.1), such issues as targeting, recognition of competitors, positioning, image-associated matters, research at various stages of the promotional programme and embeddedness of the promotional campaign within the wider development strategy arguably determine place's promotional success.

Targeting location's activity increases chances for internal coherence of the promotional activity, raises the efficiency of often limited disposable funds by, in an FDI context, directing investment flows into priority sectors (Harding & Javorcik, 2012; Wells & Wint, 2000) and avoiding the situation when everything is promoted to everybody (Kotler et al., 1999). Recognising competitors (potential and actual) and their activities allows the regional authorities to prepare a distinctive and unique offer for the targeted investors. It also helps to position place's offer, and appraise reasons behind its popularity with the target groups in relation to its competitors (Capik, 2007). Given the vast investment location possibilities at the MNEs' disposal, a clear positioning must be included in place's pro-

Table 3.1 Factors of successful place promotion

Organisation	Implementation
• Partnership and cooperation	• Coherence with (wider) regional development goals
• Wide participation (groups: business, citizens groups, art, sports, etc.)	• Image grounded in reality; coherent message
• Leadership	• Targeting
• Commitment	• Competition recognition
	• Positioning
	• Research (pre, during, and post campaign)

Source: compilation based on Kotler et al. (1999), Florek (2005a), Metaxas (2010), Monaghan et al. (2014), Almond et al. (2015)

motional efforts. By setting out to the targeted group a superiority claim and reasons why those claims should be believed, positioning also helps places to avoid competing merely on price reductions, that is, incentives (Quelch & Jocz, 2005).

Image-related matters have been discussed earlier, and so at this point it is important to stress only selected issues. In order to be convincing, a place's image must match the observable reality (place product). Also, a successful creation of an image depends on the coherence and consistency of the messages that are being communicated to the target groups. Yet, the communication to a variety of targets should not be divergent, as those diverse audiences are distinct but not separate. As people tend to merge their various exposures and experiences of a country (place) into one general impression—good, bad or indifferent—paying attention to possibly many aspects of the customer experience can be an important source of the differential advantage (Kotler & Gertner, 2002; Quelch & Jocz, 2005).

All of the above-mentioned "factors" in order to bring success must be underpinned by proper research conducted before, during and after the implementation of the promotional programme (OECD, 2015). Research activity should encompass a broad scope of issues, including awareness levels and perceptions (favourable or not, gaps between image and reality) held by the target audiences, the competitors' position, actions and successes, the unique advantages (and disadvantages) of the place with regard to targeted audiences and potential benefits and risks associated with the promotional campaign (Fitzsimons, 1995; Kotler et al., 1999; Quelch & Jocz, 2005).

Finally the promotional campaign can be considered successful when it contributes to the development of the area. To secure this, it needs to be linked to local circumstances and development goals of the place (Rainisto, 2003; World Bank, 2012), which seem to be particularly significant in the context of FDI attraction. For example, China and Ireland, while granting the investment incentives, require investors to recruit high-skilled workers locally and to cooperate with local research institutes and universities (Zanatta et al., 2006). As indicated in previous parts of the chapter the awareness and image-building activities should go hand in hand with the "product improvement", that is, infrastructural investments, labour force training, property provision and so on (Cleave et al., 2016).

Focusing on inward investment attraction and in line with the earlier identified promotional objectives, Loewendahl (2001) provides the following determinants of a successful strategy, which correspond to the conditions discussed above and support the applicability of the framework proposed here (Fig. 2.1 and Table 2.3):

- Coherent objectives set by the major stakeholders, underpinned by thorough analysis of location's competitive position; coordination between industrial policy and FDI promotion on various administrative levels.
- Investment generation is most effective when long-term relationship building with targeted investors (in priority sectors) is supported by focused communication activities.
- Effective facilitation is essential if leads are to be transformed into actual projects; this requires professional approach to project handling and coordinated provision of quality services on various levels of administrative hierarchy.
- To secure long-term benefits from FDI, and to maintain and further develop the competitive position of a location, aftercare and product improvement activities should form an integral part of investment promotion.

Typically for the subject of place promotion the discussed success determinants come from two major areas—regional development (e.g. wide participation, trans-policy links) and marketing theory (e.g. positioning, perception research). The presented list is arguably neither full nor static but confirms the applicability of the developed approach as summarised in Fig. 2.1 and Table 2.3. As other issues in promotion of broadly defined place, the usefulness and importance of particular factors would vary with the scale and characteristics of a place.

3.6 Conclusions

The marketing approach offers a set of principles, methods and tools that could be used in effective place promotion aimed at FDI attraction. The process resembles business-to-business promotional practices, hence it cannot solely rely on image creation, but needs to make use of other available measures. Despite popular claims in the literature suggesting the opposite, the decisive role of place image in MNEs' location decision-making is overstated. The promotion process needs to include phases pre- and post-image building, that is, awareness creation, and negotiations, tailored offers and services—or organisation, lead generation and post-investment services provision. From the location decision perspective it is not only important what comprises places' offer (e.g. communication infrastructure, investment incentives), but also who might be interested in it and crucially who knows about it and how was it conveyed to them that matters. In this sense the understanding of promotion should not be limited, as often is the case in the current literature, to advertising and PR techniques. Instead it needs to be extended to include other promotion mix elements enabling a holistic approach to the process of FDI promotion that would allow satisfying its threefold aims: image creation, investment generation and the provision of services. The compound character of the process is further emphasised by its inherent links to place product and an array of agents involved with its planning and implementation—on both providing and receiving ends.

Naturally place promotion aimed at FDI attraction is a long-term exercise which often does not provide immediate (measurable) outcomes. It is for this reason that, amongst other factors, coherence and consistence are most important in its successful execution.

Despite the long documented history of investment promotion, current academic knowledge and theoretical underpinnings of the concepts remain limited. It is clear that the scale affects the process; however, due to the lack of empirical evidence of regional approaches it is far from obvious if promotion can successfully be practised on a regional level, and if so, what kind of organisational setting would provide best links with the local and national scales. Comparably, current literature provides only limited evidence of promotion in other than post-industrial settings. Furthermore, the existing studies are heavily focused on image-building practices (often in a tourism context), neglecting the wider scope of promotion activities. Finally the most important issue for both sceptics and supporters of place promotion is its effectiveness. So far the emerging evidence of various promotional activities' usefulness and efficiency remains fragmented. One of the reasons for this is the lack of reliable and systematic methods of assessment. On the other hand, however, there is no empirical proof that would allow the definitive rejection of promotion as one of the policy tools.

While filling all of these gaps is beyond the scope of this book, the forthcoming chapters will provide answers to the remaining research questions posed in the opening chapter, and offer insights into a selection of issues that until now remained unexplored or have been only discussed in the literature only superficially.

References

Almond, P., Ferner, A., & Tregasis, O. (2015). The changing context of regional governance of FDI in England. *European Urban and Regional Studies, 22*(1), 61–76.

Anholt, S. (2006). Is place branding a capitalist tool. *Place Branding and Public Diplomacy, 2*(1), 1–4.

Anholt, S. (2010). *Places: Identity, image and reputation*. Basingstoke: Palgrave Macmillan.

Anholt, S., & Hildreth, J. (2005). Let freedom and cash registers ring: America as a brand. *Place Branding and Public Diplomacy, 1*(2), 164–172.

Ashworth, G. J., & Voogd, H. (1990). *Selling the city: Marketing approaches in public sector urban planning*. London: Belhaven Press.

Ashworth, G. J., & Voogd, H. (1994). Marketing and place promotion. In J. R. Gold & S. V. Ward (Eds.), *Place promotion; the use of publicity and marketing to sell towns and regions*. Chichester: John Wiley & Sons.

Barke, M., & Harrop, K. (1994). Selling the industrial town: Identity, image and illusion. In J. R. Gold & S. V. Ward (Eds.), *Place promotion; the use of publicity and marketing to sell towns and regions*. Chichester: John Wiley & Sons.

Belloso, J. C. (2011). The city branding of Barcelona: A success story. In K. Dinnie (Ed.), *City branding: Theory and cases*. Basingstoke: Palgrave Macmillan.

Bickl, M. (2004). *Image management in old-industrial regions: Policy learning, governance and leadership in North East England and the Ruhr*. PhD Thesis, University of Durham, Durham.

Borchert, J. G. (1994). *Urban marketing: A review, Abhandlungen—Antropogeographie Insitut für Geographische Wissenschaften, Band 52*. Berlin: FU Berlin.

Bradley, A., Hall, T., & Harrison, M. (2002). Selling cities: Promoting new images for meeting tourism. *Cities, 19*(1), 61–70.

Burgess, J. (1982). Selling places: Environmental images for the executive. *Regional Studies, 16*(1), 1–17.

Burgess, J., & Wood, P. (1988). Decoding Doklands; Place advertising and decision-making strategies of the small firm. In J. Eyles & D. M. Smith (Eds.), *Qualitative methods in human geography*. Cambridge: Polity Press.

Capik, P. (2007). Organising FDI promotion in Central-Eastern European regions. *Place Branding and Public Diplomacy, 3*(2), 152–163.

Charlton, A., & Davis, N. (2006). *Does investment promotion work?* Retrieved April 11, 2007, from http://personal.lse.ac.uk/CHARLTOA/IP.pdf.

Charlton, A., Davis, N., Faye, M., Haddock, J., & Lamb, C. (2004). *Industry targeting within foreign investment promotion*. Oxford Investment Research Working Paper, Oxford.

Cleave, E., Godwin, A., Sadler, R., & Gilliland, J. (2016). The role of place branding in local and regional economic development: Bridging the gap between policy and practicality. *Regional Studies, Regional Science, 3*(1), 207–228.

Clow, K. E., & Baack, D. (2018). *Integrated advertising, promotion, and marketing communications* (8th ed.). New York: Pearson.
Daniels, J. D., Radebaugh, L. H., & Sullivan, D. P. (2019). *International business: Environment and operations* (16th ed.). New York: Pearson.
Dinnie, K. (Ed.). (2011). *City branding: Theory and cases*. Basingstoke: Palgrave Macmillan.
Domański, T. (Ed.). (1997). *Marketing terytorialny; Strategiczne wyzwanie dla miast i regionów*. Łódź: Uniwersytet Łódzki.
Fitzsimons, D. S. (1995). Planning and promotion: City reimaging in the 1980s and 1990s. In W. J. V. Neill, D. S. Fitzsimons, & B. Murtagh (Eds.), *Reimaging the pariah city; urban development in Belfast and Detroit*. Aldershot: Avebury.
Florek, M. (2005a). The country Brand as a new challenge for Poland. *Place Branding and Public Diplomacy, 1*(2), 205–214.
Florek, M. (2005b). Struktura i możliwości aplikacji instrumentów marketingu terytorialnego. In H. Szulce & M. Florek (Eds.), *Marketing terytorialny—możliwości aplikacji, kierunki rozwoju*. AE Poznań, Poznań.
Fretter, A. D. (1993). Place marketing: A local authority perspective. In G. Kearns & C. Philo (Eds.), *Selling places; the city as cultural capital, past and present*. Oxford: Pergamon Press.
Gardiner, B., Martin, R., & Tyler, P. (2004). Competitiveness, productivity and economic growth across the European regions. *Regional Studies, 38*(9), 1045–1067.
Gilmore, F. (2002). A country—Can it be repositioned? Spain—The success story of country branding. *Brand Management, 9*(4–5), 281–293.
Go, F. M., & Govers, R. (Eds.). (2013). *International place branding yearbook 2012: Managing smart growth and sustainability*. Basingstoke: Palgrave Macmillan.
Gold, J. R., & Ward, S. V. (1994). Forward. In *Place promotion; the use of publicity and marketing to sell towns and regions*. Chichester: John Wiley & Sons.
Gudjonssen, H. (2005). Nation branding. *Place Branding and Public Diplomacy, 3*(1), 283–298.
Guglielmetti, C. (2009). Local development in a European Union perspective: Cohesion and regional policies in Central and Eastern Europe. In P. Blokker & B. Dallago (Eds.), *Regional diversity and local development in the new Member States*. Basingstoke: Palgrave Macmillan.
Hall, D. (2002). Brand development, tourism and national identity: The reimaging of former Yugoslavia. *Brand Management, 9*(4–5), 323–334.

Harding, T., & Javorcik, B. (2012). *Investment promotion and FDI inflows: Quality matters*. University of Oxford Department of Economics Discussion Paper Series, No. 612.

Herodes, F. (2011). The regional institution's dilemma—How regional organisations adapt to EU membership. In T. Herrschel & P. Tallberg (Eds.), *The role of regions? Networks, scale, territory*. Kristianstad: Kristianstads Boktryckeri.

Jobber, D. (2007). *Principles and practice of marketing*. London: The McGraw-Hill Companies.

Klijn, E. H., Eshuis, J., & Braun, E. (2012). The influence of stakeholder involvement on the effectiveness of place branding. *Public Management Review, 14*(4), 499–519.

Kotler, P., Apslund, C., Rein, I., & Haider, D. H. (1999). *Marketing places—Europe: How to attract investments, industries, residents and visitors to cities, communities, regions and nations in Europe*. London: Financial Times-Prentice Hall.

Kotler, P., & Armstrong, G. (2005). *Marketing: An introduction*. Upper Saddle River, NJ: Pearson-Prentice Hall.

Kotler, P., & Gertner, D. (2002). Country as brand, product and beyond: A place marketing and brand management perspective. *Brand Management, 9*(4–5), 249–261.

Kulchina, E. (2014). Media coverage and location choice. *Strategic Management Journal, 35*(4), 596–605.

Lodge, C. (2002). Success and failure: The brand stories of two countries. *Brand Management, 9*(4–5), 372–384.

Loewendahl, H. (2001). A framework for FDI promotion. *Transnational Corporations, 10*(1), 1–42.

MacKinnon, D., Dawley, S., Pike, A., & Cumbers, A. (2019). Rethinking path creation: A geographical political economy approach. *Economic Geography, 95*(2),113–135.

Madsen, H. (1992). Place marketing in Liverpool: A review. *International Journal of Urban and Regional Research, 16*, 633–640.

Markowski, T. (1997). Miasto jako produkt—wybrane aspekty marketingu miasta. In T. Domański (Ed.), *Marketing terytorialny; Strategiczne wyzwanie dla miast i regionów*. Łódź: Uniwersytet Łódzki.

Markowski, T. (2002). Marketing miasta. In Marketing terytorialny (Ed.), *Studia KPZK*. Warszawa: PAN.

Metaxas, T. (2010). Place marketing, place branding and foreign direct investments: Defining their relationship in the frame of local economic development process. *Place Branding and Public Diplomacy, 6*(3), 228–243.

Monaghan, S., Gunnigle, P., & Lavelle, J. (2014). 'Courting the multinational': Subnational institutional capacity and foreign market insidership. *Journal of International Business Studies, 45*(2), 131–150.

Morgan, N., Pritchard, A., & Piggot, R. (2002). New Zealand, 100% pure. The creation of powerful niche destination brand. *Brand Management, 9*(4–5), 335–354.

Mudambi, R., Li, L., Ma, X., Makino, S., Qian, G., & Boschma, R. (2018). Zoom in, zoom out: Geographic scale and multinational activity. *Journal of International Business Studies, 49*, 929–941.

Multilateral Investment Guarantee Agency (MIGA). (2006). *FDI Promotion*. Retrieved November 29, 2006, from www.fdipromotion.com/toolkit/user/content_page.cfm

Myant, M., & Smith, S. (2006). Regional development and post-communist politics in a Czech Region. *Europe-Asia Studies, 58*(2), 147–168.

Navaretti, G. B., & Venables, A. J. (2004). *Multinational firms in the world economy*. Princeton, NJ: Princeton University Press.

OECD. (2003). *Checklist for foreign direct investment incentives policies*. Paris: OECD Publications.

OECD. (2015). *Policy framework for investment 2015 edition*. Paris: OECD Publishing. Retrieved from https://doi.org/10.1787/9789264208667-en

OECD. (2018). *Mapping of investment promotion agencies in OECD countries*. Retrieved from http://www.oecd.org/investment/Mapping-of-Investment-Promotion-Agencies-in-OECD-Countries.pdf

Papadopoulos, N., & Heslop, L. (2002). Country equity and country branding: Problems and prospects. *Brand Management, 9*(4–5), 294–314.

Parkerson, B., & Saunders, J. (2005). City branding: Can goods and services branding models be used to brand cities? *Place Branding and Public Diplomacy, 1*(3), 242–264.

Pasquinelli, C. (2013). Competition, cooperation and co-opetition: Unfolding the process of inter-territorial branding. *Urban Research & Practice, 6*(1), 1–18.

Pasquinelli, C., & Teräs, J. (2013). Branding knowledge-intensive regions: A comparative study of pisa and oulu high-tech brands. *European Planning Studies, 21*(10), 1611–1629.

Pike, A. (2011). Placing brands and branding: A socio-spatial biography of Newcastle Brown Ale. *Transactions of the Institute of British Geographers, 36*(2), 206–222.

Pike, A., Rodríguez-Pose, A., & Tomaney, J. (2016). *Local and regional development* (2nd ed.). London: Routledge.

Quelch, J., & Jocz, K. (2005). Positioning the nation-state. *Place Branding and Public Diplomacy, 1*(3), 229–237.

Rainisto, S. K. (2003). *Success factors of place marketing: A study of place marketing practices in northern Europe and The United States*. Espoo: Helsinki.

Rzeczpospolita. (2005, February 18). *Słowacja: Już brakuje specjalistów—Koncerny podkupują pracowników*.

Saleh, M. A. E. (2001). The changing image of Arriyad City; the role of socio-cultural and religious traditions in image transformation. *Cities, 18*(5), 315–330.

Schatz, R. (2013). Overcoming the risk of stereotypes: How strategic communications can facilitate sustainable place branding. In F. M. Go & R. Govers (Eds.), *International place branding yearbook 2012: Managing smart growth and sustainability*. Basingstoke: Palgrave Macmillan.

Skinner, H. (2005). Wish you were here? Some problems associated with integrating marketing communications when promoting place brands. *Place Branding and Public Diplomacy, 1*(3), 299–315.

Slater, S., Paliwoda, S., & Slater, J. (2007). Ethnicity and decision making for internationalisation. *Management Decision, 45*(10), 1622–1635.

Supphellen, M., & Nygaardsvik, I. (2002). Testing country brand slogans: Conceptual development and empirical illustration of a simple normative model. *Brand Management, 9*(4–5), 385–395.

Szromnik, A. (1997). Marketing terytorialny—geneza, rynki docelowe i podmioty oddziaływania. In T. Domański (Ed.), *Marketing terytorialny—strategiczne wyzwania dla miast i regionów*. Łódź: Uniwersytet Łódzki.

UNCTAD, 2017, World investment report: investment and the digital economy. Geneva: United Nations.

van den Berg, L., Braun, E., & Otgaar, A. H. J. (2002). *Sports and city marketing in European cities*. Rotterdam: Euricur.

Ward, S. V. (1998). *Selling places, the marketing and promotion of towns and cities 1850–2000*. London: E&FN Spon.

Wells, T. L., Jr., & Wint, A. G. (2000). *Marketing a country—Promotion as a tool for attracting foreign direct investment*. FIAS Occasional Paper 13, IFC-MIGA, Washington.

World Bank. (2012). *Investment climate: Global investment promotions best practices*. Washington, DC: The World Bank Group.

Young, C. (2005). Place marketing for foreign direct investment in Central and Eastern Europe. In D. Turnock (Ed.), *Foreign direct investment and regional development in East-Central Europe and the former Soviet Union*. Kent: Ashgate.

Young, C., & Lever, J. (1997). Place promotion, economic location and the consumption of city image. *Tijdshrift voor Economische en Sociale Geografie, 88*(4), 332–341.

Zanatta, M., Costa, I., & Filippov, S. (2006). *Foreign direct investment: Key issues for promotion agencies*. UNU Policy Brief, No. 10, UNU-MERIT, Maastricht.

Zimmerbauer, K. (2011). From image to identity: Building regions by place promotion. *European Planning Studies, 19*(2), 243–260.

4

Regional Authorities Attracting Investors

4.1 Introduction

Previous chapters examined the importance of foreign direct investment (FDI) for Central-Eastern European (CEE) regional economies and provided a rationale for why regional authorities may be interested to engage with investment promotion. While exploring the nature and extent of the process, it has been argued that actions of the National Investment Promotion Agencies, which often are ascribed a decisive role in FDI promotion, do not guarantee an even distribution of FDI projects and flows across the Central-Eastern European Countries. In these circumstances it seems appropriate to expect the regional institutions to take action in order to redirect the discriminative FDI flows. This chapter investigates in what ways regional authorities engage with investment promotion process, and how their engagement is conditioned by the socio-economic circumstances they operate within.

The discussion presented here explores the activities of the Czech, Polish and Slovak regional authorities and offers insights into the levels of their involvement in FDI promotional activities in the context of regional socio-economic conditions. By cross-examining the approaches and the

P. Capik, *Foreign Investment Promotion*, https://doi.org/10.1007/978-3-030-13658-1_4

level of development of the area, existing FDI stock and recent flows, the chapter explores the factors determining why some areas' promotion is more erratic while the activities of others have a more comprehensive and systematic character.

Utilising original survey data and secondary socio-economic statistics the chapter scrutinises how is investment promotion linked with regional development in CEEC. It aims to establish if promotion comprises a set of conscious actions and policies, in line with the framework suggested in Chap. 2 (Fig. 2.1 and Table 2.3) or rather is an extravagant act of regional governance performed in response to the promotional activities of other regions. At another level, the chapter explores whether investment promotion is a component of wider policies aimed at tackling some of the regional problems including unemployment and outdated industrial structure, or if it comprises a set of spontaneous actions disassociated from developmental goals, stimulated by fashion or consultancies' willingness to help. Therefore, the chapter provides answers to particularly the second and third set of research questions (p. 32) as it scrutinises the role of investment promotion in the development and governance of the CEE regions.

The discussion progresses as follows. The opening sections explore the position of investment attraction in the context of wider regional promotion, and its links with the broader developmental agenda. Next, the organisation of FDI promotion and subsequently its implementation is discussed before concluding observations are offered.

4.2 Foreign Investors Amongst Other Promotion Addressees

Before analysing particular activities associated with investment attraction it is useful to have an overview of regional authorities' attitudes and general promotional activities directed to other key target groups. This will provide a wider background and put FDI attraction in the context of broader promotional activities. In order to achieve this it is useful to review the importance of individual target groups in the overall promotion and its connection with regional development strategy (RDS).

For Central-Eastern European regional authorities, tourists are the main targets addressed by promotion. Over 80% of regions assign this group first priority (Table 4.1); however, national variations can be distinguished. More than 90% of Czech regions predominantly engage with promotion aimed at tourists, while the same is true for just over 80% of Polish and 62% of Slovak regions. This is an early indication of Czech regional promotion. Coupled with the minor role of FDI amongst other target groups already at this initial stage of analysis it suggests the Czech regional authorities' approach to investment attraction.

The level of importance assigned by regional authorities to promotion aimed at foreign investors also varies between the countries. In general 14 regions consider FDI promotion to be of the highest priority, but it is the second highest priority that is most common across CEE. Together the two highest levels of priority have been indicated by over 75% of the regions. While first priority dominates in Slovakia (50%) and Poland (44%), the majority of Czech regions (71%) assign less importance to FDI promotion as only one-fifth of Czech regions consider FDI promotion to be the most important.

Comparably diverse, albeit concerning the opposite end of the scale, is the situation with promoting the region to new inhabitants. While generally over a half of the regions consider this target group of least impor-

Table 4.1 Target groups prioritising

	New Inhabitants		Tourists		FDI	
	First (number of responses)	Category with majority of responses (%)	First (number of responses)	Category with majority of responses (%)	First (number of responses)	Category with majority of responses (%)
Czech Republic	0	4 (64)	13	1 (93)	3	2 (71)
Poland	0	NT[a] (75)	13	1 (81)	7	1 (44)
Slovakia	1	4 (50)	5	1 (62)	4	1 (50)
Total	1	4 (53)	31	1 (82)	14	2 (39)

'All and few equal' included
[a]NT—not targeting this group
Source: Own research

tance, 75% of Polish regions do not target it at all. In fact only the authorities of one Slovak region (Prešovský kraj) deem it of top priority in line with tourists and FDI.

The relative popularity of 'tourists' as a target group comes as no surprise. Regions are convinced about the attractiveness of their cultural heritage, natural environment and historic legacy. Respectively 71%, 66% and 58% indicate these features as the reason for their national fame. Furthermore, tourism promotion is the longest practised and best established practice around the world (Ward, 1998) and equally some form of tourist destination promotion has been also exercised in CEE for numerous years (Florek, 2003). As a result, tourism promotion is often perceived to be a straightforward process—typically limited to occasional release of a series of glossy flyers and brochures.

Promoting the region to potential new inhabitants ranks lowest on the regional authorities' promotion agenda. This is partially associated with the unemployment rate to which the incoming population could only add, but also reflects the fairly stable demographic situation of the regions. Although in half of the areas between 1999 and 2005 population numbers decreased, none of the regions suffered serious loss of residents. An increase of population is rather perceived as a secondary effect reflecting good economic performance and environmental attractiveness of the area, and examples of worldwide practice of attracting new residents are actually few and far between.[1]

These results point to two important features of CEE promotion that will reoccur throughout the forthcoming analysis. Firstly, the tourists comprise the group most often targeted in promotion. Secondly, as far as the FDI promotion is concerned Polish and Czech regions usually present opposite views and consequently adopt contrasting approaches, while the Slovak regions tend to oscillate between the two.

[1] One such rare example is the 2006 campaign run by Wrocław authorities in London attempting to convince post-EU enlargement migrants to come to live and work in the Dolnośląskie Voivodeship capital city.

4.3 Regional Authorities' Familiarity with Target Groups

One of the indicators showing how seriously and systematically the authorities approach promotion is the level of their familiarity with the selected target groups. It relates to segmentation possibilities and conditions the choice of relevant promotional activities (Florek, 2003; Harding & Javorcik, 2012).

Least important of all promotion addressees, the inhabitants unsurprisingly constitute the most familiar group. Still, on a scale of 1 to 5 regional authorities assess the level of information they possess about the inhabitants at somewhat mediocre 3.5. The level of their knowledge about tourists, current and potential investors is judged at 3.3, 3.0 and 2.7 respectively. Polish regions claim to be better informed about all target groups than their Czech and Slovak counterparts. They indicate to have the most adequate levels of information on inhabitants and current investors, both graded at 3.9. In contrast, the Czech regions are best informed about their highest priority target group, tourists (3.2), and assess their knowledge about both current and potential investors at 2.4.

What these results show is the regional authorities' awareness of their incomplete knowledge of individual target groups, specifically those that they are most interested in attracting. Relatively more complete knowledge of current investors as compared to the potential ones hints towards existence of some forms of investment monitoring systems and sustained contacts between the authorities and companies, which could signal the emergence of broader than image only promotional activities (as advised by for Loewendahl, 2001; Wells & Wint, 2000; World Bank, 2012; OECD, 2015).

4.4 FDI Promotion and Regional Development

Previously it was stressed that FDI promotion cannot be disassociated from wider development goals and strategies. To be internally coherent and effective, promotion needs to be linked to and embedded in the RDS

(OECD, 2018, 2003; Zanatta, Costa, & Filippov, 2006). In the conducted survey the authorities have been asked to indicate the groups they are targeting and which are included in their regional development strategies. Table 4.2 presents the results.

The majority of regions (55%) declare to have promotion to all target groups included in their development strategies. Simultaneously almost a quarter of authorities claim their strategies explicitly include promotion to solely tourists and investors, while every fifth region admits to not having promotion included in their RDS at all. This is naturally diverse in the individual countries. In Poland, one region does not show links between promotion and regional development strategy, while the same is true for almost 36% of Czech and a quarter of Slovak ones. Conversely, three-quarters of Polish regional authorities claim to have all target groups included in their strategy, but it is the case with 43% of Czech and 37% of Slovak ones. All regions which declare having promotion to some groups included in their RDS (21%, 19% and 37% in Czech Republic, Poland and Slovakia) point to the two target groups which have been ascribed highest priority, namely tourists and foreign investors.

Even if the above results are considered to be overly optimistic (a check of randomly selected strategy documents show that some of the regions over-exaggerated the inclusion of target groups in their RDS), and in reality not as many regions utilise promotion to execute their development strategies, still this can be treated as an indication of a wider trend. Consequently, Polish regions present a more systematic approach to promotion, while in the Slovak, and even more so the Czech, regions promotion is dominated by less strategic, rather ad-hoc actions.

Table 4.2 Inclusion of promotion to target groups in RDS (% of answers)

	All target groups included	Some target groups included[a]	No target groups included
Czech Republic	43	21	36
Poland	75	19	6
Slovakia[b]	38	38	25
TOTAL	55	24	21

[a]All regions named tourists and foreign investors
[b]The total exceeds 100 due to rounding up of the figures
Source: Own research

Nevertheless, despite not in all regions the embeddedness of FDI promotion in the development plans is clear, the vast majority of the areas admit their future to be closely associated with the inflows of foreign investments.

The economic and social importance of foreign direct investments for the regional economies of CEE has been widely agreed (e.g. Bradshaw, 2005; Dogaru, Burger, Karreman, & Van Oort, 2015). It is not surprising therefore that the majority of the regional authorities assign considerable importance to this particular target group. In almost 95% of cases the RDS considers FDI to be 'very important' or 'important' to the future of the region. While in the strategies of Polish regions FDI is more often considered to be very important (56.3), in Slovakia and Czech Republic FDI it is rather referred to as 'important', 62.5% and 64.3% respectively. This further underlines the dissonance between the knowledge of potential investors, their position amongst other target groups and their importance to the regional economy as declared by the authorities.

Interestingly the unemployment levels or the current stock of foreign capital in the region does not influence the level of importance assigned to FDI. Given the lack of further data that could shed more light on this issue, it could be argued that attractiveness of FDI to the regional authorities appears to be underpinned by 'fashionability' rather than the perceived capacity to solve long-term problems or a proven track record of doing so.

Whatever their motivation FDI remains an important focus of regional authorities' activities and within the three-year period post-survey, they expected to attract between 2 and 60 new investors. Polish areas, more involved in FDI promotion and approaching it more systematically, were more optimistic about the number of investment projects they can attract—on average 16, which matches the average number of greenfield projects actually completed in the country's regions in 2005 alone (consult Table 1.1).

Slovak and Czech regions are less confident, expecting to attract five projects on average. Their caution however is often unfounded. Between 2002 and 2005 the number of greenfield projects in Slovakia has increased more than twofold. In the Czech Republic, despite the slight decrease over a two-year period, in 2005 alone they exceeded the three-year total expected by the regional authorities. The careful approach presented by the Czech and Slovak authorities partially reflects the prolonged dominant position of the capital city regions as FDI destinations, and the resulting disbelief in the possible immediate success of other areas, but it also points towards involvement of other organisations in FDI attraction process. Next the organisation of investment promotion is examined.

4.5 Multidimensional Organisation of Investment Promotion

Organisation capacity conditions the scope of investment promotion, hence it can determine the overall success of the activities performed (Almond, Ferner, & Tregasis, 2015; Bickl, 2004; Monaghan, Gunnigle, & Lavelle, 2014). A brief study of the regional authorities' web portals reveals the differences in organisational setting for regional promotion. Usually within the structure of the authorities there is a department responsible for general promotion including PR activities; however, how FDI promotion is organised is usually far less clear.

Based on survey results, in over 60% of the regions FDI promotion is handled by a purpose-created division within the regional authority structures. In four cases (one in Poland and the Czech Republic, two in Slovakia) the same office is also responsible for tourism promotion, hence it can be treated as a general promotion office. Another three regions operate single-person offices, rather than departments. An important fact, however, is that regional authorities investment sections (RAISs), in some form, can be found in the majority of the regions across CEE. Comparably to some of the matters discussed above this vary considerably across the three countries.

While almost 90% of regions in Poland have an FDI-dedicated promotion office, such activities are incorporated into agendas of different departments within regional authority in 50% of Czech and over 60% of Slovak regions. Promotion is not only a 'privilege of the rich' (regions) and the majority of Czech and Slovak areas operating RAISs are the ones where GDP per capita does not exceed the country's average. To the contrary, it is mainly the more prosperous Polish regions that operate such offices. However, on average the regions with RAIS are the ones where GDP per capita does not exceed the country's average,[2] which may suggest, contrary to results discussed above, that promotion is treated as a tool with the potential to improve the wealth of the region rather than a set of fashionable activities and policies.

However, the mere existence of a purposeful office responsible for the attraction of foreign investors does not guarantee appropriate execution of it. It is often highlighted that one of the main factors compromising effectiveness of place promotion is the lack of appropriate resources (Almond et al., 2015; Cleave, Godwin, Sadler, & Gilliland, 2016; Florek, 2003; Kotler & Gertner, 2002). Yet, as far as the human resources are concerned the cases of CEE regions provide contradicting evidence. The majority of the RAISs employ between one and three staff members, while only just over a tenth is staffed with seven and nine people. The size of the office is not clearly associated with the priority given to investors amongst other target groups. The majority of authorities predominantly promoting their regions to this group dedicate to this aim not more than six people. Simultaneously, investment offices with between seven and nine staff members operate in regions assigning investors a lesser priority amongst other targeted groups.

Comparably, unemployment does not seem to have a definitive impact on the office personnel capacity. In most regions where the unemployment rate exceeds the national average no more than three people are responsible for FDI attraction; however, in Poland and Slovakia such regions also have the country's biggest FDI promotion offices. Thus, again the relationship between regional problems and involvement in securing one of its solutions is unclear.

Furthermore, the size of the RAISs does not appear to be influenced by the region's contribution to the country's FDI stock. Small offices operate in regions with both high and low shares of the country's investment stock (which may be reflective of the varying levels of their efficiency—discussed later).

[2] Excluding capital city regions, which largely distort the average income per capita in their respective countries. Notably it is only the region of the Polish capital that operates an FDI promotion office.

Regardless of the amounts of the foreign capital inflows, half of the regional authorities indicate that given their responsibilities, the promotional offices are not adequately staffed. Less than 40% of the regions present the contrary opinion, while the remaining few find it hard to assess. Comparable distribution of views is noticeable amongst the Czech and Polish regions, while the Slovak authorities univocally complain about inadequate staff levels.

The number of discontents is large but not overwhelming. Considering that a relatively high proportion of CEE regional authorities are comfortable with the capacity of their RAIS, the often-quoted argument about lack of resources inhibiting promotion seems less relevant. It is made even clearer by the fact that only half of the regions dissatisfied with the staffing levels would like to expand their offices if they had the financial resources at their disposal.

Such findings stress the importance of qualitative aspects of RAIS that does not allow them to utilise their full potential. The majority of the regions, including those dissatisfied, would use the additional resources for extending RAIS activities (including wider advertising, and fairs and exhibition participation) and staff training. Thus, instead of unambiguous insufficient human resources, the situation is far more complex and reveals the underutilisation of staff capacities, but also imperfect staff qualifications.

Table 4.3 presents assessment of RAIS staff qualifications. The average grades for the three countries in the fundamental areas of FDI promotion, namely economic development and marketing, are relatively good. However, this is due to considerably higher scores awarded to RAISs in Poland, while Czech and Slovak regions assess their offices at levels below the CEE average. Staff training is graded generally higher than their experience, which reflects a relatively short history of RAISs' operations.

Considering this, the regional authorities' intentions to utilise additional resources for staff training need to be interpreted as plans to improve staff practical skills rather than their academic qualifications. Such training should be expected in marketing and promotion, since commonly RAIS staff seems to have pursued education in (regional) economics or cognate disciplines.

Table 4.3 Assessment of selected aspects of RAIS quality

	Marketing and promotion				Regional economic development			
	Czech Republic	Poland	Slovakia	Average	Czech Republic	Poland	Slovakia	Average
Training	3.16	4.33	3.5	3.66	3.66	4.83	3.5	3.99
Experience	3.66	4.09	3.0	3.58	3.66	4.08	3.0	3.58

Average score (1 lowest, 5 highest grade)
Source: Own research

Reflecting the limitations in their abilities and the importance of adequate qualifications staff of almost 80% of RAISs participate in training courses. While the exact merits of the courses vary, their main focus remains FDI servicing and external promotion activities. Such training courses are usually organised and led by the relevant National Investment Promotion Agency (NIPA). Occasionally the staff also partakes in courses on EU fund acquisition for promotional purposes, delivered either by NIPA or consultants.

Another remedy to the regional authorities' inadequate investment promotion capabilities is to utilise external agents including academics and consulting companies. Just under 65% of all regions claim to be using advice from either of the two sources, and rarely, only in 15% of the cases, both sources are used. The use of university experts in general is somewhat more popular than consulting firms; this however varies between the countries. While over 60% of Polish and half of the Slovak regions use advice and services of academics, a comparable proportion of the Czech ones rely on the expertise of consultants.

Regional authorities' internal arrangements are only one dimension of investment promotion organisation. The operations of RAISs do not take place in a vacuum, but the nature of FDI promotion is such that naturally regional authorities will have to cooperate, consult and sometimes compete with external agents at various spatial and administrative levels (Almond et al., 2015; Monaghan et al., 2014; Young, 2005). It is this multi-scalar networks and relationships of RAISs that are explored next.

4.5.1 Horizontal Cooperation for FDI Promotion

Contrary to the impression one may get studying some of *place marketing* and investment promotion literature, investment attraction is a multi-agent process requiring regional authorities to develop relationships with a variety of partners in the region and beyond it (Cleave et al., 2016; Malvestito, 1997; OECD, 2015). The type of such relations will be purpose-driven. Whereas it has a more cooperative character with organisations influencing the business climate, its nature will be rather top-down (or consultative at best) with local communities or business services organisations. Alternatively, the relationship may be more competitive, or may be limited to mere use or exchange of experiences. The main objective of the cooperation would be to consult and coordinate those 'under' regional authorities, and influence those 'above' and parallel. Whatever the nature of existing relations, the ability to generate spontaneous associations and joining in more permanent networks oriented towards achieving strategic objectives arguably remains a key to a successful promotion effort (Domański, 2011; Pasquinelli, 2013).

Apart from regional authorities there often exist a number of other public and private agencies involved either directly or indirectly in regional promotion aimed at FDI attraction or targeting other groups. For example in Britain the councils remain the main organisations, formerly often supported by the Urban Development Corporations. Around them would gather other public or semi-public agents (e.g. airports, trade fairs, convention centres) and private organisations such as Chambers of Commerce and other ad-hoc organisations whose role most often would be minor (Ward, 1998). While naturally, the regional authorities are not necessarily cooperating closely with all of such organisations they need to be aware of their existence and operations to try to effectively coordinate the promotional activities (Bickl, 2004; Klijn, Eshuis, & Braun, 2012; Young, 2005).

In CEEC the number of cooperating organisations varies as does the nature of their relationships with the regional authorities. With the average number of three cooperation partners, the Polish regions operate within wider networks than their Czech and Slovak counterparts who usually co-function next to two other institutions.

Contrary to Loewendahl's (2001) argument the wider networks (up to four organisations in the Czech Republic, six in Poland and five in Slovakia) are not stimulated by factors directly linked with perceived investors' preferences. Equally small and large, wealthy and less well-off regions, those with high and low unemployment rates and proportions of country's FDI stock, operate within both larger and smaller networks. Instead, as will be discussed later, the existence of wider networks seems to be conditioned by less tangible cultural factors and often reflects regional political arrangements.

Most commonly, the promotion networks, apart from regional authorities, include other public organisations, particularly regional development agencies (RDAs). Notably, also in this respect Polish regional authorities differ from their Czech and Slovak partners in that none of them considers the National Investment Promotion Agency as part of their network. Instead, with the exception of two, in all Polish regions RDAs are involved with FDI attraction, while it is the case in 50% of Czech and Slovak regions. The dissimilarity of Polish practice is further emphasised by the fact that one in two regional authorities, but one in three of Czech, and one in four of Slovak ones, mention regional tourist boards as their partners. Additionally, special economic zones and technological parks are more common promotion collaborates of the authorities in Poland than is the case in the other two countries.

More commonly found, however, is the sporadic representation of private capital within the promotional networks. Inclusion of Chambers of Commerce by a total of four regions and fairs and exhibition companies by another two serves as a rare exception. Another underrepresented group is civil society. Only two regions (Dolnoslaśkie voivodeship in Poland and Karlovovarský kraj in the Czech Republic) point to civic organisations involved with promotion. Such a situation is distant from the ideal scenario presented by Kotler, Apslund, Rein, and Haider (1999), suggesting very broad participation in promotion ranging from taxi drivers, individual tourist agents and industrial associations, to societal groups and investment promotion agencies.

Notably not all the organisations indicated by the authorities are directly involved with FDI promotion, nonetheless the fact that regional authorities recognise their activities could suggest coordination between promotion to the different target groups. However, the coherence between the actions and messages transmitted by different agencies is often only superficial. In fact even in the views of the regional authorities the level of coordination of promotional efforts between themselves and the various organisations is rather satisfactory (43%) than very good (26%). Typically Polish and Czech regions differ also in this respect. While 54% of Czech regions assess the coordination as satisfactory, 64% of the Polish ones judge it to be good and very good. This view is shared by a comparable percentage of Slovak regional authorities. Seemingly then neither the size of the networks nor their composition impacts the level of coordination between its members. Furthermore, regional authorities' assessment is not conditioned by the regional share of a country's FDI stock, or the region's economic performance. The reasons for more overall synchronised actions must therefore lie elsewhere, possibly in the nature of individual relationships.

However, when asked to indicate the best and worst collaborators, the CEE regional authorities mainly refrain from providing information. Over 80% of them did not indicate the organisation with which the cooperation is worst, and 60% failed to name the best ones. Those which provided the information in the Czech Republic and Poland most commonly praise the regional development agencies, and in Slovakia the national tourism board. Comparably there is no individual type of organisation which the Czech and Polish authorities complain about, while univocally for the Slovak regions the National Investment Promotion Agency remains the most troublesome partner.

4.5.2 Vertical Dimension of Cooperation

The networks discussed above stretch horizontally, that is, involve agencies operating on a regional level. Their vertical dimension is limited to the inclusion of the National Investment Promotion Agencies and the national tourist boards. This needs to be complemented by the 'downward' extension of the FDI promotion networks to incorporate the organisation on a sub-regional level. Local communities are possibly the most important such organisations. They hold influence and powers, have real interest in FDI attraction and often play an active role in the process (Drahokoupil, 2007; Jarczewski, 2007). For example Young and Kaczmarek's (2000) research shows that 63% of Polish local communities, particularly the larger and urban ones, undertake some form of promotional activity, while over 80% see attracting FDI as their main function. Complementarily, Florek's (2003) study indicates that over 70% of local communities consider investors to be their most important target group.

As the results of this study demonstrate CEE regional authorities seem to be aware of the communities' significance and 30% of them claim to consult with the urban and rural localities on their promotional activities.

Further, 47% consult some local jurisdictions (up to half of them), while the authorities of every fifth region do not involve localities in their promotional activities—a quarter of Polish and Slovak regions, and a fifth of Czech ones. The existence (or a lack) of consultations is not related to the size of the region or the number of communities within it. Regions comprised of smaller number of communities are no more likely to consult some or all of them, than the areas consisting of higher numbers of localities.

As before this practice differs between the three countries. Expectedly, it is in Poland that the involvement of all localities is most common (in 44% of regions). In contrast, a vast majority of the Czech regions (71%) are selective in their choice of partners for local cooperation, and on average consult just over 10% of local communities. In Slovakia, both approaches are equally popular, but the more selective regions on average consult 30% of localities. The number of localities which the regions involve in their FDI promotion shows no relation to the number of collaborators on the regional level. The CEE regional authorities are equally likely to develop their promotional networks horizontally and vertically.

However, these results should be treated with caution. On average, each region in the Czech Republic comprises 446, and 366 *obce* (municipalities) in Slovakia, and 154 *gminas* (communes) in Poland. Considering such multiplicity, it is difficult to assume real and equal participation of all local communities in the promotional actions of their region. Nevertheless, the Polish regions, consistent with earlier findings and previous research into other aspects of regional policy formulation and governance (e.g. Myant & Smith, 2006), seem to be more outward oriented and are more likely to cooperate with other organisations than their Czech and Slovak counterparts.

Some more dynamic localities not only may have significant impact on region's promotional strategies but can overshadow images of others and the whole region (Madsen, 1992; Pasquinelli & Teräs, 2013). Therefore the main objective of involving localities in the regional authorities' FDI promotion is twofold. Firstly, it should guarantee that local needs are fairly represented. Secondly, by exerting control over localities' actions it helps to assure the coherence of the promotional efforts—arguably one of the main success factors (Kotler & Gertner, 2002; Loewendahl, 2001).

Just over 50% of the regions believe no single locality dominates its promotional activities. A comparable amount, however, claim that some local areas either dominate or significantly impact their promotion. Most usually it is the regional capitals or other large cities, while rural areas have no major influence on the activities of the regional authorities (Young & Kaczmarek, 2000).

The importance of regional capitals is further emphasised in the context of image and promotional spending. Some of Polish regional capitals and other big cities often spend more on general promotion than do the regional authorities. For example, Szczecin and Warszawa promotional spending in 2007 reached $7.3 million, while Poznań expenditure totalled $992,000 (*Rzeczpospolita*, 2007c). Comparably in 2004 the FDI promotion budgets of corresponding regional authorities totalled $54,000, $292,000 and $81,000 respectively.

Over 45% of regional authorities studied believe the perceptions of their region are dominated by those of their capitals. Additionally, further 11% state that their capital city's image significantly overshadows the regional one, and another 14% claim this to be the case with other big cities in the region.

The communities (cities) having a major impact on a region's image are typically consulted by the regional authorities (80% of cases). However, despite their significant influence on the perceptions of the region, they do not automatically dominate their promotion. Only in six cases do the regional authorities admit their promotion is subjugated to the capital city, which also overshadows the image of the region.

Generally then, the two objectives of 'representation' and 'control' are met, albeit at different levels. The involvement of localities in the regional promotion is biased towards the bigger urban communities, and for the most part, it seems, none of the individual communities, including the regional capitals, is overrepresented in regions' promotion.

4.5.3 International Networks for Investment Promotion

Regional authorities' cooperation networks frequently extend beyond the country borders. While such collaboration is initially dominated by educational and cultural agenda (especially within the EU), progressively other issues come to the fore (e.g. environmental protection). In preparation for EU membership, CEE regions became increasingly involved in networks and partnerships fostering economic development, be it by the means of export promotion or twinning for public policy design. Such cooperation can either be institutionalised and legally sanctioned (e.g. Euroregions, Association of European Regions) or come in the form of less structured associations and initiatives (e.g. partner regions, Innovating Regions in Europe). Invariably, these groups offer potential for promotion and FDI attraction (Young, 2005). Therefore, it is important for regions to participate in such groupings, as it increases regions' international visibility, extends the networks of potential partner institutions and provides the platform for exchange of experiences and use of expertise.

Central-Eastern European regions are involved in bilateral partnerships, but also in multilateral associations. In fact, all regions report having mutual partnership arrangements and four in five participate in alliances of usually pan-European reach. Amongst the latter type the most popular is the Assembly of European Regions, and Committee of Regions. Both are characterised by intense political involvement in the European process. Another popular grouping indicated by the regional authorities is the Euroregions. With the exception of individual interior areas in the Czech Republic and Poland, all of the CEE regions constitute a part of some Euroregion (in several cases more than one) fostering transnational collaboration in environmental protection, cultural exchange and economic affairs.

In addition, all regions surveyed report involvement in economic cooperation with other areas. Some of those partnerships are utilised to foster trade or exchange promotional experience, while others serve as a promotion tool in themselves. From the perspective of target markets and competition explored in the latter part of the chapter it is interesting to examine the geographical span of such relations.

The CEE regions cooperate economically with areas in numerous different countries, including the EU, other European nations and some Asian states. However, the most popular associates (between 45% and 50% of cases) are the regions in large and strong European economies, namely France, Germany and Italy. Areas in the neighbouring countries score second in popularity, albeit with significantly less regions indicating this direction of cooperation (18%–30%).

The geographical coverage of economic partnerships varies between the three countries. While Polish regions operate within more diverse networks—on average each Polish region has partnership arrangements with areas in six different countries—cooperation of Slovak and Czech ones are usually limited to respectively four and three countries. Additionally, Polish regions more keenly maintain cooperation with areas in countries further afield (including China, India and South Korea) and in Eastern Europe (notably Ukraine, but also Russia).

As far as inter-regional dimension is concerned the last mode of association varies in popularity between the three countries and is the most popular in Poland. There is no individual region, either within respective countries or on the European scale, which serves CEE regional authorities as the benchmark example of best practice. Instead, they claim to be using established partnership networks of various kinds as the source of information and reference for the purpose of investment promotion.

The majority of Polish regional authorities identify a few regions in different European countries whose FDI promotion practices and experiences they use—most commonly in France and Germany, but also Austria, Belgium, Denmark and Sweden. Czech regions more often rely on each other's experience, but also use practices of other regions in Germany and the UK. Slovak regional authorities most commonly draw examples from neighbouring countries which, as will be discussed later, they also consider to be their main competitors.

4.6 Funding Investment Promotion

Comprehensively understood investment promotion must be underpinned by reliable and predictable budgetary commitments (Lodge, 2002; OECD, 2018). Yet, the multiplicity of agents involved and variety of the tasks performed under the heading of "promotion" means that tracing the sources of finances and their actual volume often proves difficult (Cleave et al., 2016; Ward, 1998).

Comparably to the UK and contrary to the USA, CEE regions' investment promotion budget predominantly comes from the public sources.

To pay for investment promotion CEE regional authorities exploit their own resources, make use of grants provided by the central government or utilise the Structural Funds (Table 4.4). Matching all three sources is relatively common and more popular in Poland than in the other two countries.

Most often (74%) promotion is funded with sources from various departments within the regional authorities, which may reflect attempts at a comprehensive approach, but also the relative inadequacy of the RAIS budgets. Only 16% of the regions rely solely on RAIS resources, while for a further 34% it is only one of the sources funding their investment promotion. Notably it is the Polish regions, operating bigger and often better prepared RAISs, that indicate their budget as one of the main sources of investment promotion funds. Additionally the Polish regions seem to have access to a bigger central government support than their Czech and Slovak counterparts. On the other hand, nearly 30% of Czech regions conduct their promotion using also EU funding—a source used by one in five of the Polish regions, and so far overlooked by the Slovak regional authorities. Meaningfully, but considering previous findings unsurprisingly, private capital is not utilised, which re-emphasises its lack of involvement in investment attraction process.

Table 4.4 Sources of promotion budget (% of answers)

	Regional authority investment section budget	Various departments' budgets	Central government purposeful funding	Other[a]
Czech Republic	37.5	78.6	28.6	28.6
Poland	75.0	75.0	56.3	18.8
Slovakia	25.0	62.5	25.0	0.0
TOTAL	50.0	73.7	39.5	18.4

Sum exceeds 100% as the respondents were asked to indicate all relevant answers

[a]Most commonly budget provided through projects funded by the EU Structural Funds

Source: Own research

Table 4.5 Promotion average spending in 2004

	Spending ($)				
	Average spending	Total	Spending per capita	Spending as % of regional GDP	Index 2004–2005
Czech Republic	193,183	1,931,831	0.26	0.0022	118
Poland	238,375	3,813,993	0.13	0.0023	186
Slovakia	52,708	368,655	0.08	0.0009	295
CEE average	185,296	6,114,780	0.16	0.002	185

Four Czech regions and one Slovak region did not provide the data regarding their 2004 or 2005 spending or both

Source: Own research, calculations based on online data of NBP, GUS, NBS, ŠÚSR, NBCz, ČSÚ

Despite a reasonably broad base of financing sources CEE regional authorities execute their investment promotion with the support of limited budgets—both in absolute and relative terms (Table 4.5). On average in 2004 regions spent just over $185,000 on their promotional activities, or 16 cents per one inhabitant. This amounted to 0.002% of the average volume of the regional GDP. Even when a predicted 85% increase in 2005 spending is considered, the sums fall short of promotional spending in other countries. For example, in the UK even historical spending of some areas has been substantially higher, and London Docklands Development Corporation between 1993 and 1994 spent nearly £4 million on Docklands promotion. In the same period, Birmingham's promotional spending reached £7.42 per inhabitant, and was highest among the six English main metropolitan areas, whose average spending totalled £2.85 per capita[3] (Ward, 1998).

These numbers show how, despite the earlier signalled importance of investment promotion on CEE regions' development agenda, it remains a secondary practice rather than a mainstream policy supported with adequate means.

This is additionally emphasised when national tourism promotion budgets are considered. According to *Rzeczpospolita* (2007a) the budget

[3] While these sums include promotion directed to groups other than foreign investors, they provide a useful comparative context for FDI promotional expenditure of CEE regional authorities.

for tourism promotion of Poland in 2007 totalled around €10 million, and was three times higher for the promotion of the Czech Republic. However, investment promotion is gaining importance, and quickly, as illustrated by the regions' intentions to increase their expenditure in 2005—on average by 85%.

The difference between 2004 spending and expenditure planned for 2005 varies somewhat between the three countries. A brief comparison of the national averages complies with some of the earlier findings, where Polish regions usually show deeper commitment to the promotional process than their Slovak and Czech counterparts.

Earlier it was argued that promotion is not only a privilege of the wealthy. As far as the budget is concerned, however, this finding needs to be put in the national contexts. The promotional budgets of Czech and Slovak regions are related to the regional GDP volumes and that makes them more comparable to Polish local communities (see Florek, 2003), but dissimilar to Polish regions. This further validates the previously suggested more holistic involvement of the Polish regions in the promotional process and its wider popularity in the country, while in 2004 it remained a novelty in the Czech Republic and, to a lesser extent, also in Slovakia. However, this was expected to change, as the planned budgetary changes between 2004 and 2005 shows no connection to the volume of regional GDP, that is, not only the wealthier but equally poorer regions were planning to significantly increase their expenditure on FDI promotion.

The links between promotional budget and regional potential in the Czech Republic is further stressed by its dependence on population size, that is, the more populated the region, the more it spends on promotion. This relation however does not exist in Poland or Slovakia.

An average investment promotion budget of Polish regional authorities is only slightly lower than that of Czech and Slovak ones combined—respectively $238,000 and $245,000. But there is a considerable difference between the highest and lowest spenders in Poland—almost $775,000, and over 60% of the regions spend less than the national average. This means there exists a smaller group of 'big spenders'. With the promotional budget of $810,000, Łódzkie voivodeship ranks top amongst the Polish areas. While it would be unjustified to draw any definite conclusions, it would also be wrong not to match this with the recent increase of Łódzkie's popularity among foreign investors. During the three years between 2002 and 2005 the region attracted many key investments from globally recognised brands including Dell, Gillette, Bosh-Siemens, Philips and less well known but comparably big companies such as Spanish fabric producers Alibérico and German company Häring supplying components to Mercedes and Volvo engines (*Rzeczpospolita*, 2004, 2007b).

On the other end of the scale investment promotion spending of Podlaskie voivodeship in 2004 was so insignificant that it could be better compared to local community resources dedicated to general promotion. For example, the majority of Wielkopolskie voivodeship communes do not spend more than €34,500 (Florek, 2003), and Podlaskie also fits into this bracket. Recognising this, in 2005 the voivodeship planned a threefold increase of its FDI promotional budget, which exceeds the national average of 86%.

The Czech regions in 2004 on average spent 20% less money on promotion than their Polish counterparts, but almost four times as much as the Slovak ones. With the budget close to $1 million Praha metropolitan region is by far the Czech Republic's and indeed Central-Eastern Europe's biggest spender. Promotion of other Czech regions is supported by much lower budgets, on average not exceeding $110,000.

As far as the 2005 spending plans are concerned, the Czech regions are the most conservative, planning a mere 18% rise in their promotional expenditure. This average is distorted by a few more progressive areas, while 70% of the regions declare their promotional spending will increase only by 7%. Such unanimity reflects an average increase in regional authority total budgets—the main source of promotional expenditure (Table 5.4)—rather than a change of priorities or the acquisition of additional purposeful funding.

Slovak regions spend the least amount on their investment attraction activities—on average less than $53,000 in 2004 and even an average threefold increase planned for 2005 does not take this amount beyond the $100,000 mark. Similarly, to the other two countries regional promotional budgets vary significantly. Alike in the Czech case the capital city region remains the biggest spender over the two-year period, but it is other areas, which reveal plans for the highest increases of promotional budgets.

Considering the cases of Bratislavský kraj, Praha and Łódzkie voivodeship, it is possible to suggest that there is a relationship between FDI stocks and flows and resources dedicated to regional promotion. However, it is impossible to unambiguously assess the strength and direction of such relationship. At this stage, it could be suggested that the relationship might be circular in nature. Growing investment inflows encourage regional authorities to even greater promotional activity, which in turn results in sustained or increasing inflows of foreign capital to the region.

Overall, considering the budgetary commitments, investment promotion in CEE is an emerging rather than an established activity. Merely individual regions command big enough budgets to allow them prolonged and far-reaching activities—which still only optimistically could be called 'campaigns'.

The CEE regional authorities are aware their actions are under-funded. This is reflected by both their plans to increase spending, but also by their direct opinions. More than half of the regions perceive their promotional

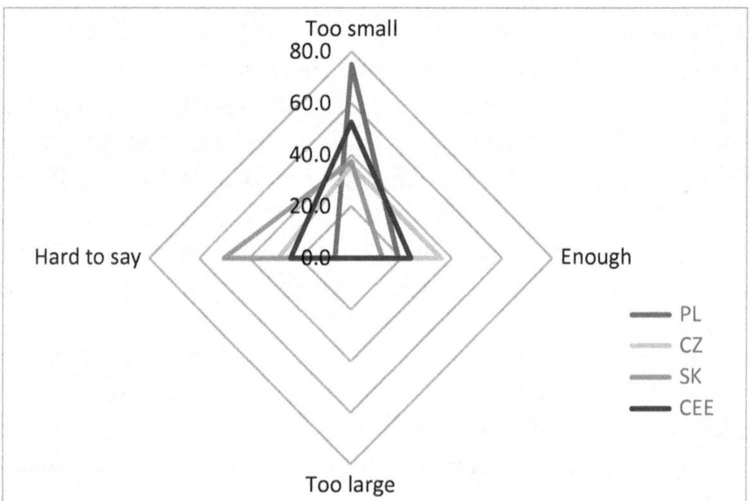

Fig. 4.1 Regional authorities' opinions on their promotional budgets. *Source*: Own research

budgets to be too small when considered in the context of their needs (Fig. 4.1). None of the regions consider it to be too large, but for almost a quarter it remains satisfactory. Equally, around a quarter of the regional authorities find it difficult to determine.

In line with the emerging picture, the more proactive Polish regions constitute the largest group displeased with their promotional spending, while over a third of the Czech ones claim the budgets satisfy their needs. This corresponds with earlier findings indicating planned higher increase in spending by the Polish regions, and more conservative plans of their Czech counterparts. Despite plans for considerable increases in promotional spending, half of the Slovak regional authorities do not have an opinion on the sufficiency of their present promotional budgets, which arguably reflects their inconsistent approach to the promotional process.

Interestingly, regional authorities across CEE know how they would utilise bigger budgets if they were available. Figure 4.2 displays the most desired ways of allocating the additional resources. It should not be treated simply as an indication of what kind of activity is currently most under-funded. Instead, high response rates for some categories often signpost the popularity and straightforward introduction of some actions and promotional tools, such as, for example, advertising, participation in fairs and exhibitions (Florek, 2003; Wells & Wint, 2000; World Bank, 2012), rather than the current lack of expenditure in this area.

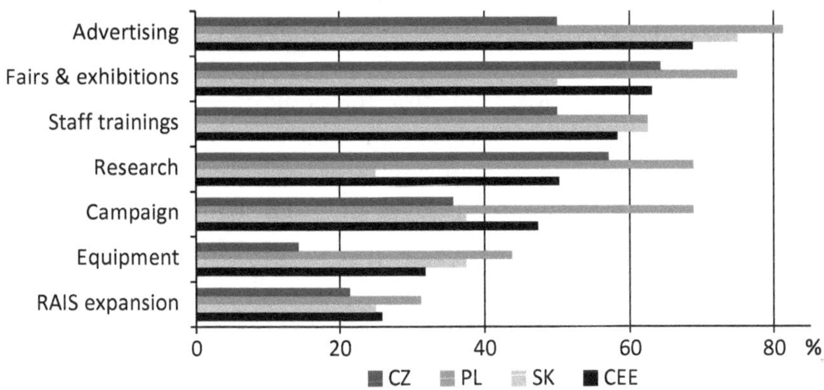

Fig. 4.2 Preferential allocations of hypothetical budgets. *Source*: Own research

Most of the regions would like to expand the visible aspects of investment promotion, namely advertising, but also increase participation in investment-focused trade fairs and exhibitions, 68% and 66% respectively. The popularity of advertising and some of the personal selling channels amongst the institutions has been observed in earlier studies, albeit the perceived attractiveness of these varies from institution to institution. Between 14% and 17% of the Polish local communities would dedicate additional resources to those two areas (Florek, 2003), while their status amongst world investment promotion agencies is much higher (Wells & Wint, 2000; World Bank, 2012).

The remaining activities on which the regions would spend additional resources reflect current inadequate spending in those areas or indeed a lack of such an activity conditioned by the insufficient level of resources.

Despite the earlier identified dissatisfaction with the staffing levels just over a quarter of regions would expand their RAIS. Instead, the authorities would rather develop their quality by improving staff capabilities and to a lesser extent modernising office equipment.

Over 55% of the regions would increase their spending on research and learning more about their competitors and potential investors, which as the forthcoming sections will show, reflects current low level of such activities.

Just over a half of CEE regional authorities would use the extra funding to launch a new promotional campaign. This confirms suggested earlier inconsistent execution of the promotional process, a lack of strategic approach and preference for ad-hoc actions. A fact further emphasised by the lack of individual ideas on how the additional budget could be spent—none of the authorities made an effort to indicate how else they would have spent additional resources.

These results vary between the three countries. Reflecting their more comprehensive approach to the promotional process, Polish regions usually score significantly higher in all categories than the Czech or Slovak ones. Comparably Slovak regional authorities in five out of seven categories score above their Czech counterparts, whose engagement with investment promotion remains irregular.

4.7 Regional Authorities' (Self-)Evaluation

Budget is one of the vital factors shaping the scope and quality of regional promotion aimed at investment attraction. Its importance increases further in circumstances when the resources are limited, as is often the case in Central-Eastern European regions. Thus, proper allocation, effective use of the funds and efficiency of the performed actions become of paramount significance.

To assure appropriate standards the authorities need to monitor and evaluate their actions—yet a paradox is observed. Despite short experience of the RAIS and existing deficiencies in staff qualifications, promotion activities of only a quarter of CEE regional authorities are being monitored and evaluated, and a mere fraction undergo external appraisal. Over a half of the regions do not evaluate their performance at all. Remaining 25% did not provide answer to the question which, we can speculate, may suggest a lack of such practice.

Lesser involvement with promotion of the Czech and Slovak regions is scrutinised more often than the more comprehensive actions of the Polish areas. Almost 40% of Slovak and 30% of the Czech regions report their promotion activities are evaluated, while this is the case in less than a fifth of the Polish areas.

The general low levels of monitoring and evaluation of the efficiency and quality of the activities presented by the CEE regional authorities can only partially be explained by the presumed high standards of the performed actions. Merely 30% of the regions which do not have evaluation mechanisms in place, involve academics and professional experts in their promotion.

In literature such attitudes are not uncommon as public authorities' promotional process is rarely scrutinised especially by external auditors (Almond et al., 2015; Ashworth & Voogd, 1994; Bradley, Hall, & Harrison, 2002; Paddison, 1993). For example 95% of local authorities in the Polish region of Wielkopolska do not have ways of assessing their promotional actions (Florek, 2003). And in any case such evaluation usually comes only after the failure of a particular campaign, as was the case with the unsuccessful promotion of Ontario in Canada (Lodge, 2002).

However, the use of external experts is more popular, particularly for general and tourism promotion purposes as illustrated by "Glasgow's Miles Better" campaign conducted by Saatchi & Saatchi (Ward, 1998). More recently the use of advertising consultancies in promotion increased as evidenced by the growing number of companies offering place promotion and branding services.

Study results also demonstrate CEE regional authorities' conviction that the current level of regional promotion is adequate, that is, the quantity of promotion is satisfactory. As illustrated by Fig. 4.3 the majority of the studied areas consider their promotional efforts to be sufficient, while the authorities in every fourth area are aware they are not doing enough to promote their region. Yet, a more detailed analysis of the data reveals a less bold and more consistent approach presented by the authorities.

Expectedly the lowest percentage of positive answers and highest proportion of negative answers is amongst the Czech regions, which matches earlier findings suggesting their limited involvement with the promotion process. However now it is put into a new context, as it shows Czech regional authorities are conscious of existing deficiencies. On the opposite end of the 'positive' scale are the Polish regions, 70% of which judge

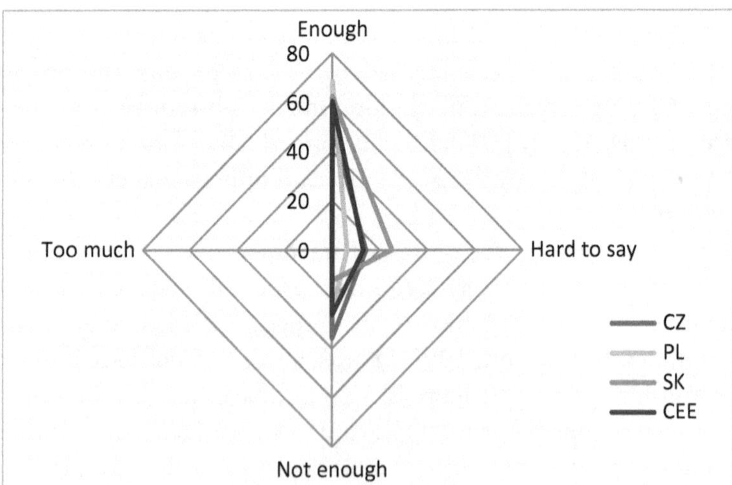

Fig. 4.3 Assessment of the volume of promotion. *Source*: Own research

their efforts as sufficient. As was often the case in earlier discussion, the Slovak regional authorities are placed in the middle and just under two-thirds of them believe they are doing enough to promote their areas, while a quarter avoided providing an answer.

Apart from involvement in promotion, budget is another factor determining the levels of regional authorities' self-assessment. Those authorities that claim to operate 'sufficient' promotional budgets do not perceive their promotion to be inadequate. Complementarily 35% of those indicating satisfactory promotion levels are the authorities satisfied with their promotional spending. The contrary is true for the same proportion of areas.

Generally then the approach to quality assessment and budgetary aspects of promotion matches the emerging depiction of three different approaches to promotion existing in Central-Eastern Europe.

Despite generally underdeveloped mechanisms for quality assessment but positive opinions about the levels of promotion, the majority of Polish and almost all of Slovak regional authorities[4] are aware of existing room for improvement and point to a number of particular insufficiencies. They often highlight deficiencies in qualitative aspects of promotion and call for improvements in research, strategic approach, increased internal coherence but also closer relationships leading to an increased coordination between RAIS and local authorities and regional development agencies. Further, the regions recognise the need of private capital involvement as either a subcontractor or a co-financier of promotion.

Additionally a number of authorities mention inadequate volume of their promotional actions, that is, they want to improve the quantity of promotion. Most notably they would like to increase regions' international visibility and more frequently participate in investment trade fairs and exhibitions.

Contrary to the claims made by some literature (e.g. Brown, 2006; Czornik, 2000; Kotler et al., 1999), the mere existence of some kind of assessment mechanism is neither a warrant of increased awareness of deficiencies nor a guarantee of an improved performance. Despite the highest proportion of the Czech regional authorities' promotion undergoing assessment, they usually cannot name the existing deficiencies, while the

[4] Only a few Czech regions identified issues they would like to improve. Those are in line with the concerns of other regions.

Polish regions, where evaluation is least common, have no difficulty with pointing out things to be improved. It appears that at this initial stage of CEE regions' involvement in promotion common sense, self-criticism and a willing attitude is more important than systematic evaluation procedures.

4.8 Investment Promotion Planning and Implementation

4.8.1 Market Research Sources and Results

Good knowledge of the region, permitting the identification of characteristics superior to those of the competitors as well as an accurate understanding of the investors as a target group are arguably some of the staples of effective promotion. Thus, research is often listed as key amongst factors determining successful promotion (Florek, 2005; Metaxas, 2010; Go & Govers, 2013). It provides the information about target groups' trends and product requirements therefore enabling the creation of distinct, targeted offer and desirable messages communicating its qualities (Charlton & Davis, 2006; Clow & Baack, 2018; Loewendahl, 2001). Perhaps the most important, though, is the initial assessment of the current situation in the region and recognition of a region's position (and perception) amongst its national and international competitors.

The CEE regional authorities appear aware about the position of their regions on the national and European mental map. As discussed earlier, the authorities are conscious that their nationally and internationally recognised assets are often biased towards tourism-oriented characteristics. Additionally more regional features have broad national range, while the recognition of regions' qualities in the wider Europe is limited. In fact, almost 20% of regional authorities believe their region is not known in Europe at all.

The level of familiarity with the foreign investors target group is somewhat less satisfactory (Table 4.6). On the scale between 1 and 5, CEE regional authorities assess it at 2.7, with the marks of the Czech and

Table 4.6 Level of familiarity and data sources on two target groups

	Existing investors					Potential investors				
		Data sources (%)					Data sources (%)			
	Level of knowledge[a]	Own research	Secondary resources	Consultancies	Not gathering information	Level of knowledge[a]	Own research	Secondary resources	Consultancies	Not gathering information
Czech Republic	2.4	36	57	36	7	2.4	29	50	21	14
Poland	3.9	38	69	50	13	3.1	25	50	56	19
Slovakia	2.5	38	50	0	13	2.4	38	63	0	13
CEE	3.0	37	61	34	11	2.7	29	53	32	16

[a]Scale from 1 (low) to 5 (high)

Source: Own research

Slovak regions below this number. The low score partially results from a limited variety of information sources used by the authorities. Research of more than half of the regions relies on secondary data provided by other public institutions including national banks, NIPAs, regional development agencies and to a lesser extent also national statistical offices.

Consultancies' services and reports, in line with earlier findings, are used by one in three regions, and are significantly more popular in Poland (56%) than in the Czech Republic (21%). Slovak authorities seemingly do not use the information provided by this source. Instead, they rely on their own primary research more often (38%) than their counterparts in the other two countries (Czech Republic 28%, Poland 25%).

Investment and aftercare services are integral parts of the promotion process, therefore acquiring information on existing investors, their needs and satisfaction levels, should be high on the regional authorities' research agenda. The knowledge of this group is assessed 0.3 points higher than is the case with potential investors, but the differences between the countries is even greater. Polish regions assess their familiarity with current investors at 3.9, and the Czech and Slovak ones at 2.4 and 2.5 respectively. Higher average score reflects the use of a wider variety of information sources and more primary research conducted by the authorities. Almost 37% of regions claim to be collecting data directly from the investors. This is partially reflective of the extent of sustained contacts between the authorities and the companies and suggests the existence of some form of feedback mechanism. Sustaining contacts with the current investors and gathering information from them is relatively cheaper than ordering studies on potential investors, which is significant considering frequent budgetary constraints.

Further, it is more common for the regions to use any kind of information source on existing companies than on potential investors, and while 16% of authorities admit to not gathering data on future investors, this is true for 11% when existing investors are considered.

Surprisingly the highest proportion of those not collecting information on either existing or potential investors exists amongst the Polish regions. This reveals inconsistencies in their approach to the promotional process, which so far appeared to be more comprehensive than those of the Czech and Slovak regional authorities.

4.8.2 Identifying Intra-national Competition

Research also involves identifying competitors and their advantages, which then allows for competitive positioning of the region and identification of region's unique selling points, that is, peculiar characteristics from the perspective of the target markets (Clow & Baack, 2018; Dinnie, 2011; Loewendahl, 2001). Yet, while it is competition which constitutes the very basis of authorities' involvement in promotion, and despite widely agreed benefits of thorough knowledge of competitors, places usually do little to understand them (Pasquinelli, 2013).

The identification of competitors, arguably, should to be guided by two principles: (1) characteristics of the places and the levels the similarity of offered products, and (2) the choice of the target market. As demonstrated by analysis of CEE regions' target markets below, the majority of the areas are interested in attracting investments in any and every industrial sector and branch from whichever country. Such situation suggests an 'all-out-war' where the regions will command their contention on general principles rather than particular, target-specific aspects of the place products.

Despite a substantial concentration of FDI in capital city regions, only a quarter of CEE regional authorities identify their national capital as their main competitor (Table 4.7). The differences between the countries are far less significant than the disparity in FDI concentration (Tables 1.3 and 6.1). However, those results should not be interpreted collectively as they reflect different attitudes prevailing in the three countries. Czech and Slovak regions consider Praha and Bratislavský kraj, respectively, to be their, what Kotler et al. (1999, p. 83) term, "superior competitors". Conversely, the two capital city regions (plus Středočeský kraj, surrounding Praha in the Czech Republic) recognise their superior or indeed beyond-the-reach position and claim they do not have any national competitors.

On the other hand, the low proportion of the Polish regions indicating Mazowieckie voivodeship as their main competitor reflects less dominating levels of FDI stock concentration in the capital region than in the Czech and Slovak instances. Consequently, there is no gradation of com-

Table 4.7 Main national competitors (% of answers)

	Neighbouring region(s)	Capital city region	Other regions	No national competition	Difficult to say
Czech Republic	14	36	7	21	14
Poland	44	19	31	0	6
Slovakia	38	25	0	12	25
CEE	32	26	16	10	13

Source: Own research

petition amongst the Polish regions, which all seem to consider one another as "peer competitors" (Kotler et al., 1999, p. 111). Indeed Polish regions express the highest level of competition awareness, with merely 6% of them having difficulty identifying rivals and 75% able to name them.

Generally, every third CEE region, particularly in Poland and Slovakia, recognises its immediate neighbours as the main national competitors. It could suggest equal spread of current FDI stock across the countries and a very gradual change in regional conditions and locational attractiveness, if any at all. While to some extent this might be true, as demonstrated in earlier parts of the book, significant differences persist in the levels of development between the regions within particular countries as well as between them (Blokker & Dallago, 2009; Dogaru et al., 2015; Domański, Guzik, & Micek, 2003). Therefore, the identification of competitors, rather than being based on systematic research, tends to reflect the regional authorities' common knowledge of their neighbours. Only a minority of the areas (16%; mainly in Poland) make more effort to identify their national rivals to the extent as to be capable of providing their names.[5]

4.8.3 International Competitors

The lack of a structured approach to the identification of rivals and their awareness based predominantly on common knowledge is even clearer

[5] Four out of five Polish regions in this category name Dolnoślaskie voivodeship, which in 2003 with the share of 7% was investors' fourth most favourite destination in Poland.

when international competition is concerned. Only 10% of CEE regions are capable of identifying competitors, while the vast majority can name merely the countries where their rivals are located.

Just over a half of the CEE regional authorities recognise neighbouring states as the main source of competition (Table 4.8). However, only one indicates an Austrian region, (Bratislavský kraj authorities identify Vienna region as their rival) two point to Germany, and another two regions claim to be competing with areas in Ukraine.

Consequently, the dominant view between the Czech, Polish and Slovak regional authorities is that competition takes places mostly between the areas of those three countries, and sporadically with areas in wider Central-Eastern Europe, including Lithuania, Romania, Serbia and Russia.

Such results seem to be in line with the earlier research findings (e.g. Dogaru et al., 2015; Helinska-Hughes & Hughes, 2003; Meyer et al., 2005) identifying stark competition for FDI between the Central-Eastern European Countries. But bearing in mind regional authorities' limited ability to accurately identify competitors, it should be considered as reflective of their presuppositions, that is, knowledge of existing state of affairs, rather than the objective confirmation resulting from a systematic research process.

Consequently, a type of a paradox in CEE investment promotion becomes clear. International dimension of competition for mobile investment is perceived to be the dominating aspect the rivalry (Phelps & Raines, 2003). Yet, if anything, it is the intra-national dimension of com-

Table 4.8 International competitors (% of answers)

	Regions in neighbouring countries	Regions in CEE	Regions in Western Europe	Regions in other countries	No international competition	Difficult to say
Czech Republic	50	21	0	0	7	29
Poland	44	6	13	13	0	38
Slovakia	75	13	0	0	0	13
CEE	53	13	5	5	3	29

Source: Own research

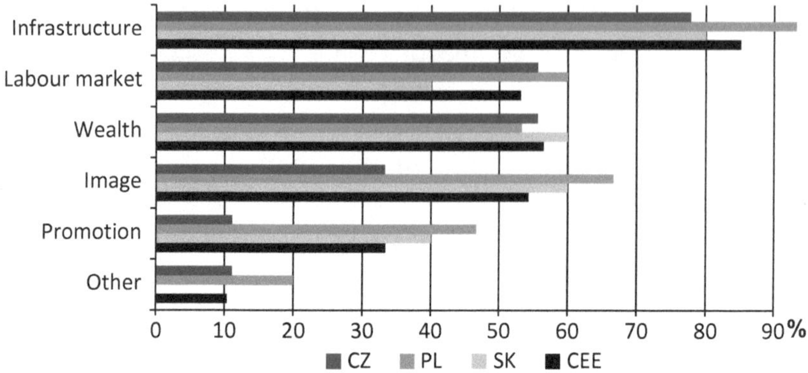

Fig. 4.4 Basis for national competition (% answers). The authorities which claim not to have national competitors or found it difficult to identify them did not have to respond to the question. *Source*: Own research

petition that is more acknowledged by the CEE regions, who make little effort to become familiar with and understand foreign rivals. It is noticeable not only in mere (in)ability to name the regional competitors abroad, but it also becomes clear when the qualitative basis for such competition are explored. The authorities find it easier to identify the reasons why investors are more likely to invest in the areas governed by their national rivals (Fig. 4.4), while their knowledge of international (European) competitors' comparative advantage generally remains restricted (Fig. 4.5). More regions are able to identify a set of features that puts them in a disadvantaged position vis-à-vis their national competitors than the European ones.

4.8.4 CEE Regions' Competitive Positioning

The issues indicated by the authorities should be understood in two corresponding ways. Firstly, indirectly they show the authorities' understanding of variables affecting FDI location, and secondly, and more directly, they indicate their self-criticism and awareness of limitations of their regions.

Reflecting often insufficient infrastructural conditions prevailing in Central-Eastern Europe (Ascani, Crescenzi, & Iammarino, 2017; Blokker

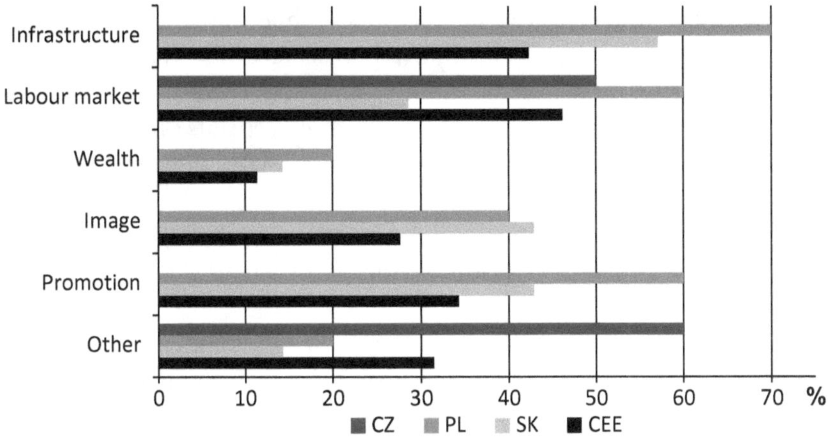

Fig. 4.5 Basis for European competition (% answers). The authorities which claim not to have European competitors or found it difficult to identify them did not have to respond to this question. *Source*: Own research

& Dallago, 2009; Chidlow, Salciuviene, & Young, 2009) a vast majority of the CEE regions believe their national competitors' infrastructural networks are superior to their own (Fig. 4.4). The two subsequent most important set of issues (specifically for the Czech and Polish authorities) that put regions in disadvantaged position against their national rivals are associated with the labour market characteristics and economic condition of the region.

Almost 60% of CEE regional authorities express the opinion that their rivals are characterised by better labour market circumstances and superior economic capacity. Interestingly, the same proportion or regions claim to have problems with their image, although this is more varied between the three countries. Most likely, this should not be understood as regions suffering from negative images, but rather experiencing a lack of distinctive image which is often overshadowed by the perceptions of the whole country (*Instytut Marki Polskiej*, 2004).

The authorities rarely link promotion to merely image-related activities, and despite the alleged inferior perceptions, the majority of CEE regions express satisfaction with their own promotional activities and only about 35% perceive them to be of lower standards than those of both national and European competitors. While this broadly confirms earlier findings, it also shows that regions are aware that even well-performed promotion does not bring immediate effects in the form of improved image. Further, it presents authorities' general conviction about the importance of regional image and promotional actions in FDI location process.

When considering the international competition the regional authorities of the three countries prioritise the particular (dis)advantages in a slightly different order (Fig. 4.5).

Infrastructure remains Polish regions' biggest disadvantage on the European scale. But it is the issues associated with the labour market, particularly the costs, quality and accessibility of labour, that most CEE regions feel put them in an inferior position against their competitors. The wealth of the region and its economic capacity seems to be relatively insignificant.

One other noteworthy distinction from the national context is the regional authorities' ability to name a selection of additional criteria that should be considered. The authorities point to the significance of a stable legal environment and the perceived lesser amount of bureaucracy in their competitor countries.

Investment incentives is another often-quoted matter. Particularly the Czech regions are convinced that their rivals offer better financial and fiscal incentives, which shows how, despite questionable effectiveness and vague impact on actual investors' location decision (Dunning & Lundan, 2008; Navaretti & Venables, 2004), this policy tool remains high on the promotional agenda of regional authorities.

Analysis of opinions on image and promotion in the context of national and international competition reveals two main facts. Firstly, the authorities assign different roles to promotion depending on the scale of competition. On the national market of localisations, according to the CEE regional authorities, regional image plays a more important role than on an international scale. Once the country has been shortlisted or even better, selected by the investor, the regions consider it to be more important to have a clear, positive and distinctive image. Secondly, when competition takes place amongst the national regions, promotional activities need to be chosen accordingly. Consequently, on the international level, where the regional image is of lesser importance, the regional authorities suggest the use of other than image-building techniques.

This is a distinctive feature of regional promotion as compared to activities performed by NIPAs on behalf of countries, which initially tend to concentrate on image-building activities, and only subsequently engage with other forms of investment promotion (OECD, 2015; Wells & Wint, 2000; World Bank, 2012).

4.8.5 Targeting Foreign Investors

An intensive competition for the FDI projects and often limited resources at the disposal of the regional authorities require them to assure efficiency of their promotional measures. One important factor conditioning higher returns on investment in promotion is targeting (Charlton, Davis, Faye, Haddock, & Lamb, 2004; Harding & Javorcik, 2012; Loewendahl, 2001).

The various targeting strategies discussed in Chap. 3 indicate the importance of research, knowledge of one's own assets, recognition of competitors' advantages and consistency in adopted approach as key features of comprehensive targeting (Clow & Baack, 2018; Kotler et al., 1999; Wells & Wint, 2000).

National Investment Promotion Agencies across the world widely adopt various targeting strategies and organise their structures and promotional activities accordingly (Charlton et al., 2004; OECD, 2018). While naturally organisational arrangements of regional authorities are constrained, they can and should recognise the need of targeting their actions leading to an increased awareness of location amongst the identified groups and providing chances for relationship building with the potential investors (Harding & Javorcik, 2012; Loewendahl, 2001).

The two fundamental approaches to segmentation of the investors' market are based on country of origin and sectoral characteristics. Recognising the distinctive nature of investors' national cultural backgrounds allows to tailor a set of investment services and to utilise the personal selling techniques accordingly. It enables to adequately design the promotional message and convey it via the relevant channels. This is also an advantage embedded in sectoral targeting. However, while geographical targeting guides 'how' various promotional tools should be used, the sectoral or branch targeting informs 'why' and encourages the consideration of more technical-managerial aspects of targeted industries. Subsequently the second group can be further divided into sub-segments characterised by particular qualities such as size, growth rates, trade intensity, capital and labour intensity, technological advancement and so on. In reality such precise targeting rarely occurs, more often NIPAs adopt direct marketing approaches and target individual companies instead (Wells & Wint, 2000; World Bank, 2012).

This however remains a time-consuming and labour-intensive practice (Loewendahl, 2001) which CEE public authorities due to their limited promotional capacities cannot afford. For example Florek (2003) has found that only 5% of Wielkopolska local communities demonstrated the direct marketing approach, while in the study discussed here only one region revealed using the direct marketing approach. The authorities of Středočeský kraj in the Czech Republic were attempting to attract Changhong, a Chinese TV sets manufacturer.[6]

In fact the targeting of CEE regional authorities' promotion in the majority of cases falls short of any more precise definition than 'foreign investors'. As illustrated by Table 4.9 the activities of over 60% of regions are guided neither by sectoral nor geographical targeting principles. Thus while earlier research has shown that NIPAs' targeting is usually sector oriented (Charlton et al., 2004; World Bank, 2012), the CEE regional authorities reveal little preference in their target group selection criteria. If anything they are just slightly more likely to define their targets based on the nationality of the investors.

The Czech regions constitute a group presenting the least targeted approach. Slovak authorities are more careful and a quarter of them aim to attract investment in a particular industrial sector, and further 13% target investors from selected countries. On the other end of the spectrum the majority of Polish areas claim to have target markets defined more carefully—38% based on sectoral characteristics and 44% on geo-

[6] This reflects the negotiations ongoing at the time of the study, rather than conscious direct marketing activities performed by the Středočeský kraj authorities. Ultimately the project was successful and in March 2007, having invested 15 million USD, Changhong opened its factory creating 300 jobs in the town of Nymburk (CzechInvest, 2007).

Table 4.9 Targeting of foreign investors (% of answers)

	Sectoral targeting	Geographical targeting	No targeting
Czech Republic	7	14	86
Poland	38	44	44
Slovakia	24	13	63
CEE	24	26	63

Source: Own research

graphical features. A quarter of Polish regions define their target groups based on both principles.

The CEE regions use previous experiences and target their promotion at investors from countries they are more familiar with. Amongst the areas whose promotion is geographically targeted, 70% aim to attract German investors. The next most popular source of FDI is France and Sweden—respectively 40% and 30%. The regions attempt to attract investors from the EU-15, rather than from further afield; however, the USA and China were also named amongst the target countries. Such choice broadly reflects the existing structure of foreign investment stock in the three countries. While the exact order of the national origins of the capital may vary, the European countries, notably Germany, France, the Netherlands and Austria, until mid-2000s have provided CEEC with the highest amounts of foreign money (Bradshaw, 2005). Furthermore, the structure of the FDI stock nationality seems to be stable over the years, which considering the relatively short history of investment attraction in Central-Eastern Europe, suggests the existence of measures which maintain the status quo rather than explore new markets.

In the broader context of this study, from the perspective of regional development, the motivations underlying CEE regional authorities' targeting approaches suggest that regional promotion is rather an effect than a causative factor of development. The analysis of sectors targeted by the regional authorities largely confirms this.

The sectoral composition of targeted investors is varied but more dispersed than it was the case in geographical targeting. Predictably, the most popular (44%) is the automotive industry, followed by the electronic industry (33%). The next most sought-after industries include environmental protection and wood processing—each targeted by a fifth of regions. Most desirable service investments comprise tourism and the IT sector—targeted by every third region.

Comparably to geographical targeting structure, the configuration of industrial targets to a considerable degree also reflects the established state of affairs.[7] Only the composition of desired service sectors varies from the FDI sectoral trends observed in the three countries in mid-2000s. However, it is in line with the global tendencies. In 2004 a UNCTAD survey of world investment promotion agencies found that the majority of them target computer services, tourism, hotels and restaurants. In Central-Eastern Europe 80% of NIPAs targeted IT services, and a further 50% aimed to attract investments in the tourism sectors (UNCTAD 2004a). On the one hand it indicates growing mobility of those sectors, on the other however, and more importantly from the perspective of this stud, it signifies the attractiveness of such investments and resulting from it vivid competition between the countries in attracting them.

As for the industrial sectors, the CEE regions' targets do not match those of other highly developed economies. Charlton and Davis (2006) have found that the majority of OECD countries target telecommunications, chemical and plastic manufacturing and business services. This does not mean that there is no competition for the branches targeted by the CEE regions, but rather illustrates that the competition is located elsewhere, namely in less developed nations (as well as appearing between the three countries themselves).

In summary then, considering targeting, the investment promotion of the majority of CEE regions resembles shooting in the dark rather than the operations of a counter-sniper. Those that employ a more consistent approach seem to be extending the reasoning of the Multilateral Investment Guarantee Agency (2006) to include geographical targeting. The CEE regions reflect the opinion that "if your location already receives investment from a particular sector and country, investors from this country and sector are more likely than not to have better than average information on your location" (MIGA, 2006).

[7] Sectoral targeting should identify the sectors in which the host region is best placed to attract FDI and which meet the developmental objectives of the area (Potter & Moore, 2000; World Bank, 2012). Due to the lack of data on the regional level the analysis has to rely on country level data, which prohibits making a reliable connection between the sectors chosen by the authorities and the structure of industrial activity in particular regions.

4.9 Conclusions

The chapter aimed to offer a detailed picture of regional promotion in Central-Eastern European regions, with special focus on investment attraction. Through the analysis of the purposefully gathered survey data, it provided insights into the extent of CEE regional authorities' involvement in the process of investment promotion. By providing such "regional" perspective it complements other research focusing on single agent studies at urban, community or national scales (e.g. Florek, 2003; Madsen, 1992; Paddison, 1993; World Bank, 2012; Young, 2005). Additionally, by exploring perspectives guided by the research questions, it advances the current debate by examining the promotional approaches adopted by CEE regional authorities within the context of levels of development of their areas.

The discussion presented allows drawing a number of conclusions in relation to the research questions.

The promotion of CEE regions tends to be generic or tourism oriented, rather than targeted at investors. This is in contrast with the esteem and importance assigned to FDI throughout the transition process, but arguably partially explains concentration of investments in more recognised, though usually less promotionally active, capital city regions.

Robust investment promotion, embedded in regional development strategies, is still to materialise. Currently the activities performed by the regional authorities remain unstructured and unsystematic, and the adopted approaches are characterised by a high degree of improvisation and fragmentation, and at times contradiction. For example, while generally inward investments are deemed important to the regional economy, only half of the regions make relevant provisions in their development strategies. Further, whilst the majority of CEE regional authorities admit promotion is high on their agenda, it is recognised in development strategies of only some, and considered in the budgets of a few. Consequently, as found by other studies, it is the resources which significantly impede the promotional process (Brown, 2006; Cleave et al., 2016; Madsen, 1992; Pasquinelli, 2013). In half of the cases the offices of regional authorities investment sections remain understaffed, and a mere third have adequate financial resources at their disposal. This impacts not only the scope of the activities performed, but perhaps more importantly also the preparatory stages of the promotional process including research. In turn this leads to imprecise targeting (potentially resulting in the misuse of already limited resources) of promotion.

Analysis of targeted sectors indicated by the regional authorities reveals their conservative approach to development. For the most part the sectors which have been indicated are those which have a history of operations within the area. Thus, arguably promotion cannot be seen as a tool changing the state of current affairs, as suggested by some literature (OECD, 2015; Wells & Wint, 2000), but rather one which helps to strengthen them. It is not used to strategically diversify the regional economic base, but rather to reinforce it.

Optimistically regional authorities are aware of the flaws in their promotional efforts regarding both its qualitative and quantitative aspects, and they acknowledge the deficiencies in staff qualifications and poor coordination of the process.

Thus, investment promotion on a regional level in Central-Eastern Europe is an emerging phenomenon, as evidenced by fragmented actions, underdeveloped cooperation networks and restricted budgets, amongst others. However erratic as it may seem, there are signs of more comprehensive practices appearing in some regions which decided to go beyond the naïve production of leaflets, and began adopting a process-like approach to investment attraction.

The overall confusion and lack of structure guiding much the CEE regional promotion efforts vary between the countries. Polish regional authorities tend to present more systematic and comprehensive approaches as compared to their Slovak, and particularly Czech, counterparts. The divergent approaches are not determined by developmental variables such as wealth and economic capacity, human potential or FDI stock. Neither can it be attributed to differences in legal prerogatives of the regions, as each of the countries has at least one regional authority whose approach to investment promotion appears more comprehensive than others.

In such circumstances, a question arises about the reasons conditioning such situation. This will be answered in the next chapter which identifies the wider promotional networks regional authorities operate in, and explores their nature and division of powers and responsibilities.

References

Almond, P., Ferner, A., & Tregasis, O. (2015). The changing context of regional governance of FDI in England. *European Urban and Regional Studies, 22*(1), 61–76.

Ascani, A., Crescenzi, R., & Iammarino, S. (2017). The geography of foreign investments in the EU neighbourhood. *Tijdschrift voor economische en socialte geografie, 108*(1), 76–91.

Ashworth, G. J., & Voogd, H. (1994). Marketing and place promotion. In J. R. Gold & S. V. Ward (Eds.), *Place promotion; the use of publicity and marketing to sell towns and regions*. Chichester: John Wiley & Sons.

Bickl, M. (2004). *Image management in old-industrial regions: Policy learning, governance and leadership in North East England and the Ruhr*. PhD Thesis, University of Durham, Durham.

Blokker, P., & Dallago, B. (2009). Introduction: Regional diversity and local development in new Member states. In *Regional diversity and local development in the new member states*. Basingstoke: Palgrave Macmillan.

Bradley, A., Hall, T., & Harrison, M. (2002). Selling cities: Promoting new images for meeting tourism. *Cities, 19*(1), 61–70.

Bradshaw, M. (2005). Foreign direct investment and economic transformation in central and Eastern Europe. In D. Turnock (Ed.), *Foreign direct investment and regional development in east Central Europe and former soviet union*. Aldershot: Ashgate.

Brown, J. (2006). *Attitudes and experiences of the rebranding of Liverpool: the Liverpool08 local experience*. CIRM 2006 Proceedings, Manchester Metropolitan University, Manchester.

Charlton, A., & Davis, N. (2006). *Does investment promotion work?* Retrieved April 11, 2007, from http://personal.lse.ac.uk/CHARLTOA/IP.pdf

Charlton, A., Davis, N., Faye, M., Haddock, J., & Lamb, C. (2004). *Industry targeting within foreign investment promotion*. Oxford Investment Research Working Paper, Oxford.

Chidlow, A., Salciuviene, L., & Young, S. (2009). Regional determinants of inward FDI distribution in Poland. *International Business Review, 18*(2), 119–133.

Cleave, E., Godwin, A., Sadler, R., & Gilliland, J. (2016). The role of place branding in local and regional economic development: Bridging the gap between policy and practicality. *Regional Studies, Regional Science, 3*(1), 207–228.

Clow, K. E., & Baack, D. (2018). *Integrated advertising, promotion, and marketing communications* (8th ed.). New York: Pearson.
CzechInvest. (2007, March). *Monthly newsletter*. Praha: Czechinvest. Retrieved November 15, 2007, from http://www.czechinvest.org/en/monthly-newsletter-march-2007.
Czornik, M. (2000). *Promocja miasta*. Katowice: AE.
Dinnie, K. (Ed.). (2011). *City branding: Theory and cases*. Basingstoke: Palgrave Macmillan.
Dogaru, T., Burger, M., Karreman, B., & Van Oort, F. (2015). Functional and sectoral division of labour within central and eastern European countries: Evidence from greenfield FDI. *Tijdschrift voor economische en socialte geografie, 106*(1), 120–129.
Domański, T. (Ed.) (2011). *Marketing terytorialny; Strategiczne wyzwanie dla miast i regionów*. Łódź: Uniwersytet Łódzki.
Domański, B., Guzik, R., & Micek, G. (2003). Zróżnicowanie regionalne krajów Europy Środkowowschodniej i jego zmiany w latach 1995–2000. *Biuletyn Komitetu Przestrzennego Zagospodarowania Kraju PAN, 204*, 125–142.
Drahokoupil, J. (2007). *The rise of the competition state in Central and Eastern Europe: The politics of foreign direct investment*. PhD Thesis, Central European University, Budapest.
Dunning, J. H., & Lundan, S. M. (2008). *Multinational enterprises and the global economy*. Cheltenham: Edward Elgar.
Florek, M. (2003). Territorial marketing: Theoretical issues and empirical survey in wielkopolska communes. *Quaderno di ricerca, 2*, 1–28.
Florek, M. (2005). The country brand as a new challenge for Poland. *Place Branding and Public Diplomacy, 1*(2), 205–214.
Go, F. M., & Govers, R. (Eds.). (2013). *International place branding yearbook 2012: Managing smart growth and sustainability*. Basingstoke: Palgrave Macmillan.
Harding, T., & Javorcik, B. (2012). *Investment promotion and FDI inflows: Quality matters*. University of Oxford Department of Economics Discussion Paper Series, No.612.
Helinska-Hughes, E., & Hughes, M. (2003). Joining the competition: Central and eastern European challenge to established FDI destinations? In N. Phelps & P. Raines (Eds.), *The new competition for inward investment*. Cheltenham: Edward Elgar.
Instytut Marki Polskiej. (2004). *Fragmenty Raportu z Realizacji Projektu Marka dla Polski*. Warszawa: Diagnoza i Idea Przewodnia, IMP.
Jarczewski, W. (2007). *Pozyskiwanie inwestorów do gmin*. Warszawa: Wolters Kluwer.

Klijn, E. H., Eshuis, J., & Braun, E. (2012). The influence of stakeholder involvement on the effectiveness of place branding. *Public Management Review, 14*(4), 499–519.

Kotler, P., & Gertner, D. (2002). Country as brand, product and beyond: A place marketing and brand management perspective. *Brand Management, 9*(4–5), 249–261.

Kotler, P., Apslund, C., Rein, I., & Haider, D. H. (1999). *Marketing places—Europe: How to attract investments, industries, residents and visitors to cities, communities, regions and nations in Europe*. London: Financial Times-Prentice Hall.

Lodge, C. (2002). Success and failure: The brand stories of two countries. *Brand Management, 9*(4–5), 372–384.

Loewendahl, H. (2001). A framework for FDI promotion. *Transnational Corporations, 10*(1), 1–42.

Madsen, H. (1992). Place marketing in Liverpool: A review. *International Journal of Urban and Regional Research, 16*, 633–640.

Malvestito, G. (1997). Marketing terytorialny w świetle włoskich doświadczeń. In T. Domański (Ed.), *Marketing terytorialny—strategiczne wyzwanie dla miast i regionów*. Łódź: Uniwersytet Łódzki.

Metaxas, T. (2010). Place marketing, place branding and foreign direct investments: Defining their relationship in the frame of local economic development process. *Place Branding and Public Diplomacy, 6*(3), 228–243.

Meyer, K. E., Ionascu, D., Kulawczuk, P., Szczesniak, A., Antal-Makos, Z., Tỏth, K., & Darskuvenie, V. (2005). *The changing patterns of foreign direct investment in EU accession countries: Insights from a new survey*. CEES Working Papers, no.57.

Monaghan, S., Gunnigle, P., & Lavelle, J. (2014). 'Courting the multinational': Subnational institutional capacity and foreign market insidership. *Journal of International Business Studies, 45*(2), 131–150.

Multilateral Investment Guarantee Agency (MIGA). (2006). *FDI promotion*. Retrieved November 29, 2006, from www.fdipromotion.com/toolkit/user/content_page.cfm

Myant, M., & Smith, S. (2006). Regional development and post-communist politics in a Czech region. *Europe-Asia Studies, 58*(2), 147–168.

Navaretti, G. B., & Venables, A. J. (2004). *Multinational firms in the world economy*. Princeton, NJ: Princeton University Press.

OECD. (2003). *Checklist for foreign direct investment incentives policies*. Paris: OECD Publications.

OECD. (2015). *Policy framework for investment 2015 edition.* Paris: OECD Publishing. Retrieved from https://doi.org/10.1787/9789264208667-en

OECD. (2018). *Mapping of investment promotion agencies in OECD countries.* Retrieved from www.oecd.org/investment/Mapping-of-Investment-Promotion-Agencies-in-OECD-Countries.pdf

Paddison, R. (1993). City marketing, image reconstruction and urban regeneration. *Urban Studies, 30*(2), 339–350.

Pasquinelli, C. (2013). Competition, cooperation and co-opetition: Unfolding the process of inter-territorial branding. *Urban Research & Practice, 6*(1), 1–18.

Pasquinelli, C., & Teräs, J. (2013). Branding knowledge-intensive regions: A comparative study of Pisa and Oulu high-tech brands. *European Planning Studies, 21*(10), 1611–1629.

Phelps, N., & Raines, P. (Eds.). (2003). *The new competition for inward investment; companies, institutions and territorial development.* Cheltenham: Edward Elgar.

Potter, J., & Moore, B. (2000). UK enterprise zones and the attraction of inward investments. *Urban Studies, 37*(8), 1279–1311.

Rzeczpospolita. (2004, March 26). *Za Gillette pójdą inni.*

Rzeczpospolita. (2007a, November 14). *Polska wschodzącą gwiazdą turystyki.*

Rzeczpospolita. (2007b, March 02). *Nowe fabryki wyrosną pod Łodzią.*

Rzeczpospolita. (2007c, November 20). *Więcej na reklamę miast.*

UNCTAD. (2004a). *What services do IPAs target?* UNCTAD Investment Brief, no.1/2004.

UNCTAD. (2004b). *World investment report 2004: The shift towards services.* Geneva: United Nations.

Ward, S. V. (1998). *Selling places, the marketing and promotion of towns and cities 1850–2000.* London: E&FN Spon.

Wells, T. L., Jr., & Wint, A. G. (2000). *Marketing a country—Promotion as a tool for attracting foreign direct investment.* FIAS occasional paper 13, IFC-MIGA, Washington.

World Bank. (2012). *Investment climate: Global investment promotions best practices.* Washington: The World Bank Group.

Young, C. (2005). Place marketing for foreign direct investment in central and Eastern Europe. In D. Turnock (Ed.), *Foreign direct investment and regional development in east-Central Europe and the former Soviet Union.* Kent: Ashgate.

Young, C., & Kaczmarek, S. (2000). Local government, local economic development and quality of life in Poland. *GeoJournal, 50*(2–3), 225–234.

Zanatta, M., Costa, I., & Filippov, S. (2006). *Foreign direct investment: Key issues for promotion agencies.* UNU Policy Brief, No.10, UNU-MERIT, Maastricht.

5

Governance and Implementation of Investment Promotion in Central-Eastern European Regions

5.1 Introduction

Previous chapter examined promotional practices and the degree of involvement in the process of the Czech, Polish and Slovak regional authorities, the principal agents of regional governance. While the issues discussed exceeded the scope of existing literature and offered original insights into the regional promotion process, by focusing on an individual agent it broadly reflected the approach presented in other studies (e.g. Harding & Javorcik, 2012; Madsen, 1992; Paddison, 1993; World Bank, 2012; Young, 2005; Young & Kaczmarek, 1999). However, from the analysis as well as wider literature it is apparent that investment attraction is a complex process involving a multitude of organisations and transecting various administrative and spatial scales.

Regional authorities operate within wider networks, and while the degree of their involvement in the process varies in the three countries studied, it usually remains low. It is therefore necessary to identify the sources of, and forces driving, investment promotion and explore the different institutional arrangements guiding the process in Central-Eastern Europe (CEE). Using the examples of selected regions, Jihomoravský kraj in the Czech Republic,

P. Capik, *Foreign Investment Promotion*, https://doi.org/10.1007/978-3-030-13658-1_5

Wielkopolskie voivodeship in Poland and Košický kraj in Slovakia, the objective of this chapter, in line with the fourth set of research questions (p. 32) is to identify those and examine the inter-organisational relationships and their implications. The discussion presents analysis of the interview data complemented with information sourced from printed and online materials published by the organisations concerned.

The organisation and governance of regional promotion can be crucial for its success (Almond, Ferner, & Tregasis, 2015; Cleave, Godwin, Sadler, & Gilliland, 2016; Monaghan, Gunnigle, & Lavelle, 2014; van den Berg, Braun, & Otgaar, 2002). Throughout the investment process, investors come in contact with a variety of actors on various administrative levels. They are subjected to regions' promotional communiqué in diverse forms and meet the promotion actors in diverse situations: from trade fairs and exhibitions to personalised, investor-tailored events and circumstances. All of which makes the division of responsibilities between the different promotion actors crucial to avoid overlaps, or indeed competition, facilitate the efficient use of often limited funding and also in order not to make false promises and have a coherent message, combining to create a positive impression and consequently secure the investment project.

The chapter proceeds as follows. Firstly, it identifies the institutions actively involved in the promotion of the regions, that is, the regional promoters. Apart from common core organisations, those vary between the regions. Next, by exploring the relationships between them, the chapter identifies the various promotion governance frameworks. The fundamental feature differentiating the governance set-ups is the degree of power and initiative centralisation within the National Investment Promotion Agency (NIPA). The literature for the most part argues for strong NIPAs, which act as guarantors of the professionalism and coherence of the process (Loewendahl, 2001; MIGA, 2006; OECD, 2015; World Bank, 2012). This assertion is put to the test in the subsequent parts of the chapter where the internal coherence and consistency within the promotional frameworks are examined. By comparing and contrasting individual agents' approaches to place product, image staples, targeting and competition, it is observed that greater coherence and consistency can be found in more decentralised frameworks.

The innovative nature of this is chapter lies in its comprehensive approach connecting the institutions, which are consciously (whether by choice or obliged by the law) engaged in one form or another in investment promotion. A thorough examination of their activities allows scrutinising of the dependencies between governance models and operational choices of the individual actors.

5.2 Regional Promoters

Regional authorities are not the only agents of promotion. Indeed, in some cases they seem to play a minimal role in the process, while operating in wider networks. Hence, it is axiomatic that there will be other 'promoters' both on the regional level and higher and lower in the administrative hierarchy, some of which are expected to fill in the void resulting from the limited involvement of the regional authorities. Alternatively, the opposite causative dependency might exist, and the minimal engagement of the regional authorities might be conditioned by the dominance of other organisations.

Ideally, the organisations should create a system of closely cooperating partners, for the key to successful promotion lies with the ability to create temporary and lasting network connections (Domański, 1997; Metaxas, 2010; Pasquinelli, 2013). However, in reality, as demonstrated by Parkerson and Saunders' (2005) review of activities performed by various agencies promoting an area, operating within networks often proves difficult and uncoordinated.

The organisation and governance of regional promotion activities, including cooperation networks, responsibilities and duties of particular agencies, stand among the crucial factors determining the success of the performed actions. Yet, those directly engaged with it, the place promoters, regardless of the administrative level, can be difficult to identify. Regional promotion—predominantly managerial—is also a political process often involving an array of organisations and agencies, posing questions about responsibilities, interdependence and coordination of actions. It is a multi-scalar process and its organisation and administration differs greatly (e.g. Almond et al., 2015; Bickl, 2004; Burgess & Wood, 1988; Lever, 2001; Monaghan et al., 2014; Young & Kaczmarek, 1999).

A variety of institutions and organisations in CEE regions claim to be involved in investment promotion. Industrial associations, special economic zones, business incubators and civic organisations all list involvement in FDI promotion amongst their primary activities. But in fact, usually their actions remain limited to directing interested investors to organisations actually engaged with FDI attraction. In the three regions under study here, a number of such organisations exist: regional authorities (promotion department), regional development agencies and regional branches of National Investment Promotion Agency. Additionally, in Jihomoravský kraj and Košický kraj, the involvement of private capital is more visible than in Wielkopolskie voivodeship. However, the nature of this involvement varies between the Czech and Slovak regions. While in Jihomoravský kraj CTP Invest is a privately owned company whose business operations explicitly include attracting investors, the Economic Development Centre (EDC) operating in the East of Slovakia could rather be likened to a privately run investment promotion agency.

However, private organisations, while often prevailing in the USA, rarely feature in the FDI attraction landscape in Europe (Ward, 1998), and with a few exceptions (including the examples discussed here) are even less prominent in Central-Eastern European Countries. Regional promotion aimed at investment attraction remains predominantly the domain of public organisations. It requires vertical cooperation of agents at different administrative levels, and calls for horizontal links between agents on the same level.

Two organisations, operating on a national and local scale common in the regions studied, can be identified: regional capital city authorities (promotion office) and the National Investment Promotion Agency. Variations of the organisations involved in the process include, in the Czech Republic (on the national level), a group of internationally renowned consulting and manufacturing companies in the form of the Association for Foreign Investment (AFI). In the Polish case, the Institute for Polish Brand (IPB) plays an increasingly significant role in shaping the country's brand image but does not participate directly in investment attraction.

To the organisations directly involved in FDI promotion, an even larger number of collaborators can be added. While the number of partner institutions and the nature of relationships between them and any of the main agents vary, the main collaborators usually are regional and national chambers of commerce, industrial associations, regional and national tourism boards, local development agencies, national embassies abroad.

The relationships between the regional and national agents vary considerably across the countries, as do their responsibilities and strategy-setting powers (Table 6.1). The forthcoming sections explore the characteristics of selected promoters—the National Investment Promotion Agencies and private enterprises. While NIPAs often remain dominant players in FDI attraction, the modes of private capital involvement are in some cases unprecedented, and therefore interesting also from a theoretical point of view.

5.2.1 The Ambiguous Leadership of National Investment Promotion Agencies

The National Investment Promotion Agencies are often mistakenly perceived as sole operators of the country or regional promotion aimed at FDI attraction (e.g. UNCTAD, 2004; World Bank, 2012). As demonstrated in previous chapters and the sections above this is clearly not the case in Central-Eastern Europe, where a number of other organisations, notably the regional authorities, also participate in the process. NIPAs, however, acting as quasi-governmental organisations, often attempt to dominate the investment promotion landscape, and their success rate varies between the three countries.

Usually, it is expected that NIPAs' mission will include the cultivation of the country's positive image abroad, dissemination of information about investment opportunities in the country, provision of investors' services and contribution to the improvement of the overall investment climate (World Bank, 2012). Additionally, apart from attracting and facilitating relations with foreign investors, NIPAs' tasks may extend to export promotion, industrial development, fostering entrepreneurship and SME development. To successfully achieve this, NIPAs need to operate along business lines and have a significant degree of autonomy, sufficient resources and links to the private sector and government, enabling them to influence policy (Loewendahl, 2001; OECD, 2018; Zanatta, Costa, & Filippov, 2006).

CzechInvest, established in 1992 as an investment promotion agency with the main objective of increasing investors' awareness of the opportunities in the Czech Republic, subsequently evolved into such a comprehensive national development agency (Young, 2005). By mid-2000s, over 170 of the agency's staff focused on two main pillars of its activity—investment attraction and business development through administration of SME-oriented programmes funded by the EU Structural Funds. Regarding the former, the agency is exclusively authorised to manage the investment incentives schemes, as it files the applications with the adequate governmental bodies and prepares draft offers for the investors. Its task is also to provide potential investors with up-to-date information on investment opportunities, and the general business climate in the Czech Republic. It offers comprehensive services for potential investors, including business properties and supplier identification and aftercare services. A network of regional offices was established in 2005 in order to foster closer connections to the regional and local authorities and provide the headquarters with regional knowledge. At the time of research, however, as the subsequent parts of the chapter will demonstrate, both of these objectives were yet to be met.

CzechInvest also operates a network of offices around the world, which in the period 1993–2006 contributed to the agency successfully attracting to the Czech Republic 661 investment projects creating over 150,000 new jobs. In 2006 the agency's representatives made over 430 business trips and in addition to 40 events it organised, they have participated in 80 events worldwide (CzechInvest, 2008). Despite already by mid-2000s being a multi-award-winning agency,[1] on several occasions CzechInvest

[1] Best Practices in Promotion 2004, presented by the steering committee of the World Investment Forum; WAIPA Awards 2003—'Best Advertisement by an IPA' (third place); Best Investment Promotion Agency in the EU Accession Countries of the Year 2002; European Investment Promotion Agency of the Year 2000 and 2001.

has become caught up in disputes between the main political parties, resulting in as much as one-third of its staff leaving or being dismissed (Drahokoupil, 2007a).

Of the three national agencies, Slovenská agentúra pre rozvoj investícií a obchodu—SARIO, the Slovak Investment and Trade Development Agency, is probably the least affected by the political process. This is not because of the agency's apolitical nature, but rather due to the relative importance of FDI to the Slovak economy the agency is not treated as a bargaining chip or a war trophy after a change of government. The agency is also the youngest of the three NIPAs studied, created in 2001 in effect of a U-turn from the hostile stance towards FDI taken by Slovak governments throughout the 1990s (Artisen-Maksimenko, 2000). While investment promotion remains the agency's main focus, the other two core activities include supporting Slovak companies' exports and management of selected EU Structural Funds programmes. The FDI division is actively involved with promotion and performs various publicity activities and searches for investors by participating in trade and exhibitions and direct mailing campaigns. Additionally, comparably to CzechInvest, the agency acts as a one-stop shop and offers comprehensive investment services including mapping out and creating databases of available real estate and industrial parks, support in investment incentives acquisition, and assisting with the completion of investment projects (SARIO, 2004). In three years of its operations SARIO successfully concluded 61 investment projects creating over 22,000 jobs. In 2006 alone, the agency's representatives gave nearly 190 presentations and participated in multiple conferences and seminars worldwide.

Apart from addressing its promotional activities to investors, through a network of regional offices the agency also maintains contact with regional and local authorities and occasionally provides information and training programmes whose main objective is to make the authorities aware of SARIO's activities and potential benefits resulting from cooperation with the agency (SARIO, 2007).

The Polish NIPA, Polska Agencja Informacji i Inwestycji Zagranicznych (PAIiIZ, the Polish Information and Foreign Investment Agency), attempts to remain visible and active on the regional level. The agency operates a network of Investor Service Centres (ISCs)—institutions run in cooperation with regional authorities or regional development agencies in each of the 16 Polish voivodeships. Prior to 2005 the ISCs had no formal explicit links to the agency; however, they are now closely related to it and often rely on its expertise and support.

The creation of closer ties to the regions was only one in many reforms the agency underwent since its inception. PAIiIZ officially began its operations in 2003; however, the existence and actions of its two component predecessors, the Polish Foreign Investment Agency and Polish Information Agency, date back to 1992 and 1991, respectively. The creation and initial operations of the former were supported by a generous grant from the PHARE fund; however, since then PAIiIZ has been mainly relying on the state budget and since 2004 support from the EU Structural Funds.

Unlike its Czech and Slovak counterparts, PAIiIZ is not a one-stop shop for investors, yet it performs a wide range of activities, including offering access to complex information on economic and legal business environments, assistance in finding appropriate partners and suppliers, and suitable investment locations and advice during each phase of the investment process. In 2004 agency representatives participated in a range of international events including conferences, trade fairs and exhibitions. The agency has also organised many publicity-oriented events in Poland including press conferences and 64 media study visits. Perhaps the most noticeable activity, however, was the awareness-raising campaign conducted in the international press and television, including articles in the *Financial Times*, *The Economist*, and advertisements on BBC World and CNN (PAIiIZ, 2005).

5.2.2 Private Sector in Investment Promotion

Private capital has an important role to play in various aspects of regional promotion. Firstly, it can provide its expertise in the formulation and implementation of promotion plans. Secondly, since firms' export volumes are expected to benefit from a region's positive image, they should contribute to its creation and reaffirmation (Kotler, Apslund, Rein, & Haider, 1999). Consequently, sometimes local enterprises willingly contribute to the promotional spending budget (Parkerson & Saunders,

2005). Thirdly, the involvement of private capital in the investment promotion makes the process more believable for potential target markets, as the companies involved are the living proof of opportunities existing in the area and the good treatment investors can expect from the authorities (Loewendahl, 2001; Schotter & Beamish, 2013; Wells & Wint, 2000).

While the participation of enterprises, private or state-owned, in CEE regional promotion is uncommon, there are some interesting cases of private capital involvement in the investment attraction process.

In mid-2000s CTP Invest was the biggest commercial property developer in the Czech Republic, expanding rapidly into other Central-Eastern Europe countries. It specialises in the development and financing of large-scale, built-to-lease industrial facilities as well as A-class office space, retail and mixed-use facilities. From its humble beginnings of 10 hectares in 1996, a decade later CTP owned 650 hectares of land and managed over two million square metres of built properties (CTP Invest, 2006). In 2006 40% of its income was generated by manufacturing, 30% by logistics, 20% by office and 10% by retail properties.

In the same year the company became the market leader in industrial property development in the Czech Republic with a 65% share of the market. From its initial site in Humpolec (Vysočina kraj) CTP grew to operate a network of various types of sites throughout the Czech Republic prepared to host manufacturing and logistics (CTPZones, including build-to-order—CTPoint and short-term lease flexi-space facilities), business services (CTParks) and retail activities. In 2007 the company had operations in almost 50 locations throughout the country, with the main centre in Jihomoravský kraj. The intrinsic nature of CTP's offer is such that the company, through creating and managing the clusters of regional sub-products, has a direct impact on the regional mega-product. The commercial character of those makes CTP's role in regional promotional activities a very peculiar and uncommon one. While the CTP's offer does not explicitly exclude Czech companies, its business is primarily focused on providing facilities for the foreign investors.

The operations of the Košice-based Economic Development Centre (EDC) are less explicitly commercially driven, that is, the rationale for investment attraction is not directly underpinned by sustaining the economic existence of the organisation.

The US Steel acquisition of the East Slovakian Steelworks in Košice (VSŽ) was conditional upon the creation of an organisation that would engage in attracting other foreign investors to the region. From its foundation in February 2001 the EDC's primary objective was regional promotion and investment attraction to Eastern Slovakia. Although initially, in accordance with the Memorandum agreed between the Slovak government and US Steel, the Centre was meant to function for a two-year period, thanks to its successful operation it continued to operate and, in 2007, extended the scope of its involvement to include educational and knowledge transfer activities.

While the EDC could be sceptically perceived as part of US Steel's corporate branding strategy and an extension of its sales department, considering the scope of the Centre's activities (discussed later), it is hard to deny its role in the promotion of the region. During the six years of its operation the Centre claims to have assisted 27 foreign companies in initiating their activities in Eastern Slovakia, creating almost 5000 new workplaces.

Clearly then, in addition to the means of private capital participation in regional promotion aimed at investment attraction highlighted in earlier studied, some new mode needs to be added. Local enterprises can have a significant impact on various aspects of the place product, most importantly individual facilities and their groupings. Moreover, private companies can fill in the void caused by limited (or a lack of) involvement of public organisations and take on some of their responsibilities and activities.

5.3 Emerging Frameworks of Investment Promotion Governance

In order to develop understanding of how promotion actually occurs, that is, to understand the various aspects, stages and channels of the process, it is crucial to investigate dealings between the different agencies, and explore their mutual relationships.

As highlighted in various studies (e.g. OECD, 2003; World Bank, 2012; Young, 2005) the implementation of FDI promotion is frequently at the discretion of NIPAs. Despite direct supervision of policy-makers, ideally such organisations should enjoy considerable levels of autonomy (Loewendahl, 2001; OECD, 2015). At the same time, due to the operational complexity of the promotional process entailing direct and indirect involvement of a variety of other institutions, in some countries varying levels of decentralisation could be anticipated.

CzechInvest, focusing on the Czech Republic as a whole, plays the dominant role in the preparation and execution of the overwhelming majority of investment promotional activities (Table 5.1 and Fig. 5.1). Consequently, the regional and local agents in the Czech Republic are allowed little independence and their involvement in the process is usually submissive and restricted.

Public officials are 'used' by the Association for Foreign Investments, the NIPA's close ally, in a series of PR events 'Investors' Breakfast with the Governor'. Generally, however, the regional and local authorities' role is often reduced to information provision and occasional participation in events organised or attended by CzechInvest, which believes the regions are too small to effectively compete for FDI alone:

> The regional authorities are not really getting involved in activities we [CzechInvest] perform. No, it's not a common practice. It's not useful, it doesn't make sense, because we take part in events where Czech regions are too small to be seen.[2]

Young (2005) also argues that the size of the country is the main factor allowing CzechInvest to effectively act on behalf of the regions. Interestingly, despite the fact that in reality the agency hardly does, the regional agents seem content with the situation and name CzechInvest as the institution with which their cooperation is the best. Yet, paradoxically, they tend to focus on cooperation between themselves, which stresses the existence of psychic distance to the centre and may be reflective of political tensions between the region and the centre.

CzechInvest also utilises an array of other institutions, public and private, national and regional, including Confederations of Industry,

[2] Interview with the CzechInvest representative.

Table 5.1 Regional promotion governance frameworks

	Jihomoravský kraj (Czech Republic)	Košický kraj (Slovakia)	Wielkopolskie voivodeship (Poland)
National Investment Promotion Agency	Country focused promotion; strategy setting and execution; one-stop shop: complete investor services provider	Country promotion with limited regional dimension; strategy setting and execution; complete investor service provider	Country promotion with regional focus; limited service power; guidance and consultancy services provision
Regional authorities	Activities chiefly dependent on NIPA and RDA; negligible own initiative	Increasing involvement in promotion; presently relying on NIPA	Promotion as a strategic tool in regional development; close, systematic cooperation with regional and local agents
Regional development agency(ies)	Servicing smaller investors; limited own initiative	Local focus; sporadic FDI promotion, rather tourism-oriented activities	Executing regional authorities' strategies
NIPA regional representative	Newly established; fully HQ-dependent	Fully HQ-dependent; evolving links with regional (and local) agents	Largely independent of HQ
Regional capital city authorities	Activities fully dependent on NIPA and RDA; incidental cooperation with regional authorities	Initial involvement; reliant on NIPA and regional agents	Active promotion; occasional cooperation with regional authorities
Private capital	Single company, business oriented; nationally: in form of association acting nationwide, largely dependent on NIPA	Individual case of serious involvement; activities complementary to NIPA	Not active; as cooperation networks only
Regional population	No active involvement	No active involvement	No active involvement
Overall	Centralised	Centralised with regional perspective	Regional (decentralised)

Source: Own research

Chamber of Commerce and CzechTourism in the way it deems necessary—mostly for information and provision of business contacts. The agency also invites their representatives to networking sessions and other events organised in the Czech Republic.

While other promotion agents name the same organisations as their partner institutions, the strength of links, scope of cooperation and frequency of contact is far less intense than in the case of CzechInvest.[3] Instead, the amount and strength of contacts with various municipalities is more apparent.

Brno and Jihomoravský kraj authorities engage with occasional external promotion, commonly participating in selected trade fairs and exhibitions (e.g. MIPIM in Cannes), and also co-produce selected promotional materials.

Jihomoravský kraj RDA, initially CzechInvest representative in the region and partly funded by the national agency, supports regional and Brno authorities (the remaining founders) together with smaller municipalities in their promotional efforts and based on its links with the NIPA offers services for the potential investors.

CTP Invest, the only private capital representative actively and directly involved in investment promotion, based on the principle that both organisations "chase the same investors"[4] remains in regular contact with CzechInvest. The company participates in NIPA's activities in the Czech Republic and abroad, including investment seminars and road-shows. The company also maintains good working relationships with the regional authorities, with whom it occasionally prepares promotional seminars, and shares the costs of participation in fairs and exhibitions. It also sustains contacts with various municipal authorities, but those are more often related to the company's business rather than regional promotion (e.g. feasibility studies, compliance with local development plans, certification process). CTP's relations with Jihomoravský kraj RDA remain similarly business-driven.

[3] With the exception of Jihomoravský kraj RDA which maintains strong ties with the Chamber of Commerce.

[4] Interview with the CTP Invest representative.

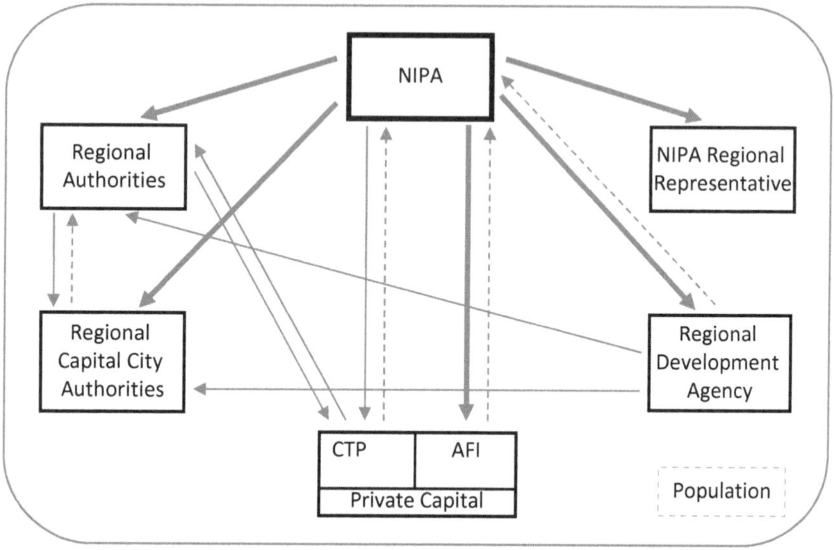

Fig. 5.1 Czech regional investment promotion governance framework. The thickness of the lines of the boxes representing individual organisations reflects the level of their overall engagement with promotion (dotted line indicates lack of direct involvement). The direction of arrows between the organisations shows the dominant course of initiative and influence, while their thickness reveals the strength of these relations (dotted line signifying very low and thick line revealing high levels of intensity). *Source*: Own research

The level of involvement in the promotional process, as well as the initiative and influence relations between the agents as discussed above, are summarised in Fig. 5.1 illustrating the governance framework in the Czech region (Fig. 5.2 for the Polish and Fig. 5.3 for the Slovak regions). The thickness of the contours of rectangles representing individual organisations reflects the level of their overall engagement with promotion (dotted line indicates lack of direct involvement). The direction of arrows between the organisations shows the dominant course of initiative and influence, while their thickness reveals the strength of these relations (dotted line signifying very low and the thick line reflecting high levels of intensity).

CzechInvest plays the central role within the framework and dominates the relationships with all other agents whose involvement in invest-

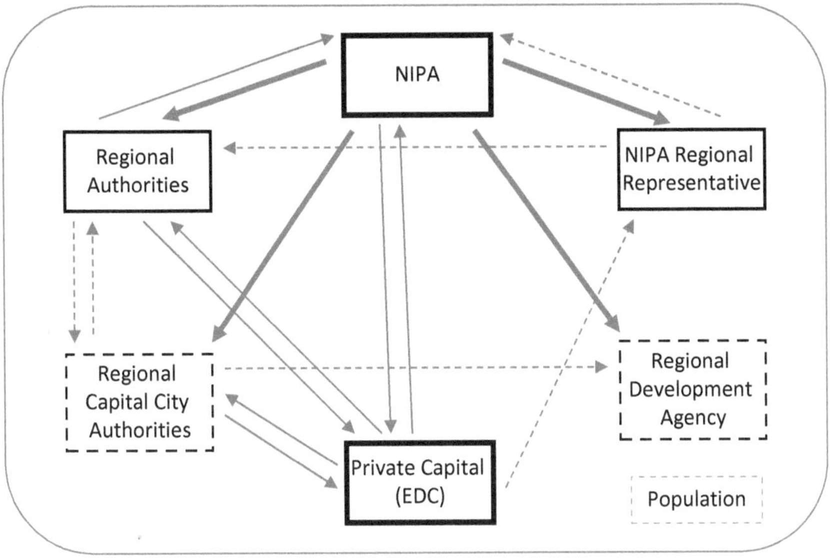

Fig. 5.2 Slovak regional investment promotion governance framework. The thickness of the lines of the boxes representing individual organisations reflects the level of their overall engagement with promotion (dotted line indicates lack of direct involvement). The direction of arrows between the organisations shows the dominant course of initiative and influence, while their thickness reveals the strength of these relations (dotted line signifying very low and thick line revealing high levels of intensity). *Source*: Own research

ment promotion is less significant. Regional agents including Brno and Jihomoravský kraj authorities and the regional development agency have little or no influence over the initiatives pursued by the national agency. On the regional level the RDA leads the relationships with regional and city authorities, with the latter also dominated by all other organisations. The regional office of CzechInvest serves mainly as its extension and has no clear connections to any other organisation in the region.

Regional population involvement in the FDI promotional process, while recommended in theory (e.g. Klijn, Eshuis, & Braun, 2012; Kotler et al., 1999; Quelch & Jocz, 2005), in reality is very limited and equally indirect. The populations of the Czech Republic, Poland and Slovakia generally, and the inhabitants of the three regions studied in particular, have only two ways to shape the promotion of their area, both of which

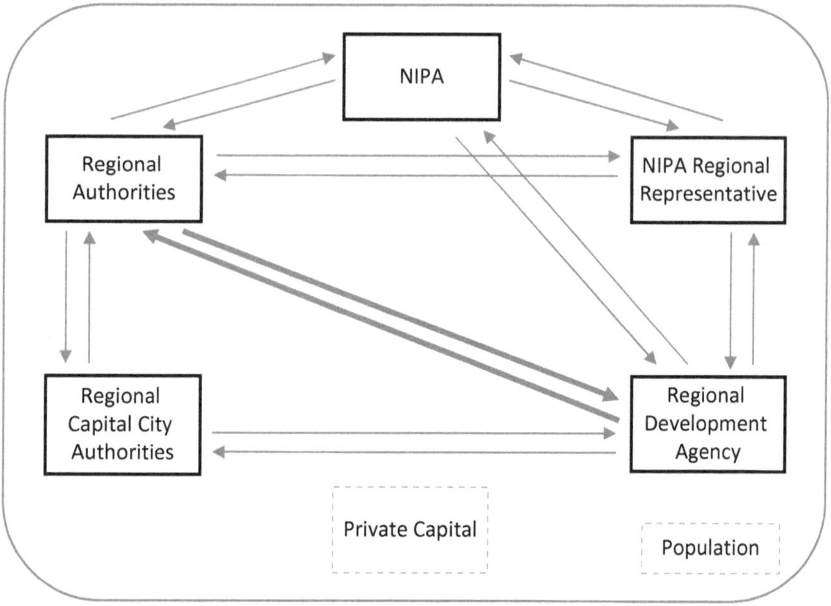

Fig. 5.3 Polish regional investment promotion governance framework. The thickness of the lines of the boxes representing individual organisations reflects the level of their overall engagement with promotion (dotted line indicates lack of direct involvement). The direction of arrows between the organisations shows the dominant course of initiative and influence, while their thickness reveals the strength of these relations (dotted line signifying very low and thick line revealing high levels of intensity). *Source*: Own research

are largely indirect. Firstly, and very generally, by voting for their representatives to the elected governing bodies, and secondly when the regional development strategy undergoes the process of public consultations.

As indicated in Table 5.1 and illustrated by Figs. 5.1, 5.2, and 5.3, to a large degree this is also true of the other two regions (countries) investigated. The populations of neither Košický kraj nor Wielkopolskie voivodeship get any more actively and directly involved with the investment promotion process. Across the CEE there are occasional civic organisations of a regional or local nature, attempting to contribute to the general promotion of their respective areas (e.g. Association for the

Promotion of Dolny Śląsk[5]); however, their efforts are often ephemeral and rarely extend internationally.

As far as the involvement of private capital is concerned, based on the case of Jihomoravský kraj, a three-level gradation of increasing passiveness could be distinguished. The single most actively involved (level 1) private company is CTP Invest, whose business objectives underpin its regional promotion activities. Level 2 comprises the Association for Foreign Investments consisting of exclusively well-recognised private companies operating in the Czech Republic and primarily acting as potential service providers and suppliers to foreign investors. Such flagship brands serve also as evidence of the positive investment climate in the country. The most passive (level 3), nevertheless still potentially valuable, is the involvement of the most numerous group, namely private capital representations (e.g. industrial associations and chambers of commerce, Confederation of Industry), which are used by the active promotion agents, notably CzechInvest, as information sources and less frequently serve as potential supplier base.

Despite clear dominance of the National Investment Promotion Agency—SARIO, as illustrated by Fig. 5.2, the Slovak regional investment promotion framework is more decentralised than the Czech one, with the apparent involvement of several of the regional organisations. SARIO controls the majority of its relationships; however, some regional agents actively engage and attempt to influence the activities of the Slovak NIPA. Furthermore, the involvement of private capital is strong on the regional level with the Economic Development Centre maintaining equal partner relations with Košický kraj and Košice city authorities.

Reflecting the level of decentralisation SARIO attempts to maintain the regional focus of its operations and thus, to a larger extent than its Czech counterpart, involves the regional agents in its operations (Table 5.1 and Fig. 5.2). It recognises the need for the participation of regional and municipal authorities, for "they also have their ways of promotion"[6] and

[5] Existing since 1996 the Association comprises public authorities, local businesses (including newspapers) and local non-government organisations. Its main activities focus around tourism promotion, local produce promotion and cultural activities. The Association also serves as a forum for exchange of experiences and best practices in promotion between the local authorities.

[6] Interview with the SARIO representative.

its regional offices are apparently the means for engaging regional and local authorities in the promotional process. However, the evidence gathered does not fully support this, since as the Košický kraj regional authorities claim SARIO's regional office is a "'one person office', and it's not *important*"[7] thus indicating that they would rather have direct access to the headquarters. Furthermore, because of poor organisation on their part, the contribution of local and regional governments remains generally limited, especially in the case of Košice city authorities, to meetings with investors for PR purposes.

While Bratislava-based headquarters deals with strategy setting and implementation, and performs the bulk of promotional activities (ranging from publicity to aftercare services), the regional authorities, through contacts with SARIO's offices, can (at least potentially) influence some of the agency's actions. Similar to the Czech Republic, the authorities take part in the events organised by the agency—a gesture which SARIO willingly reciprocates.

The Slovak NIPA maintains relationships with a comparably wide range of organisations as its Czech equivalent, and for the same reasons—mostly as information and reference providers, and potential suppliers. It uses various chambers of commerce (including the Swedish and American ones) to access required information and further its cause amongst their members. The SARIO activities remain mainly investor driven, and the agency is keen to involve a wide range of organisations in its FDI attraction activities as long as "it's useful for the investors".[8] Often such contacts are project-specific, and their intensity increases on an ad-hoc basis.

Somewhat contrary to the Czech Republic, the cooperation relationships on the regional level seem to be less strong. The majority of the regional and local actors indicate SARIO as their main partner, and while the horizontal dimension of collaboration is evident, the vertical dimension appears to be the dominant one. The regional authorities operate within wide networks, but usually these are not explicitly oriented towards FDI attraction. The same is true for Košice city authorities,

[7] Interview with the Košický kraj representative.

[8] Interview with the SARIO representative.

which with regard to investment promotion additionally complain about the unsatisfactory relations with the regional government.

Spišska Regional Development Agency, as indicated in Table 5.1, is mostly preoccupied with tourism promotion and only occasionally gets directly involved with investment attraction. It acts as an information provider for SARIO, and also sporadically supports municipal authorities' promotional efforts by, for example, fostering their contacts with places abroad interested in the exchange of experiences.

Comparably to the Czech case, in the Slovak region private capital remains largely inactive as far as the promotion process is concerned. The usual collection of private organisations and representations, specifically the various chambers of commerce, are used by the more active promoters as the sources of information, references and potential suppliers' database. The activities of the Economic Development Centre, which effectively plays the role of corporate-run investment promotion agency, is a notable exception of otherwise passive involvement of private enterprises. This makes the EDC an outstanding example of private capital participation in the investment attraction process, and a unique one in Central-Eastern Europe. The EDC developed an extensive network of partners including public institutions such as SARIO, local and regional authorities, and universities. Furthermore, being a part of US Steel, the EDC utilises the company's far-reaching, international commercial contacts while preparing and performing a variety of promotional activities ranging from publishing of the promotional materials to organisation of road-shows. Through its actions EDC fills up a gap left by limited involvement of Košice city and a number of regional development agencies predominantly occupied with tourism promotion. The model developed by the EDC has subsequently been emulated in other parts of Europe. Upon the purchase of the Serbian steelmaker, Sartid, US Steel opened a comparable Economic Development Centre in Belgrade.

The involvement of population is as minimal and indirect as in the case of Jihomoravský kraj and Wielkopolskie voivodeship, discussed next.

The Polish case differs from both the Czech and Slovak ones in the degree of power concentration and regional initiative (Table 5.1 and Fig. 5.3). This is conditioned by the two interlinked factors. Firstly, the authority of the Polish NIPA is more limited than that of the Czech and

Slovak ones. Secondly, the regional agents in Wielkopolskie voivodeship seem to be much more proactive in their approaches to investment promotion. The result of this, as illustrated by Fig. 5.3, is a decentralised investment promotion governance framework with participating agencies involved in the process to a similar degree, and where the initiative and influence relationships between them are predominantly equal. The core of the framework comprises regional authorities and the regional development agency, connected to each other by a strong relationship, and maintaining equal, partner links with all other agents.

The Polish NIPA does not act as a one-stop shop, but is rather a free-of-charge advisory and consulting body guiding potential investors through the investment process. Perhaps for this reason PAIiIZ goes beyond the usual, already wide cooperative networks, and is interested in having good relations with regional and local authorities.

The agency sustains close contacts with its owner and coordinator, the Ministry of Economy, which provides its annual budget and occasional ad-hoc, project-related resources. Additionally, PAIiIZ cooperation with the Agencja Rozwoju Przemysłu (Industrial Development Agency) and Polska Agencja Rozwoju Przedsiębiorczości (Polish Agency for Enterprise Development) is often project-specific and includes joint participation in events and training activities. The Polish NIPA also maintains working contacts with the Polish Tourism Promotion Agency and Polish embassies around the world. While the relationships with the latter often prove uneasy, due to unclear legal and administrative arrangements, the agency points to the Polish Embassy in Tokyo as an exemplar partner.

PAIiIZ regional representatives, in the form of a network of Investor Service Centres, often have been created as a cooperative arrangement between the regional authorities, regional development agency and local communities' representatives. The ISCs provide services on PAIiIZ's behalf but remain financially and, to an extent, also operationally independent from the agency.

ISCs are not the only mode of cooperation between the Polish NIPA and regional and local authorities. PAIiIZ appreciates its long-established relationships with both levels of the public administration, nevertheless it recognises the differences in approaches existing throughout the country. While some authorities are increasingly active and professional about promoting their areas and preparation of the place offer, others are more passive and expect the agency to provide for them.

Wielkopolskie voivodeship regional authorities are clearly in the former group. They closely cooperate with the RDA in a variety of promotional activities, including management of an extensive, regional web portal, tailored to investors; participation in fairs and exhibitions; and the preparation of the materials. While regional authorities are responsible for strategy setting, the RDA supports its execution. The authorities also sustain contacts and occasionally participate in initiatives instigated on the ministerial level, for example, Polish Year in Sweden (in 2003) or Germany (in 2005/2006); however, these are not explicitly oriented towards investment promotion and put emphasis on trade, cultural and tourism activities.

Wielkopolska RDA, in addition to officially coordinating the activities of the ISC,[9] operates within a considerable network of collaborators including the Wielkopolska Tourism Board, regional chambers of commerce and industrial and crafts associations, and local governments.

While these contacts often do not have an explicit investment promotion focus, the agency uses them as such when necessary.

Perhaps for this reason the city of Poznań authorities are the only regional agent to indicate some discomfort with the relationship with the other institutions. Poznań operates its own FDI attraction policy; however, the city authorities often cooperate with other regional and local agents, including various municipalities, especially with regard to participation in international promotional events and production of publicity materials.

Comparably to Jihomoravský kraj and Košický kraj, the population of Wielkopolska does not get involved in the investment promotion process. Also, the involvement of private capital in the Polish case is even less prominent than in the Czech and Slovak regions. In fact, it remains only passive in nature, especially on the regional level. Nationally the Institute for Polish Brand, within the Polish Chamber of Commerce, attempts to influence and coordinate the activities of various governmental and par-

[9] ISC has existed in Wielkopolskie since 2003, however only since June 2005 has it comprised an official part of the PAIiIZ network.

liamentary working groups, in an attempt to create a comprehensive and coherent branding strategy for Poland.

In addition to a considerable level of regional and local agents' involvement in the investment promotion process, another significant distinctive feature of the Polish set-up is the willingness of regional actors to undertake active lobbying of PAIiIZ, trying to ensure FDI inflows to the region, or as ISC representative puts it:

> One can say we lobby with NIPA for Wielkopolska region and its different parts. If we receive an offer, a folder, some investment information we make sure we pass them on to PAIiIZ and that they recognize and consider it.

Interestingly, such activities are implicitly encouraged by the agency itself, which believes that "the regional and local authorities always win when they are more active because we remember more about them, and they can learn more from us".[10]

The governance frameworks of investment promotion presented above differ along the two major interdependent fault-lines. Firstly, in the level to which the process is dominated by the NIPA, and secondly in the approaches pursued by the regional agents.

Such organisation and characteristics of promotion correspond to and complement the findings discussed in earlier chapter. Considering the multi-agent perspective the Polish region seems to be more active, and the Slovak and the Czech ones less so. This suggests that there is a link between the level of NIPA hegemony and participation of regional promoters in the process.

The initially raised research question re-emerges are these three differing organisational arrangements of regional investment promotion reflected in operations, that is, is this apparent consensus in division of responsibilities and powers reproduced in operational and strategic choices made by individual agents?

[10] Interview with the PAIiIZ representative.

To answer this question, the remaining parts of the chapter identify and analyse the set of activities performed by the individual agents and investigate the consistency of their strategic choices.

5.3.1 The Pervasive Lack of Strategic Approach

The literature advises that as one of the promotion addressees, the foreign investors should be clearly identified in the promotional strategy. Such strategy should comply with the area's wider developmental goals and be universally implemented by the network of agents responsible for place governance (Almond et al., 2015; Cleave et al., 2016; OECD, 2003; Pasquinelli, 2013). The evidence gathered in the course of this study suggests none of these conditions is fully met.

The issue of power and initiative centralisation is fairly accurately reflected in the pursuits of individual organisations. As far as the strategy of actions is concerned, a lack of strategic approach rather than its clear imposition from the top, or its bottom-up creation, is the dominant trend.

The majority of the promotion agents in the three regions perceive FDI as an important, if not critical (e.g. SARIO, Jihomoravský kraj RDA) developmental tool, having the potential to decrease the level of unemployment, and to contribute to further growth and prosperity of their respective areas. However, only a few organisations on a regional level seem to be approaching investment promotion in a long-term, coherent, strategic manner.

The most explicit long-term approach to FDI attraction is presented by the National Investment Promotion Agencies. Amongst the other agents only IPB in Poland attempts to "set the programme of national marketing in motion",[11] that is, prepare a long-term strategy for building and promotion of the country's brand. On the regional level, Wielkopolskie voivodeship authorities have included promotion aimed at various target groups in the Regional Development Strategy, but it lacks the FDI focus. Comparably, Poznań authorities' promotional activities are related to the

[11] Interview with the IMP representative.

City Development Strategy, but particular FDI-oriented activities are planned on an annual rather than a long-term basis.

As discussed in the previous chapter, the Czech and Slovak regional authorities operate along defined FDI attraction plans less often than their Polish counterparts. The other agents on the regional and local levels work in a similar manner, that is, while functioning in line with their respective development strategies, they do not operate systematic promotional schemes aimed at investors, or indeed any other target group. Arguably then, considering the high level of power, initiative and responsibility concentration within CzechInvest and SARIO this fact comes as the consequence of such a situation. However, as following sections illustrate, the earlier identified domination of the Czech and Slovak NIPAs on the operational level is far less evident than expected. In other words, while the lack of long-term plans could be attributed to the control and powers of the NIPAs, the actual strategic choices and operational decisions made by the individual promotion agents on the regional and local level provide evidence to the contrary.

The CTP Invest activities offer one interesting exception, since its strategic approach is driven by the company's business objectives. The company's place promotional efforts to a large degree overlap with, or in some instances are subordinated to, the promotion of the company and its core business.

5.3.2 Scale-Dependent Politics of Regional Promotion

In addition to the political dimension of general regional promotion discussed in earlier chapters, the research results disclose further issues particular to investment attraction in the CEE context. FDI attraction proves to have a political element for a number of interrelated reasons. Firstly, in its fundamental sense, it requires multiple organisations to continuously negotiate their position and cooperate with one another to reach compromise-based solutions. Secondly, NIPAs and some of the regional intermediaries as non-elected agents are subordinates to the elected authorities, that is, national and regional governments. Thirdly, the level of involvement in the promotional process and its quality seem to be conditioned by local and regional party politics.

The complex political economy of inward investment makes it a controversial subject in itself (Dunning & Lundan, 2008), with generic legislation regulating investors' activity prepared on the national level. SARIO claims that it was the lack of conviction amongst the consecutive governments that has obstructed the flow of foreign capital to Slovakia during the 1990s.

Indecisiveness and inconsistency also characterised several governments of Poland. Frequent changes of the ruling parties resulted in a multiplicity of plans and ideas concerning the Polish NIPA. However, PAIiIZ criticises each office for its lack of vision and commitment to the agency:

> One of our key concerns is the persisting lack of clear and definitive information about the role of PAIiIZ and its legal form and resulting prerogatives. The proposals keep changing, and the issue remains unresolved. PAIiIZ has been actively involved in drafting of the act clarifying its position, our lawyers prepared different variants, offered ideas based on experiences of, for example, CzechInvest, but the final decision has been postponed and we still do not know what the future holds, and how can we be more effective in our operations.[12]

Further, the agency indicates how subsequent ministers overseeing the agency are using its successes to gain popular support. Heavy dependence on the Ministry of Economy and the resulting politicisation of PAIiIZ operations is perceived by the agency as a crucial factor compromising its efficiency. This opinion is seconded by the Polish Brand Institute, which emphasises the overwhelming presence of politics in country promotion and brand building.

CzechInvest, despite being also heavily entwined in the political process (see e.g. Drahokoupil, 2007b) remains the only NIPA satisfied with its relations with the consecutive Czech governments.

---

[12] Interview with the PAIiIZ representative.

On the regional level the political dimension of investment attraction changes from what could be generalised as 'political economy' arguments discussed in earlier chapters, to more party politics, with party interests often overshadowing those of the population—hence compromising the efficiency of FDI promotion agents. For example, PAIiIZ indicates the changes of regional governments usually affect their mutual relationship in a negative way. In the other cases, while Brno authorities attribute smooth cooperation with the Jihomoravský kraj regional government to existing political links between the two, in the opinion of Košice city authorities their rocky relationship with the kraj government is underpinned by the diverse ruling parties. The EDC seems to be finding its way through these meanders of regional politics, and appreciates the involvement of the mayors of Košice and other cities in the region in the Centre's promotional events.

Better political climate and friendlier political relations on the city region axis in Jihomoravský kraj make it easier for CTP involvement in the promotion process. The company adopts a pragmatic view of politics and stresses that "[i]t's a part of our job to understand what the region wants to do, where the political support is and see how we can benefit from that."[13]

5.4 Promotion Frameworks at Work

Having established generic power and initiative generating relationships between the different organisations engaging in the investment promotion process, it is now important to examine how those are reflected in the decisions and actions of the individual agents. Presenting the relations and interdependencies, so far the chapter has explored the governance framework of Central-Eastern European regional FDI promotion as seen on the surface (Figs. 5.1, 5.2, and 5.3). It has been highlighted that generally the actions of the majority of the promotion actors in the three regions are rarely guided by a strategic vision. It differs somewhat between the areas studied, with the Polish agents seemingly adopting

[13] Interview with the CTP Invest representative.

more long-term approaches and the Czech and Slovak ones not having any longer-term plans.

To some extent such a situation is hardly surprising. In more centralised governance frameworks the initiative and leadership is expected to come from the top, which liberates the regional agents from the need of preparation and implementation of their own plans. The contrary should be true for the more decentralised arrangements.

However, as partly indicated by the forthcoming analysis of the activities performed, this does not necessarily have to be true. Consequently, referring back to the fourth set of research questions, it needs to be considered how are these governance frameworks reflected in individual agents' operations and strategic choices, what are the links between the organisation and strategy, and if similar approaches are adopted in differing settings.

5.4.1 Promotion *de facto*

As has been explored in Chap. 2 (see Fig. 2.1 and Table 2.3) those participating in investment attraction have a variety of tools at their disposal, choice of which should be guided by, amongst others, such factors as aims to be achieved, target group characteristics, budget and agents' internal capacity (Domański, 1997; Florek, 2005; Rainisto, 2003). However, the analysis of the research result indicates that those factors do not necessarily play a role in determining the agents' preference of promotional activities and tools, or at least not to any significant extent. The organisations use a plethora of promotion channels and activities largely on their own initiative, and mutual projects which could allow economies of scale advantages (and potentially increase coherence) are more often an exception than a rule, particularly in the case of the Czech and Slovak regions. Having said that, it should be stressed that it is the NIPAs which engage in promotion most comprehensively, that is, making use of the widest range of tools and channels, which is in line with the earlier studies (e.g. Wells & Wint, 2000). It is clear however that some other agents strive to achieve an all-encompassing approach and, by so doing, they compete with NIPAs and one another, and duplicate activities.

By far the most popular activities performed by virtually all agents[14] in all three regions are communication oriented. Predominantly advertising and interactive marketing but also publicity and PR tools are commonly used to raise awareness of the areas and convince about their assets (Florek, 2003; Rainisto, 2003). In general then, as stressed by Brno authorities' representative, "communication is extremely important".

Printed materials, including leaflets, posters, pamphlets and brochures presenting regional profiles or sectoral studies, are the most commonly utilised channels and bearers of the promotional message. Also the agents commonly declare the use of media for publicity and PR purposes. However, apart from the NIPAs which more frequently use the mass media of national and international reach, the majority of promoters exploit local and at most national newspapers, magazines and radios and TV channels, albeit significantly less regularly. This usually involves announcing the successful completion of negotiations leading to investments in the area, in the hope of this having a demonstration effect. Alternatively, the aim may be to highlight the benefits to the regional economy, and win public support.

The main promoters in Wielkopolska also utilise digital technology and publish CD-ROMs with appropriate presentations and materials about the region.

Another example of a common initiative is the 'Survival Kit'—a manual for potential investors prepared by Jihomoravský kraj authorities and the RDA. Such co-publishing is, however, atypical as generally the CEE regional agents tend to act individually as far as the communication activities are concerned. This is best exemplified by the lack of cooperation, or indeed consultation, regarding the use of websites—the medium that, due to its flexible characteristics, should be the easiest to cooperate on. In line with recent developments, nearly all promoters operate websites whose parts are dedicated to foreign investors. The quality of those varies greatly and with the exception of NIPAs' web portals, they are often one-way instruments characterised by mixed and often contradictory information. In this respect again the Polish region seems to perform

[14] With the exception of Košice city authorities, whose active involvement in investment attraction until recently has been minimal.

in a somewhat more organised manner. The 'wielkopolska-region.pl' web portal created and maintained in cooperation between regional authorities and the RDA offers extensive, mostly up-to-date information specifically selected for potential investors. This is, however, the closest CEE regional promoters get to the use of comprehensive interactive (two-way) marketing tools. In that sense, the passive nature of websites earlier observed by Ward (1998) is emphasised even further.

As could be expected, private capital agents' communication activities diverge from those of the public authorities. CTP Invest remains focused on its business objectives, which is reflected in the type and content of preferred tools. The company publishes leaflets exploring the various products it offers, which are also elaborated in more detail in two books authored by the firm. The same focus is upheld on the CTP Invest's interactive websites, and in the company's own monthly newsletter.

In contrast, the EDC maintains a place-based focus in its communication activities. Yet those are limited to a small number of straightforward leaflets and the website providing basic information about the region. Instead the EDC puts more emphasis on personal selling channels and regularly organises road-shows, seminars and participates in a variety of investor-oriented events worldwide.[15] The EDC regularly uses support from investors already present in Košický kraj as an endorsement and testimony to the business potential of the region.

The popularity and fragmentation of image-building focused communication measures stems from their relative cost advantages, and misconceptions about their straightforwardness and simplicity, that is, the unfounded belief that 'anybody can prepare a leaflet or a website'. This however is not true for investment generation-oriented personal selling measures, which leads to them being less popular activity but one done usually in cooperation with other promoters.

In the FDI attraction context personal selling tools often prove more expensive than communication measures. They also put more demands on staff whose abilities are tested in direct contact with potential investors. These reasons implicitly induce a closer cooperation between the various promotion agents, if not continuous at least project-oriented.

[15] Generally the EDC's activity is more focused on predefined target groups.

As before, it is the NIPAs that engage in the most comprehensive set of activities. They participate in externally organised events, particularly conferences, trade and exhibitions, but also arrange seminars and road-shows on their own. While preparing these the national agencies often encourage the participation of other agents, who usually, lacking organisational capacities themselves, respond very positively and willingly take part in NIPAs' events both in home countries and abroad.

The use of international gatherings, including sector-oriented fairs and more general exhibitions, is widespread amongst the CEE regional promotion agents. Their participation is a common initiative, and in many instances the only mode of direct cooperation.

While the Slovak regional promoters are on average less active than their Czech and Polish counterparts, out of all of the organisations it is only the Economic Development Centre that, apart from active participation in externally arranged events, regularly organises seminars and road-shows in other countries.

Another set of personal selling measures, which perhaps is the best proxy for the involvement in FDI attraction, comprises an array of investors' services. Again the NIPAs offer the most comprehensive services while the regional agents' capacities in this respect vary.

In the Slovak case, apart from SARIO, the EDC is the only regional agent offering investor services. On the other hand in the Czech framework the services are offered by the organisations closely linked to CzechInvest, namely the AFI and the Jihomoravský kraj RDA. Contrary to the two, in the Polish example it is only the regional authority which does not offer investor services, but entrusts this activity to the RDA and ISCs. In addition to this, the Poznań authorities recently started providing an unusual, extensive service for investors interested in investing in the agglomeration. The authorities created a group of consultants are at the disposal of the potential investor 24/7, helping them to cut through the red-tape and to solve problems ranging from the most trivial ones, such as dry-cleaning, through to establishing contacts with appropriate public agencies and offices (*Gazeta Wyborcza*, 2007). The scope of activities of 'the pilots', as they are officially referred to, largely overlaps with the responsibilities of project managers within PAIiIZ and representatives of Wielkopolska ISC, which implies competition between the agents, potentially leading to conflict between them. Simultaneously it also reflects the limited capacity of the latter two and the potential need for the expansion of such services in the region.

The last measure of personal selling, which also blurs into the sales promotion domain, is negotiations. Although this area in the Czech Republic and Slovakia is mainly dominated by CzechInvest and SARIO respectively, the regional and local governments are also invited to participate in the process particularly in cases of important, large investment projects. In the Polish case PAIiIZ's position and role in the process is far less dominant, but the actors remain the same.

Investment negotiations are the privilege not only of the public bodies. Driven by its business objectives, CTP Invest negotiates contracts with potential customers on a daily basis. Those relations, however, only on the most generic level can be compared with the discussions between the public authorities and potential investors.

Due to their nature and legal requirements and regulations sales promotion tools in the investment attraction context (e.g. investment incentives), as explored in Chap. 2, are the prerogative of predominantly public institutions.[16] Different countries adopt different regimes and frameworks (Navaretti & Venables, 2004; Zanatta et al., 2006) varying in the level of authority vested with NIPA and regional governments. Central-Eastern European Countries are no different in this respect. Again, however, a clear distinction emerges between the approaches adopted by the Czech, Slovak and Polish governments.

While in the case of the former two the NIPAs dominate the process, in the case of Poland some tax-incentive powers (e.g. real estate tax) lie with the local communities. However, the regional and local promotion agents in all three countries can use the spatial planning process to create favourable investment conditions.

The Czech, Slovak and Polish NIPAs and regional promotion agents of Jihomoravský kraj, Košický kraj and Wielkopolskie voivodeship use a range of different promotion tools and channels, amongst which the most popular ones are communication and personal selling. Sales promo-

[16] In order to meet its objectives CTP Invest also widely uses these measures, although this is different from the way they are utilised by the public authorities.

tion measures are sanctioned by legal regulations, while time and labour-intensive direct marketing techniques (Belch & Belch, 2004) remain largely unexploited.

The earlier identified frameworks are not unambiguously reflected in the choice of the tools used. They are perhaps the most visible in the case of sales promotion measures; however, this is legally sanctioned rather than voluntarily agreed and managed. The frameworks are completely unnoticeable in the case of communication techniques used by the regional promoters. Thus it can be expected that even the most centralised organisation of promotion does not guarantee the increased efficiency of actions which could result from the economies of scale.

Apart from the earlier mentioned unclear intensity, some questions about the quality of the activities performed remain. The forthcoming sections will shed some light on several aspects of promotion quality, namely the internal consistency of the process and coherence of choices and performed actions.

5.4.2 Approaches to Place Product

As discussed in Chap. 3 defining place product is rarely a straightforward process (Rainisto, 2003; van den Berg et al., 2002). The differentiation of scales adds to the complexity of it (Ashworth and Voogd, 1990; Capik, 2007); however, awareness of what it is that an institution actually wants to promote can significantly improve the chances of success of the investment attraction actions. In circumstances where many institutions are involved with promotion, Domański (1997) points to two crucial factors in product definition determining the interests and perceptions held by the target groups—clarity and coherence. Both guarantee that the place offer is comprehensible, so that the promotion addressee knows what kind of advantages are to be gained. For the most part the CEE regional promotion practices meet these conditions in that the definition of place product corresponds to place advantages.

CzechInvest, in line with the mega-product approach, defines the country product as "the entire business environment in the Czech

Republic".[17] One reason for such an approach is that the agency, via feedback mechanisms and direct links to the government, can influence various aspects of it, that is, effectively contribute to product development.

The dominant position of the agency in strategy setting and execution is however less visible in the definition of the regional product. The Czech regional and local agents are far more precise, and instead adopt a sub-products approach. They emphasise the tangible assets, that is, the *facilities* and *clusters* (van den Berg et al., 2002), such as the investment incentives and infrastructure with regard to the industrial parks network, and skilled labour force and research facilities in the case of Brno city.

Despite its priority being commercial products—in the case of CTP Invest primarily office, production and storage space—the company also points to certain aspects of place product. It stresses the suppliers' networks, technical infrastructure and also the less tangible industrial traditions of the area and, associated with these, the skills of the labour force.

In Slovakia, SARIO also adopts a mega-product perspective and indeed the same stand as its Czech counterpart, but in addition identifies one particular cluster of place facilities, namely the technological parks. Other regional actors have problems with clear identification of their place products, which is yet another aspect reflecting the lack of principles and plans guiding their promotional efforts (if restricted ones). Two exceptions, the Spiska RDA and the EDC, define adequately industrial parks and labour skills as the main components of the regional product.

In the Polish case, the findings suggest, PAIiIZ's place product hardly differs from the one identified on the regional level. All agents recognise the availability and quality of particular investment sites as the main components of the regional product. Additionally the regional agents stress the role of transport infrastructure, and perceive Poznań as a cluster of various place facilities and thus a vital ingredient of the Wielkopolska product.

From the perspective of place product, the identified promotion frameworks are less explicitly visible in the decisions and approaches adopted by the Czech and Slovak individual agents than in the case of Poland. In more centralised set-ups evidently the scale has a significant

[17] Interview with the CzechInvest representative.

impact on the product definition. While the Czech and Slovak NIPAs by default focus on the 'nuclear product' and treat the country as a unified, homogenous mega-product, the corresponding regional agents are far more specific and point to a line of sub-products comprising the regional nuclear product. What this indicates, and what has been so far omitted in the literature, is that the product definition corresponds to the agents' powers and authority to shape the place product, which clearly emphasises the role of scale—the issues also largely neglected in the current 'place marketing' discourse.

The decentralised Polish framework seems to further support the argument about the existing relationship between an agency's power and the identification of the place product. Having limited influence on national legislation and the business environment, and paying more attention to the regional dimension of promotion, PAIiIZ's place product definition corresponds to those of regional agents. The agency indirectly influences the various aspects of regional products, for example by organising 'Grunt na Medal' ('The Golden Site') competition and managing relationships with regional and local authorities responsible for developing aspects of place offer.

The importance of scale, highlighted by the research questions, is further confirmed in the context of the place product. Namely it is the powers of organisations particular to a national, regional and local scale that have significant influence on the way the investors' place product is defined. The promotion agents perceive the place product as the features of the place which can be influenced within the scope of their authority. Consequently commonly the organisations do not recognise the bundle-nature of the investors' place product. Some of the investors' services offered by particular organisations are thought to comprise parts of such a 'bundle', which confirms the dual nature of such services proposed in Chap. 2.

5.4.3 Regional Attractiveness and Image Staples

In order to be convincing and have the chance of succeeding (staying in the minds of the targeted audiences and changing their attitudes), projected place image should ideally be a result of analysis of place product, competition and target markets (Anholt & Hildreth, 2005; Florek, 2005). A variety of organisations involved in the promotion process cause additional difficulty in defining the image staples and projecting a coherent image.

Despite acknowledging the role of the country and regional image in FDI attraction none of the agencies in the studied regions systematically monitor, or have conducted research, attempting to find out the image of a particular place held by the potential investors.[18] PAIiIZ utilises the studies conducted in the early 2000s by the Institute of Public Affairs exploring the change in the pre- and post-EU accession image of Poland in selected European states. However these studies lack an FDI perspective and can only be considered as general guidance. To get some insights into investors' perceptions of CEE one needs to refer to consultancy reports (e.g. Ernst & Young's *European Attractiveness Survey* series) but again these tend to be general and not very comprehensive, and therefore of limited reliability and usability for the promoters.

Lack of research and knowledge of the current perceptions held by the potential investors does not prevent those responsible for investment attraction from having fairly clearly identified features which they use to create the image. Those however differ only slightly, especially amongst the National Investment Promotion Agencies, therefore only marginally contribute to the breaking away from what, with regard to Africa, Anholt (2006, p. 3) calls "continent branding effects", but what considering the area's past could be termed as "[eastern] bloc branding effect".

Staple features on which to build the desired image cause the least controversy in the Czech Republic. Both national and regional FDI promotion agents agree on the main positive characteristics that should constitute image foundations. As often happened earlier with place promotion in Britain or North America (for details see e.g. Burgess, 1982; Ward, 1998), centrality, accessibility and connectivity play a major role in the creation of country, regional and local images:

[18] This however is not only characteristic of investment promotion agents in the studied regions. Generally the studies approaching place images from the demand perspective (i.e. the different target groups) are few and far between.

> Czech Republic is a compact country well connected to other parts of Europe, to many countries, it has good infrastructure including highways, the rail network and airports.[19]

> Jihomoravský kraj is located on a highway with close proximity to other countries.[20]

> Brno is a modern city on the crossroads of main routes. [...] It is close to Bratislava and Vienna.[21]

Additionally, industrial tradition and labour force quality and quantity are stressed. 'Industrial tradition' serves as a form of guarantee, assuring a potential investor about the skills and values of industrial organisations embedded in the national (regional) mindset. Availability of labour is a negative phenomenon of unemployment turned to the advantage of a location (Ward, 1998). Future availability of workforce is ensured by stressing the numbers of university students. This factor also supports the 'quality of labour' staple, further emphasised by flexibility, technical and language skills, and most importantly labour costs. Interestingly, while CzechInvest presents the cost-efficient labour availability across the nation, Jihomoravský kraj authorities emphasise more competitive labour costs in the region as compared to Prague, which underlines their attitudes towards the competition from the capital. This however is the sole exception from an otherwise coherent picture.

In the Slovak case the consensus regarding the main characteristics on which to build the country and regional image is comparably high, particularly amongst the regional agents. Similar to the Jihomoravský kraj, they place emphasis on industrial traditions (often in particular industries including wood processing and metallurgy), together with availability and qualitative aspects of labour force such as discipline, skills, willingness to learn and cost-effectiveness. Additionally, Spišská RDA and the EDC, recognising the importance of demonstration effects, stress the importance of previous investments, and use success stories in their

[19] Interview with the AFI representative.

[20] Interview with the Jihomoravský kraj RDA representative.

[21] Interview with the Brno city authorities representative.

regional image-building efforts. SARIO, on the other hand, adopts a more general approach. Using the example of recent developments within the Slovak automotive industry, the agency strives to associate Slovakia with the favourable business environment, dynamically reforming (e.g. introduction of the flat tax system, labour code amendments) and adapting to corporate requirements. Being aware of the deficient infrastructure and somewhat peripheral location, none of the Slovak agents try to support their image with the accessibility, connectivity and centrality arguments.

PAIiIZ argues that the problem with the image of Poland is not that it is bad, but that it is hardly existent, and if it does exist it is both blurred and confused (PAIiIZ, 2005). The agency is convinced this is "a good starting point".[22] It bases the investment image of Poland on features used by its Slovak and Czech counterparts: availability of a dynamic, well-trained, competitively priced workforce and a central location. For the same reasons as SARIO it avoids the themes of connectivity and accessibility. Instead PAIiIZ puts more emphasis on size of the economy and its recent dynamics.

The Wielkopolskie voivodeship agents use area specific characteristics in the attempt to put a regional dimension on some of the features used by the national agency. They emphasise the entrepreneurial spirit embodied in the regional workforce, and stress advantages other than centrality, such as the proximity to the German border and location within the transport corridor Paris-Berlin-Warszawa-Moscow. The distinctive economic structure, with a prosperous agriculture sector, and better than national average performance according to the regional authorities, Wielkopolska RDA and Investor Service Centre, constitute the remaining image staples.

There seems to be a general internal coherence regarding the image staples between the various agents in the regions studied. This is dissimilar to the previous research conducted in another CEE country, Latvia, which concluded that image building is often fragmentary and lacked coordination (Dzenovska, 2005). However, the common use of some staples in the different countries, particularly by the three NIPAs, would

[22] Interview with the PAIiIZ representative.

suggest that it is not the level of centralisation but rather the general popularity of some features that matter the most. Those often correspond to the investment location factors as previously identified by academic research (e.g. Dawson, 2005; Domański, 2001; Hilderbrandt & Wörz, 2004) and consultancy reports (e.g. Deloitte, 2007; Ernst & Young, 2007).

And while the projected advantages broadly reflect the reality and the place product defined by the promoters, as according to Quelch and Jocz (2005) they should, they do little to allow the external perceptions of the countries to defeat the overshadowing effects of the image of the whole of the CEE region. Effectively then the promotion agents contribute to the strengthening of one of the image dimensions, namely the perceived sameness of the individual states as identified by the Safron Brand Consultants' report (2004). The emphasis put on particular features may to some extent vary, nevertheless the main message is one of indistinctiveness.

On the national level, when the NIPAs perceive countries as homogenous entities, there seems to be little motivation for differentiation between the three nations. This is countered by the regional actors, which naturally attempt to provide a more individual dimension and stress features differentiating the area from other parts of their respective countries, that is, question the homogeneity advocated by NIPAs. The levels of emphasised uniqueness vary, with the agents of the Polish region emphasising the characteristic identity of certain areas more visibly than their Czech or Slovak counterparts.

The above analysis points to two observations. Firstly, broadly speaking the image staples chosen by the promotion agents in the three regions are linked to their respective place product, which contradicts the frequent opinion about images aimed at misleading the audiences and portraying false realities. Secondly, as argued by Ashworth and Voogd (1994), place images exist through their uniqueness, yet as shown in Chap. 4, although there are more distinct features of each region then similarities between them, the qualities stressed by the promoters are hardly distinctive. Moreover it often remains unclear how the images presented are linked to the chosen target groups. More often than not the features which are being stressed seem to be aimed at any investor, rather than those in particular sectors, best suited to the regional needs.

5.4.4 Generic and Targeted Approaches

Targeting and proper recognition of the customers' needs is crucial for regional promotion activities (Fitzsimons, 1995). As discussed in Chaps. 3 and 4, it is not sufficient to perceive FDI as a unified and homogenous target group. To attract investment which can maximally contribute to the regional economy there is a need to divide the group into more precise segments. While the investment promotion agencies worldwide operate sector-based strategies (Charlton, Davis, Faye, Haddock, & Lamb, 2004), the majority of the CEE regional authorities seem not to recognise such need at all, and those that do focus rather on the investors' nationality.

Market segmentation and targeting are amongst the most strategic decisions which traverse and inform the various areas of investment promotion, including agents' internal organisation, a set of activities performed, the projected image and identification of competitors. For this reason it can be expected to reflect best the earlier identified promotional frameworks. The data gathered provides less optimistic evidence. In the context of the other issues explored here (image, competition) it can be rather concluded that segmentation and planned targeting (especially in the case of the regional agents) is largely rhetorical, and not backed up by actions, that is, reflects a desirable (wishful thinking) rather than actual (current) state of affairs.

All Czech agents' targeting is industrial sector based. However, minor as they are, there are some differences between the agents regarding the choice of the sectors. CzechInvest avoids attracting assembly plants and aims to secure investments in high value added sectors, R&D and strategic services. Jihomoravský kraj RDA and Brno city authorities' activities are additionally targeted at medical equipment producers, precise engineering and electronic branches. The design and designation of industrial parks is considered an important tool in attraction of desired investment projects. The regional authorities, in line with the findings presented in Chap. 4, tend not to target their actions at all, claiming they "welcome all investors willing to take part and benefit from our [their] promotional activities and wanting to invest in the region."[23]

[23] Interview with the Jihomoravský kraj regional authorities representative.

CTP Invest presents a more entrepreneurial approach and claims that in order to maximise profits its actions are targeted as precisely as possible. The company shows no preference for the investors' origins, in fact it has been previously successful in attracting American and Taiwanese firms from Scotland. Instead CTP Invest focuses its actions on particular service sectors including business process outsourcing, shared service centres, IT, distribution and logistics, and manufacturing sectors such as the automotive, plastic and electronics industries.

Slovak national and regional institutions mainly identify divergent target groups, although they agree on the significance of high value added sectors. Not entirely in line with this, SARIO stresses the importance of a whole range of sectors from automotive companies, call centres through leisure and tourism investments to IT and biotech. The agency attempts to attract large investments: "it is better to get one big company than 10 small ones", because "you can always better support a big company than smaller ones".[24] The Slovak NIPA's regional office is more focused and emphasises the importance of high-tech sectors, which is in stark contrast with other regional agencies. For example Spišská RDA targeting is driven by the local situation, and based on tradition, local resources and skill base the agency is interested in attracting wood processing and machinery construction industries.

To the contrary the EDC is the only agency whose promotion is geographically and sectorally targeted. The Centre conducts the majority of its activities, including road-shows, in the USA and Canada, and aims to bring manufacturing investors who would have a positive impact on the regional labour market:

> We are focusing on the manufacturing investments. At the moment we are focusing on FDI creating as much as possible of new jobs—due to the fact that region suffers from high levels of unemployment. In city of Košice and the surrounding area the unemployment rate is 15–18%. Across Eastern SK there are districts where the unemployment rate is over 30%. We are focusing to bring as much jobs as possible for people here.[25]

---

[24] Both quotes come from an interview with the SARIO representative.

[25] Interview with the EDC representative.

Simultaneously, however, the Centre admits that while it attempts to focus its activities, it treats all investors interested in locating in the region on equal terms.

PAIiIZ is the only agency recognising the need of geographical and sectoral targeting. The agency focuses on attracting FDI from countries that already are Poland's largest investors—the USA,[26] France, Germany and the UK. More recently, PAIiIZ also focused its activities on Asian investors. Successful performance at Expo 2005 in Aichi encouraged the agency to develop promotional activities in Japan and open its first overseas office in Tokyo. The agency's sectoral focus is largely similar to its Czech and Slovak counterparts and comprises automotive, IT, biotech industries and business services.

Apart from directly approaching investors, there are numerous agencies which can potentially influence the company location, but which possess diverse levels of knowledge about the region and have different needs and expectations (Fretter, 1993). Unlike the majority of the other promoters, PAIiIZ, together with the Institute for Polish Brand, recognises the need for "influencing the influential"[27] and attempts to target its activities also at various investment intermediaries.

On the regional level hardly any of the agents in Wielkopolska clearly define their targets. Both regional and Poznań city authorities are interested in attracting any kind of investor willing to come to the region. Generally, the Investor Service Centre emphasises the importance of differentiating between the tourism and FDI target groups. Only Wielkopolska RDA attempts to define target groups more precisely and indicates the need to attract investment creating jobs in technology-based sectors, including IT.

Effectively then, contrary to expectations and best practice as described by the literature (e.g. Kotler et al., 1999), there is no shared approach to targeting in any of the regions under study. In fact, a considerable degree of chaos and lack of coordination is quite evident. The level of centralisation of the promotion governance framework seems largely irrelevant.

[26] For example amongst other activities in June 2007 PAIiIZ organised the 1st Congress of Polish Diaspora in the USA and used it extensively as an investment promotion event (*Rzeczpospolita*, 2007).

[27] Interview with the Institute of the Polish Brand's representative.

Firstly, in line with earlier findings some regional agents (at least one in each of the regions) do not target their activities at all. In this respect Wielkopolskie voivodeship institutions present the most unstructured approach. Secondly, apart from the Czech region case, there is no agreement on the fundamental matter as to whether sectors, countries or both should be targeted. Thirdly, the sectors selected by the National Investment Promotion Agencies usually only at the general level overlap with those indicated by the regional promotion agents. The NIPAs aim to attract projects with higher value added and that are more knowledge-intensive, which are also chased by other countries[28] (Zanatta et al., 2006). The regional agents (especially those in Jihomoravský kraj and Košický kraj), in addition to the popular sectors, also aim to draw investment in activities complementary to the profiles of their regional economies. Fourthly, a number of sectors, popular amongst all of those agents which declare to be targeting their promotional efforts, can be identified. Automotive industries, electronics, IT, biotech and R&D activities and business services seem to be the most sought-after sectors. This situation implies the existence of competition between the studied areas, which is further emphasised by the considerable degree of similarity between the place products being offered to investors, and accordingly analogous image staples explored earlier. The issues associated with the identification of competitors are discussed next.

5.4.5 Regional Competitive Positioning

The level of competition awareness varies across the regions and between the organisations. Perhaps the only common view is that the regions of all three countries compete with other Central-Eastern European nations:

> Slovakia, and Bratislava region in particular is a strong competitor for us [Jihomoravský kraj].[29]

[28] In this respect the Czech, Polish and Slovak NIPAs are distinct from other such agencies in this part of Europe, which, as indicated in the previous chapter, usually target IT services and tourism sector investments (UNCTAD, 2004).

[29] Interview with the Jihomoravský kraj RDA representative.

> The Visegrad countries are our [Brno] key competitors, particularly cities such as Bratislava, Budapest, Eger, Kraków.[30]

> Poland, Czech Republic and Hungary are our [Košický kraj] main competitors.[31]

> As a large region we [Wielkopolskie voivodeship] are competing with entire Slovakia, and many regions in the Czech Republic and Hungary.[32]

The Czech agencies operating on the national level define competitors depending on industry sector. While for some sectors (e.g. automobile industry) the Czech Republic competes with its immediate neighbours, for others (e.g. call centres) the main competitors are located in Asia. CzechInvest, its former associate Jihomoravský kraj RDA and AFI are convinced there is no inter-regional competition within the country and argue that the authoritarian-like powers of the national agency guarantee this. As has been shown in Chap. 4, this view is contested by the majority of the Czech regional authorities, including Jihomoravský kraj. Equally Brno city authorities challenge this position. Both agents identify Praha as their superior competitor, while their opinions vary with regard to the peer rivals. Plzeň and Ostrava constitute the main national competition for Brno, while Jihomoravský kraj perceives all the other regions in the Czech Republic as its rivals. Regarding international competition, however, the view of regional actors hardly varies from the one presented by national bodies, in that there is a persistent lack of specific knowledge and ability to identify particular regional competitors abroad.

With regard to regional competition on both inter- and intra-national scale, CTP Invest finds itself in a tricky situation. While the company has a very considerable presence in Jihomoravský kraj, it also has a track record of operations in other Czech regions. More recently the company also got involved in the other CEE countries, notably Slovakia and Romania, but also increasingly in Hungary and Poland. Clearly then

[30] Interview with the Brno city authorities representative.

[31] Interview with the Spiš Regional Development Agency representative. View shared by Košický kraj regional authorities representative.

[32] Interview with the ISC representative.

there is a potential conflict of interests, and a considerable one. The company, however, presents a different point of view. It argues that the Czech regions "hardly compete with one another. It is really always a win-win situation as different companies are interested in locating in different regions".[33] This allows the company to operate a clear and precise targeting strategy as reflected by the types and characteristics of the company's offer in the different areas.[34] On an international scale CTP Invest's experience shows that while looking for the location in this part of Europe, the investors are usually most interested in one of the Visegrád countries.

The Slovak agents seemingly express the same opinions with regard to international competitors. While being unable to identify any particular regions, both NIPAs and the majority of the regional promoters agree that the Czech Republic, Poland and Hungary constitute the most serious challenge for their areas.

On the national scale SARIO, similarly to its Czech counterpart, believes there is no competition between regions. The rationale for such judgment, however, is not an authoritarian one, but supported by the view that regions in Slovakia are so diverse that each one attracts a specific kind of investment. Infrastructure-dependent projects would go to western parts of the country, while efficiency-seeking investment would locate in eastern parts where the availability of skilled and cost-efficient labour is greater.[35] Such a west/east divide is also traceable in the approach presented by other regional and local actors. The distinctive feature, however, is that they argue that Košický kraj is in, albeit unequal, competition (for investment) with the more prosperous and better infrastructurally endowed regions of western Slovakia, specifically Bratislavský kraj and those in its proximity. EDC presents a complementary view and perceives central parts of the country as the main competitors on a peer level.

Other countries of Central-Eastern Europe along with China constitute the main competition for Poland and its regions in the view of some

---

[33] Interview with the CTP Invest representative.

[34] Nevertheless the company acknowledges the existence of sectors whose location requirements are more universal, for example logistics, and it recognises that both Jihomoravský kraj and Ostravský kraj compete for those in the Czech Republic.

[35] This is in conflict with SARIO regional branch in Košický kraj which recognises each region of Slovakia as potential competition.

regional actors and PAIiIZ alike. The agency also recognises the existence of competition between the regions within the country, but argues this does not adversely affect its actions.

> The regions compete but this is not visible in our actions. We try to give attention to all regions and their needs, particularly those poorly connected, etc, and emphasise their advantages to the investors—but ultimately the decision is up to them.[36]

This is in contrast with the Investor Service Centre's lobbying activities influencing PAIiIZ's perception and actions regarding FDI location in Wielkopolska. Such activities result from the conviction of the existence of strong competition between different parts of Poland. Similar to their Czech and Slovak counterparts, some of the Wielkopolska promoters identify the national capital and its surroundings as the individual superior rival. However, as could be expected, considering survey results presented in the previous chapter, Wielkopolska authorities have a contrary opinion on this.

Additionally Małopolska and Dolny Śląsk in the south and south-west of Poland are considered to be peer competitors. Wielkopolska agents, despite recognising competition, admit they do not feel rivalry from any regions abroad, as in their view it is the national level where the direct competition really takes place.

With regard to the issue of competition, the promotional frameworks are unambiguously reflected in the mere fact of NIPAs admitting or not the existence of intra-national competition between the regions in the countries studied. It is, however, only such general level where the frameworks are evident. The presupposed coherence and consistency expected in the centralised set-up of the Czech Republic is virtually non-existent with the regional agents having ideas divergent not only from the NIPA but also from one another. In the case of the Slovak, less centralised, framework the latter divergence is less prominent, while the Polish decentralised set-up allows for substantial, albeit not complete, convergence of views with regard to both dimensions.

---

[36] Interview with the PAIiIZ representative.

Young (2005, p. 118) asserts that the "fight for inward investment [...] leads to some localities being losers in the development terms". Given the evidence presented above, the opposite seem to be more accurate. While the promotional frameworks are not exactly reflected in the perception and identification of intra- and inter-national competition, it is apparent that in a country (Poland) where the NIPA recognises the existence of such rivalry and where the regions are more free and active in their promotion the distribution of foreign capital is far more equal (see Tables 1.3 and 6.1) than it is the case in countries (the Czech Republic, Slovakia) where these conditions are not met.

5.5 Reflecting on CEE Regional Investment Promotion

It has been argued in the literature that one of the communist era legacies, namely the deficiency of institutional thickness on the local and regional levels, is to be blamed for the lack of sophisticated "place marketing" in Central-Eastern Europe (Young, 2005). The analysis presented above would suggest reinterpretation of such an argument. Bearing in mind the research questions guiding this study, the third and fourth set in particular (p. 32), the forthcoming parts offer further discussion of the findings of the study.

As far as the regional promotion aimed at investment attraction is concerned, the regions are institutionally well endowed. The abilities and capacities of individual institutions vary; however, between them a robust set of promotional activities is being performed, utilising all the channels of promotion with a comprehensive selection of promotion tools and techniques. As evidenced by the data presented above, sometimes revealing significant operational and strategic inconsistencies, CEE regional promotion suffers not from non-existence but a rather qualitative deficit in the composition of networks (i.e. limited or no direct participation of private capital and civil society) within which relationships are additionally characterised by power asymmetry (compare Figs. 5.1, 5.2, and 5.3), leading to often fragmented and incoherent approaches and actions.

Table 5.2 Trans-scalar consistency and coherence of promotional frameworks

	Jihomoravský kraj	Košický kraj	Wielkopolskie voivodeship
Place product	–	–/+	+
Image	+	+/–	–/+
Target	–	–/+	–/+
Competition	–/+	+/–	+
Activities	+/–	–/+	+/–

Source: Own research
Notes: +: good; –: bad; +/–: more good than bad; –/+: more bad than good

Table 5.2 illustrates the levels of such incoherence within the three identified promotion governance frameworks. None of the frameworks, regardless of the degree of centralisation, guarantees full operational and conceptual coherence and consistency.

On the generic level the quality of interactions and strength of relationships between the participating organisations does not condition the coherence of the approaches adopted by individual agents. In other words, even if organisation A names organisation B as its best partner (and vice versa) it does not automatically imply both will be approaching place product, competitors, targets or any other aspect in a similar way. The level of decentralisation seems to be of greater importance in this respect.

The higher level of internal consistency of the process is more visible in a decentralised framework of the Wielkopolskie voivodeship. In the more centralised set-up of Košický kraj there is consistently little interconnectedness between the main aspects of promotion amongst the agents. The most centralised framework of the Czech region is simultaneously the least coherent one.

Additionally, it remains ambiguous which particular aspects of promotion are usually approached in the most or least coherent manner. There are no apparent similarities regarding any particular aspect shared by all three regions; however, there are some parallels between two regions. For example consistency in 'targeting' is the most problematic issue for the Czech and Polish regions. Equally the complementarity of the activities performed is most evident in the same two areas.

The most divergent approaches to 'competition' are to be found amongst the promoters of Jihomoravský kraj and Košický kraj.

The 'image' issue is an interesting one in this respect. While there is a high level of coherence amongst the national and regional promoters of the Czech region regarding the image staples, the contrary needs to be said in the case of Wielkopolska voivodeship. The reasons for that, however, according to the literature (Ashworth & Voogd, 1994; Fretter, 1993) are putting the Polish region in an advantaged position with respect to its Czech counterpart. Whilst the Wielkopolska image promoted by the regional agents is based on the features particular to the region, but dissimilar to the image staples chosen by the Polish national promoters, the qualities chosen to project the image of Jihomoravský kraj are very much in line with those used by CzechInvest to create the image of the whole Czech Republic.

Considering the existing inconsistencies within the frameworks identified, but also often within the approaches adopted by individual agencies, it comes as little surprise that the promotion activities of the agents are not subject to assessment or audit. Yet, despite this, the agents have clear ideas about the advantages and deficiencies in the promotional process of their areas. Not only can they name their own weaknesses, but also express unambiguous opinions regarding the practices of others, in some instances even more boldly.

However, even when only considering the NIPAs, some divergences become apparent. CzechInvest recognises the need to be ever more proactive in investment promotion, but mostly is proud to have been the winner of multiple awards (including 'European Investment Promotion Agency of the Year' in 2000 and 2001, 'Best Practices in Promotion' in 2004 presented by the steering committee of the World Investment Forum) and perceive it as sufficient evidence of the quality of their actions. SARIO on the other hand plays down the role of 'quality'. The agency admits that currently the foreign investors' interest in Slovakia is such that the country hardly needs any promotion. Additionally, following the example of the Irish Industrial Development Agency is meant to secure the agency's excellence. Contrary to these two, PAIiIZ expresses concerns about the quality of Poland's promotion and its own activities which all too often are negatively influenced by political arrangements and processes. Consequently, whereas the Czech and Slovak NIPAs primarily stress the often-quoted financial aspect (Ward, 1998; Young &

Kaczmarek, 1999) as the main factor conditioning the improvements and expansion of promotional procedures, the Polish NIPA recommends the most comprehensive list of required changes ranging from increase in resources and powers, amendments to financing arrangements, through to multilevel cooperation and increased coordination of efforts. The latter two are also commonly recognised by the Wielkopolska promoters.

This largely reflects the NIPAs' experiences and the positions they occupy within the frameworks identified earlier, where the Czech and Slovak agencies exert considerable dominance over investment promotion but where the Polish NIPA is one of the players with considerably less powers than its counterparts in the other two countries.

While many of the other agents involved in promotion are content with their own actions, several of them also extend a wide-ranging critique of different aspects of promotion.

The Czech and Polish organisations operating on the national level criticise various aspects of country promotion. AFI points to the need for closer coordination of actions performed by the different organisation. On the other hand the Institute for Polish Brand offers a substantive critique and suggests that PAIiIZ should be less government dependent and focus solely on provision of the investors' services instead of getting involved with other aspects of promotion. Additionally, on a more general level the Institute for Polish Brand criticises the total advertising and publicity aspects of promotion of Poland as being abrupt, fragmentary and uncoordinated, leading to situations where political scandals have more serious impacts on the country's external perceptions than its international accomplishments such as NATO and EU membership. Consequently, the Institute, in line with the AFI suggestion, but extended onto promotion directed towards various target groups, postulates a more synchronised and long-term approach to the promotion of Poland.

The regional agents' opinions and suggestions for improvements for the most part only marginally diverge from those presented by the national agents. This, however, again differs between the three regions. It seems that the only two aspects on a general level common to the majority of the organisations are: (1) some level of appreciation of the existing promotional efforts, and (2) demand for increased funding.

Jihomoravský kraj RDA and CTP Invest stress the positive role CzechInvest plays in FDI attraction to the Czech Republic and emphasises the high standard of its actions. With regard to the regional level, also both organisations praise the efforts of the regional authorities, whilst admitting that there is room for improvement. In contrast Brno city authorities are more critical and condemn the regional authorities for focusing too much on smaller towns and communities throughout the region. Similar opinion, leaning towards some form of a more centralised system, is also expressed by the regional authorities themselves, who however indicate that, in order to improve effectiveness of their efforts, they would require broader powers in the management of the land belonging to local communities.

Brno city authorities are convinced that the number of incoming investment projects reflects the high quality of city promotion. Potential improvements in the process can only result from extension of the authorities' powers and increased spending. In demanding more powers Brno authorities are however isolated, for the other promoters of the Czech region, as well as the Polish and Slovak ones, regardless of the level of satisfaction with their activities, stress the need for improvements in coordination of efforts rather than the reform of administrative arrangements.

Wielkopolskie voivodeship agents offer the most comprehensive appraisal of the regional promotion effort. While there is a shared recognition and appreciation for the actions of the regional and Poznań authorities, the ISC criticises the limited degree of cooperation between the two and further denotes the varying levels of involvement of the local communities in the process—an issue earlier criticised by Florek (2003).

The other organisations additionally point to numerous shortcomings linked rather to the overall quality of the investment promotion than the activities of individual agents. Such issues as clear division of duties and responsibilities, coordination of actions (within and amongst individual agents), a strategic approach, wider involvement and increased capacity including research and the investors' services are commonly perceived as the key areas for improvement to the regional promotion process. Such recommendations are more systemic and comprehensive in nature than those offered by the organisations in the Czech and Slovak regions, which is in line with the findings presented earlier, concerning the differing approaches and governance frameworks guiding the promotion of the regions.

The promoters of Košický kraj are divided in their opinions regarding the quality of the promotion of the region. The regional and Košice city authorities both recognise that promotion plays largely a secondary role to other activities, but while the capital city suggests this should be quickly amended, the regional authorities seem to be of a contrary opinion.

The RDA and the Economic Development Centre on the other hand emphasise the recent progress in region's promotion and recognition, but also point to some persisting deficiencies. The Centre recognises the positive effects brought about by the change of Slovak government attitudes and policies towards the foreign investors. Consequently on the regional level the EDC appreciates the growing involvement and increasing capacity of promotion. At the same time the regional development agency argues this could be further strengthened by a creation of strategy and clear division of responsibilities.

In the three countries, in line with NIPAs' postulates, the regional agents universally would welcome higher spending dedicated to their promotion activities. Most of them would simply use the additional resources to fund the extension of their actions, that is, increase the amount of publicity material and increase the frequency of participation in trade fairs and exhibitions. Wielkopolska RDA and Investor Service Centre, on the other hand, would rather see the additional resources contributing to the qualitative improvements, particularly the development of research activities and increased investor servicing capacity.

The agents' judgments on the current promotional process are fairly reflective of the identified promotional frameworks. The Czech regional promoters' self-confidence is underpinned by the widely appreciated activities of CzechInvest. The agents in Košický kraj recognise their limited involvement, but also point to the recent positive developments, while the organisations in the Polish region express possibly the highest levels of self-criticism, but of a constructive nature, that is, allowing them to come up with the most comprehensive set of desirable enhancements.

Judging by the existing levels of coordination, it is hardly surprising that improvements are advocated by the majority of organisations. It remains to be seen if those claims and postulates are implemented and have any impact on the practice. The popular character of this notion allows for some optimism and permits to expect positive developments in the future.

This is however curbed by the fact that postulated coordination refers to the operational level, that is, it indicates the demand for a more clear division of labour, while the conceptual and strategic dimensions remain largely neglected. It can only be expected that the harmonisation of the latter will appear as a consequence of the successful coordination of the former.

5.6 Conclusions

Responding the fourth set of research questions, this chapter identified the governance frameworks of FDI promotion in the Central-Eastern European regions and, through examination of operations, strategic and conceptual choices made by the individual agents, investigate their internal coherence. By so doing it is adding to the general discussion about the complexity of the FDI promotion process (e.g. Wells & Wint, 2000; World Bank, 2012; Young, 2005), and more specifically to the debate about efficiency and productivity of organisational arrangements in investment promotion (e.g. Loewendahl, 2001; MIGA, 2006; OECD, 2015).

In the CEE regions, a variety of organisations get directly involved with investment promotion. An analysis of the relationships between them allows identifying governance frameworks characteristic for each country (Table 5.1, Figs. 5.1, 5.2, and 5.3). The review of activities performed and strategic choices made by the component agents discloses the political dimension of the investment promotion process and reveals various levels of internal coherence conversely proportional to the degree of power and initiative centralisation. The dominance of the National Investment Promotion Agency does not guarantee the proper flow of information between the different participants of the process, which further impedes the inter-institutional synergy.

The multiplicity of the organisations involved (particularly public sector ones) unavoidably adds a political dimension to the promotional process. The character of it differs, and to some extent seems to be scale specific. While on the national level it is rather the political economy arguments driving the process, the regional-level practice, as illustrated by the relationships between Brno and Jihomoravský kraj authorities and Košice and Košicky kraj authorities, is more dominated by 'realpolitik'. In some circumstances, particularly in the Polish case, there are strong calls for the de-politicisation of the process, which arguably can lead to its increased efficiency and effectiveness.

In many respects there are discrepancies between the promotion pursued by the regional authorities (discussed in Chap. 4) and the process conducted in a multi-scalar and multi-agent setting. The differences extend beyond the obvious organisational ones to include also strategic and operational disparities, such as the identification of competitors and target groups, and a set of activities performed. However, one particular feature of CEE regional promotion aimed at investment attraction clearly demonstrated by the dataset is confusion. Spontaneous rather than strategic approaches dominate, evidenced by poor organisation, leading to doubling of activities and contributing to conceptual incoherence of the process. Often not only the approaches adopted by various organisations differ, but also there are instances where within an individual organisation contrasting decisions and choices are made, for example regarding the targeted sectors and image staples.

The degree of centralisation of regional promotion activities in CEEC varies. However, while different frameworks can be identified, the centralisation level is not always explicitly visible in the strategic choices and actions of the regional promoters. Decentralisation does not imply a lack of coherence, but rather indicates a bottom-up approach in strategic and conceptual choice dissemination, as evidenced by the Polish example. Yet, even among closely cooperating regional agents there are divergent approaches to place product, target groups, competition and image staples. Also within a single organisation these issues are not necessarily interlinked and the image promoted is not always explicitly associated with a defined product, which indicates the lack of a systematic approach to FDI promotion characterising the actions of majority of the agents, especially, but not exclusively, those at the regional level.

It has been suggested that the organisation of promotion depends as much on the size and economic capacity of the region, as it does on the legal context and empowerment of the regional bodies (Loewendahl, 2001). Furthermore, the regions in smaller countries (e.g. Czech Republic, Slovakia) should benefit from a single, strong NIPA (Zanatta et al., 2006). This is not explicitly the case in Central-Eastern Europe. Powerful NIPAs (specifically CzechInvest but also SARIO, albeit to a lesser extent), despite their usual politically correct rhetoric, rarely involve regional agents in promotion activities, fail in steering investment projects evenly to the various regions of the countries (see Table 6.1). There is scope (and indeed the need) for more convincing involvement of regional- and local-level organisations, as demonstrated by the Wielkopolska case. The regional agents, particularly those directly in charge of the development of their areas, should not solely rely on NIPAs but also take on the promotional responsibility and in the long term they should go towards establishment of a peculiar 'division of labour' leading to increased efficiency and improved quality (and coherence) of the promotional process. In a short-term perspective, they need to become more active and exploit various modes of cooperation and influencing the NIPAs, whether directly or through the national agencies' regional representatives. In turn this can be used by the NIPAs to control the intra-national competition between the regions. Regional promotion aimed at investment attraction certainly is a multi-scalar process, where in as much as the NIPAs require international presence they need to have strong links to lower administrative levels within the country (Young, 2005).

The lack of coherence characterising the CEE regional promotion results mainly from fragmented actions and limited vertical and horizontal communication between the process participants, often underpinned (especially in the Czech and Slovak cases) by the arrogance of the National Investment Promotion Agency and wasteful, partially politically driven competition between the regional organisations.

There is a serious deficiency of citizens' participation and private capital involvement in strategy setting and operational activities. The exceptions of the EDC and CTP Invest indicate the various possibilities and gains from firms' engagement in regional promotion. The presence of a large investor in a region provides it with significant promotional potential in many respects, particularly in developing demonstration effects, and benefits from the MNE's global business networks and promotional expertise. Also, there is a scope for deeper involvement of regional capital cities, which often constitute the region's main asset (and indeed repeatedly are perceived this way by other agents).

References

Almond, P., Ferner, A., & Tregasis, O. (2015). The changing context of regional governance of FDI in England. *European Urban and Regional Studies, 22*(1), 61–76.

Anholt, S. (2006). Is place branding a capitalist tool. *Place Branding and Public Diplomacy, 2*(1), 1–4.

Anholt, S., & Hildreth, J. (2005). Let freedom and cash registers ring: America as a brand. *Place Branding and Public Diplomacy, 1*(2), 164–172.

Artisen-Maksimenko, P. (Ed.). (2000). *Multinationals in Eastern Europe.* Houndmills: Macmillan Press.

Ashworth, G.J., & Voogd, H. (1990). *Selling the city: marketing approaches in public sector urban planning.* London: Belheven Press.

Ashworth, G. J., & Voogd, H. (1994). Marketing and place promotion. In J. R. Gold & S. V. Ward (Eds.), *Place promotion; the use of publicity and marketing to sell towns and regions.* Chichester: John Wiley & Sons.

Belch, G. E., & Belch, M. A. (2004). *Advertising and promotion: An integrated marketing communications perspective.* Boston: McGraw-Hill.

Bickl, M. (2004). *Image management in old-industrial regions: Policy learning, governance and leadership in North East England and the Ruhr.* PhD Thesis, University of Durham, Durham.

Burgess, J. (1982). Selling places: Environmental images for the executive. *Regional Studies, 16*(1), 1–17.

Burgess, J., & Wood, P. (1988). Decoding Doklands; Place advertising and decision-making strategies of the small firm. In J. Eyles & D. M. Smith (Eds.), *Qualitative methods in human geography.* Cambridge: Polity Press.

Capik, P. (2007). Organising FDI promotion in Central-Eastern European regions. *Place Branding and Public Diplomacy, 3*(2), 152–163.

Charlton, A., Davis, N., Faye, M., Haddock, J., & Lamb, C. (2004). *Industry targeting within foreign investment promotion*. Oxford Investment Research Working Paper, Oxford.

Cleave, E., Godwin, A., Sadler, R., & Gilliland, J. (2016). The role of place branding in local and regional economic development: Bridging the gap between policy and practicality. *Regional Studies, Regional Science, 3*(1), 207–228.

CTP Invest. (2006). *CTP Invest*. Humpolec: CTP Invest.

CzechInvest. (2008). *Annual report 2006*. Praha: CzechInvest. Retrieved January 15, 2008, from http://www.czechinvest.org/data/files/vyrocni-zprava-ci-2006-723.pdf

Dawson, A. (2005). Foreign direct investment: A sectoral and spatial review. In D. Turnock (Ed.), *Foreign Direct Investment and Regional Development in East Central Europe and Former Soviet Union*. Aldershot: Ashgate.

Deloitte Consulting LLP. (2007). *2007 global shared services survey results*. Retrieved August 19, 2008, from http://www.deloitte.com/dtt/cda/doc/content/2007GlobalSharedServicesSurvey%20-%20Ireland.pdf

Domański, B. (2001). *Kapitał zagraniczny w przemyśle Polski*. Kraków: IGiGP Uniwersytetu Jagiellońskiego.

Domański, T. (Ed.). (1997). *Marketing terytorialny; Strategiczne wyzwanie dla miast i regionów*. Łódź: Uniwersytet Łódzki.

Drahokoupil, J. (2007a, May 7). Is CzechInvest facing extinction? *Czech Business Weekly*.

Drahokoupil, J. (2007b). *The rise of the competition state in Central and Eastern Europe: The politics of foreign direct investment*. PhD Thesis, Central European University, Budapest.

Dunning, J. H., & Lundan, S. M. (2008). *Multinational enterprises and the global economy*. Cheltenham: Edward Elgar.

Dzenovska, D. (2005). Remaking the nation of Latvia: Anthropological perspectives on nation branding. *Place Branding and Public Diplomacy, 1*(2), 173–186.

Ernst & Young. (2007). Wanted: A renewable Europe; European Attractiveness Survey 2007. Retrieved January 28, 2008, from http://www.paiz.gov.pl/files/?id_plik=8654

Fitzsimons, D. S. (1995). Planning and promotion: City reimaging in the 1980s and 1990s. In W. J. V. Neill, D. S. Fitzsimons, & B. Murtagh (Eds.), *Reimaging the pariah city; urban development in Belfast and Detroit*. Aldershot: Avebury.

Florek, M. (2003). Territorial marketing: Theoretical issues and empirical survey in wielkopolska communes. *Quaderno di ricerca, 2*, 1–28.

Florek, M. (2005). Struktura i możliwości aplikacji instrumentów marketingu terytorialnego. In H. Szulce & M. Florek (Eds.), *Marketing terytorialny—możliwości aplikacji, kierunki rozwoju*. Poznań: AE Poznań.

Fretter, A. D. (1993). Place marketing: A local authority perspective. In G. Kearns & C. Philo (Eds.), *Selling places; the city as cultural capital, past and present*. Oxford: Pergamon Press.

Gazeta Wyborcza. (2007, April 20). *Poznań ma swoja "brygadę tygrysa"*.

Harding, T., & Javorcik, B. (2012). *Investment promotion and FDI inflows: Quality matters*. University of Oxford Department of Economics Discussion Paper Series, No. 612.

Hilderbrandt, A., & Wörz, J. (2004). *Determinants of industrial location patterns in CEECs*. WIIW Working Papers, vol. 32.

Klijn, E. H., Eshuis, J., & Braun, E. (2012). The influence of stakeholder involvement on the effectiveness of place branding. *Public Management Review, 14*(4), 499–519.

Kotler, P., Apslund, C., Rein, I., & Haider, D. H. (1999). *Marketing places—Europe: How to attract investments, industries, residents and visitors to cities, communities, regions and nations in Europe*. London: Financial Times-Prentice Hall.

Lever, J. (2001). *The effectiveness of place imagery in English local authority inward investment promotion—An evaluation*. MPhil Thesis, Manchester Metropolitan University, Manchester.

Loewendahl, H. (2001). A framework for FDI promotion. *Transnational Corporations, 10*(1), 1–42.

Madsen, H. (1992). Place marketing in Liverpool: A review. *International Journal of Urban and Regional Research, 16*, 633–640.

Metaxas, T. (2010). Place marketing, place branding and foreign direct investments: Defining their relationship in the frame of local economic development process. *Place Branding and Public Diplomacy, 6*(3), 228–243.

Monaghan, S., Gunnigle, P., & Lavelle, J. (2014). 'Courting the multinational': Subnational institutional capacity and foreign market insidership. *Journal of International Business Studies, 45*(2), 131–150.

Multilateral Investment Guarantee Agency (MIGA). (2006). *FDI promotion*. Retrieved November 29, 2006, from www.fdipromotion.com/toolkit/user/content_page.cfm

Navaretti, G. B., & Venables, A. J. (2004). *Multinational firms in the world economy*. Princeton, NJ: Princeton University Press.
OECD. (2003). *Checklist for foreign direct investment incentives policies*. Paris: OECD Publications.
OECD. (2015). *Policy framework for investment 2015 edition*. Paris: OECD Publishing. Retrieved from https://doi.org/10.1787/9789264208667-en
OECD. (2018). Mapping of investment promotion agencies in OECD countries. Retrieved from www.oecd.org/investment/Mapping-of-Investment-Promotion-Agencies-in-OECD-Countries.pdf
Paddison, R. (1993). City marketing, image reconstruction and urban regeneration. *Urban Studies, 30*(2), 339–350.
PAIiIZ. (2005). *Rocznik 2004*. Warszawa: PAIiIZ.
Parkerson, B., & Saunders, J. (2005). City branding: Can goods and services branding models be used to brand cities? *Place Branding and Public Diplomacy, 1*(3), 242–264.
Pasquinelli, C. (2013). Competition, cooperation and co-opetition: Unfolding the process of inter-territorial branding. *Urban Research & Practice, 6*(1), 1–18.
Quelch, J., & Jocz, K. (2005). Positioning the nation-state. *Place Branding and Public Diplomacy, 1*(3), 229–237.
Rainisto, S. K. (2003). *Success factors of place marketing: A study of place marketing practices in northern Europe and The United States*. Espoo: Helsinki.
Rzeczpospolita. (2007, March 16). PAIiIZ—jak przyciągnąć kapitał.
Safron Brand Consultants. (2004). *A brand for Poland: Advancing Poland's national identity*. Safron Brand Consultants, (internal IMP materials).
SARIO. (2004). *SARIO—Agency profile*. Bratislava: SARIO.
SARIO. (2007). *Annual report 2006*. Bratislava: SARIO.
Schotter, A., & Beamish, P. W. (2013). The hassle factor: An explanation for managerial location shunning. *Journal of International Business Studies, 44*(5), 521–544.
UNCTAD. (2004). *What services do IPAs target?* UNCTAD Investment Brief, no.1/2004.
van den Berg, L., Braun, E., & Otgaar, A. H. J. (2002). *Sports and city marketing in European cities*. Rotterdam: Euricur.
Ward, S. V. (1998). *Selling places, the marketing and promotion of towns and cities 1850–2000*. London: E&FN Spon.
Wells, T. L., Jr., & Wint, A. G. (2000). *Marketing a country—Promotion as a tool for attracting foreign direct investment*. FIAS Occasional Paper 13, IFC-MIGA, Washington.

World Bank. (2012). *Investment climate: Global investment promotions best practices*. Washington: The World Bank Group.

Young, C. (2005). Place marketing for foreign direct investment in central and eastern Europe. In D. Turnock (Ed.), *Foreign direct investment and regional development in east-central Europe and the former Soviet Union*. Kent: Ashgate.

Young, C., & Kaczmarek, S. (1999). Changing the perception of the post-socialistic city: Place promotion and imagery in Lodz, Poland. *The Geographical Journal, 165*(2), 183–189.

Zanatta, M., Costa, I., & Filippov, S. (2006). *Foreign direct investment: Key issues for promotion agencies*. UNU Policy Brief, No.10, UNU-MERIT, Maastricht.

6

Conclusions: Between Assumptions and Reality

6.1 Introduction

The discussion and analysis presented in this volume attempted to challenge the supremacy of the image-focused studies dominating the current 'place marketing' discourse. It intended to achieve this by drawing the attention to *promotion*, and examining it in the wider regional development context of strategies and policies aimed at inward investment attraction. Such a more comprehensive understanding of regional promotion, as has been argued, better reflects the activities performed by relevant organisations and matches the complex nature of the process.

The originality of this contribution lies with its sectoral and spatial focus. Firstly, it focused on promotion aimed at foreign investors, and thus it complements earlier general and tourism-oriented promotion studies. Secondly, focusing on the regional level of analysis, it filled the 'scale' gap that exists in the literature centred on exploring national and local levels of promotion. Thirdly, it provided insights into investment promotion at the regional level in Central-Eastern Europe (CEE), a relatively new competitor for the global share of foreign investment flows, thus far largely avoided by scholars.

P. Capik, *Foreign Investment Promotion*, https://doi.org/10.1007/978-3-030-13658-1_6

The survey part of the research allowed the analysis of investment promotional activities performed by the regional authorities in the context of their socio-economic environments and developmental responsibilities. It revealed that in CEE, on the regional-level investment promotion is a largely inconsistent, under-budgeted practice dominated by fragmented actions disassociated from wider development objectives, and often performed by semi-competent individuals. A number of exceptions in each of the studied countries were observed, proving that promotion is gaining popularity and understanding of it has increased which in time may lead to further professionalisation of the process. The analysis conducted provided inconclusive answers about the relationship between regional promotion and development. Both affluent and underdeveloped regions engage in comprehensive promotion, and equally there are instances of both kinds performing it only to a limited extent.

The qualitative analysis of investment promotion activities performed by a range of organisations in selected regions confirmed earlier findings and complemented them with a range of new facts. The performance of regional authorities is conditioned by the powers and activities of the National Investment Promotion Agency (NIPA) and the intensity of efforts of other organisations involved in promotion of the region. Promotion of each of the regions studied is conducted within a distinctive organisational and governance framework (see Table 5.1 and Figs. 5.1, 5.2, and 5.3). The analysis of the actions performed by individual agents exposed the political dimension of the investment promotion process and revealed various degrees of internal coherence conversely proportional to the degree of authority centralisation. The dominance of the National Investment Promotion Agency does not guarantee coordination or the sufficient flow of information between the participants of the process, which further impedes its inter-institutional synergy.

Further to these generally critical findings, erratic as it may seem, there is evidence of a systematic, comprehensive "process" approach to investment promotion, indicating that Central-Eastern European regions are, as Ward (1998, p. 9) puts it, "joining the game" of place promotion.

The chapter draws together the main arguments and findings elaborated in the book. It summarises the key observations and answers the research questions which have guided the study. Its objective is also to explain this book's contribution to the theoretical debate, and explicate its policy implications. Finally, it identifies the deficiencies of the study and suggests directions for future research.

6.2 Revisiting the Research Questions

The study set out to investigate regional promotion efforts aimed at investment attraction in three Central-Eastern European Countries competing for inward investment. It has been guided by a set of research questions enquiring about the links between regional promotion and regional policy and the development of a region, as well as promotion governance and implementation. Specifically, the following questions directed the research:

1. *What is the nature of place promotion in the context of foreign investment attraction?*
2. *What is the relationship between regional promotion and the wider development of a region?*
3. *What is the importance of promotion in Central-Eastern European regions' development agenda?*
4. *What are the consequences of the different approaches to promotion governance on the strategy setting and implementation level, across the CEEC?*

The first question about the nature of promotion in the investment attraction context can be answered from a range of perspectives. Based on the literature reviewed in Chaps. 2 and 3, two general roles of promotion can be distinguished. First, in its generic sense some authors argue promotion should be treated as a prism through which all other policies should be viewed. In the words of Ward (1998, p. 3): "[E]very aspect of public policy from street cleaning to the provision of housing, from equal opportunities to public transport, from the award of public contracts to sewage outfalls can be made to bear the imprint of place selling ethos." The alternative approach, one reflected throughout this book, perceives promotion as a set of policies and subsequent actions in their own right, whose role is to foster developmental processes of places. In the most extreme cases promotion is assigned a critical role in regions' attempts to manage the impact of globalisation and political change (Paddison, 1993; Young & Kaczmarek, 1999). While this 'critical' role of promotion should be treated with some scepticism, the nexus between promotion process and regional policy, particularly FDI attraction measures, appears evident and is confirmed by the results of this study presented and discussed in Chaps. 4 and 5.

As is the case with other areas of public policy, so too promotion reveals the potential for conflict of interest resulting from a variety of often divergent needs of a region's many customers. Even if other target groups are excluded (e.g. tourists) and only promotion aimed at investment attraction is considered, the variety of sectoral characteristics and firms' location factors creates space and opportunities for choices and potential conflicts, particularly from the perspective of place product development. This is further emphasised when the needs of local inhabitants are added to the equation. The variety of promotion addressees is coupled by a range of regions' stakeholders and promotion agents facing persisting resource constraints, all of which adds a complex political dimension to the process of regional promotion.

Another perspective illuminating the meaning of regional promotion in a wider developmental policy context is a set of shared principles guiding the two. The literature recommends a bottom-up approach, and wide participation in strategy formulation and links with other policy areas, in order for both regional development policy and investment attraction to be successful. Considering the latter, in the studied CEE countries these principles are met to a different degree. In the Czech Republic and Slovakia, it is the National Investment Promotion Agency, administered by central government, which exercises control over investment promotion, and regional actors have limited opportunities to significantly impact the process. In Poland the situation is somewhat different, with regional initiatives granted broader opportunities. In this respect promotion reflects the wider regional policy-making arrangements prevailing in these countries, characterised by similar levels of power centralisation within national institutions.

The development of a region and regional product offers the final perspective on the meaning of promotion in a context of investment attraction. Promotion, as indeed investment projects, is not an aim in itself, but serves as a means to achieve the developmental goals of a region. In this sense, it is one of the developmental policies. However, in order to successfully attract investors, regions also need to be able to satisfy their location requirements and develop their offer by, for example, investing in infrastructure, supporting innovation, upgrading the skills of the local workforce, or provision of investment incentives.

The second research question, about the relationship between promotion and the wider development of a region, has been partially addressed above, in the response to the first research question, predominantly its latter parts discussing diversity of stakeholders, the bottom-up approach in strategy formulation and place product. Based on the nature of place product, one aspect of this relationship is its reciprocal dependence, that is, promotion, arguably, can be used to support regional development, while the development of the region can potentially make the promotional efforts easier and more efficient.

Promotion aimed at investment attraction needs to be linked to wider developmental strategies and goals pursued by regions (Cleave, Godwin, Sadler, & Gilliland, 2016; Crescenzi & Iammarino, 2017; OECD, 2003; Zanatta, Costa, & Filippov, 2006). It aims to advance development and structural change in an area by bringing in the necessary resources (capital, skills) and creating further opportunities (employment, development of supplier base). However, such a structured use of investment attraction measures aimed at meeting the strategic, developmental objectives of a region is hardly a common occurrence in Central-Eastern Europe. Half of the regional authorities across the countries studied claim to have included promotion in their regional development strategies, and the vast majority recognise FDI to be crucial to the future of their areas, yet commonly they admit to having limited knowledge and understanding of the inward investors' needs and requirements.

Further, the regional authorities' intensity of engagement, coherence and spending on promotion is rarely linked to the level and nature of structural problems in their jurisdictions. As explained in Chap. 4 the high levels of unemployment seem to neither encourage more systematic and wide-ranging promotional activities nor prevent them. Equally, the efforts of regions with unemployment rates below the national average are neither stimulated nor curbed by that fact. Similarly, neither the dynamics of growth of the regional economy nor the wealth of regions measured by GDP per capita seems to be influencing regional authorities' engagement with and scope of their promotional activities.

Research results also revealed another perspective, associated directly with policy setting. Some level of design and implementation of regional promotion occurs within wider networks, including predominantly national partners such as National Investment Promotion Agencies, regional development agencies, local communities (particularly regional capital cities). This provides a forum for regions' stakeholders but also allows for the development of relationships helpful in other policy areas. Occasionally regional authorities utilise their international networks including Euroregions, Innovative Regions in Europe, and other purposeful initiatives such as Centrop, to draw on the experience of international partners. However, their use is often limited due to other operational focus (e.g. culture, education), yet they do provide potential for exchange of experiences and knowledge, and sharing of best practice.

Approaching this question from the perspective of the national scale offers further insights. The governments have at their disposal a range of policy options (e.g. fiscal and financial incentives) and schemes supporting investments in selected regions within their countries. These are often administered by the National Investment Promotion Agencies, who ideally should attempt to steer the investment projects to the most needy areas. In this limited understanding promotion is used as a regional policy measure. This is also often accompanied by relevant place product development policies within the scope of governments' authority focusing on infrastructure or labour market.

On the regional level one other aspect of the promotion–regional development relationship needs highlighting, namely the emergence of intra-national competition. As demonstrated by the analysis in Chaps. 4 and 5, a fact often disregarded by NIPAs, regions recognise and actively compete with other areas not only abroad but within their own countries. A quarter of regional authorities point to national capital city regions as their main competitor. This view is shared by other regional promoters (e.g. Brno city authorities, Investors Service Centre in Wielkopolskie voivodeship). A further third identify neighbouring regions as rivals in investment attraction. In the context of promotion such competition can be constructive and have positive effects in the form of increased efficiency and sophistication of efforts, and focused improvements of the regional offer. Equally, in some circumstances (e.g. lack of national coordination) it can be detrimental, lead to a considerable waste of resources or race to the bottom, where investment incentives are administered regionally.

While based on the results of the study it is not possible to offer an unequivocal answer about the direct relationship between promotion and regional development, as demonstrated throughout this volume, it has been possible to identify where the links might be and offer insights into a range of aspects of such a relationship.

The answer to the third research question builds on the discussion above. When exploring the importance of promotion in Central-Eastern European regions' development agendas a distinction needs to be made between the *claimed* and *actual* levels as demonstrated by regional authorities' activities. As demonstrated by this study the former tends to be high, with 55% of CEE regional authorities claiming to have promotion embedded in their development strategies. However, as evidenced by the analysis of the actual activities, the latter tends to be much lower. Generally, the significance attached to investment promotion varies between the regions with some (particularly in Slovakia and Poland) assigning investor target group the highest priority, and others (particularly the Czech authorities) considering investors to be of secondary importance to tourists. Also, as discussed in Chap. 4, the knowledge of investors as target group remains relatively low, with regional authorities evaluating it at 3 out of 5. However, regardless of its importance and the degree of authorities' engagement with promotion, it is rarely explicitly linked to regions' wider development strategies, hence usually it is not directly connected to regional structural problems. This in turn impacts the coherence of the practice. For example, some regional promoters in Jihomoravský kraj indicate 'industrial tradition' to be the key image staple when attempting to attract business services and high-tech industry. Similarly, organisations promoting Kosicky kraj avoid using connectivity and infrastructure arguments while at the same time targeting manufacturing and assembly sectors for which those issues are important.

While FDI inflows remain central to the growth and change of the Central-Eastern European regional economies, as demonstrated in Chap. 4 only half of the regions formally recognise them as an important resource and make adequate provisions in their development strategies. Fewer still have a clearly defined investment promotion strategy supported by appropriate budgets allowing for their execution. This occurs against the background of open claims by the authorities about their interest in and dedication to promotion, as evidenced by the presence of a dedicated investment section dealing with FDI promotion in 60% of them. Such a dichotomy of 'wants' and 'reality' is further emphasised by limited resources dedicated to promotion, and reflected in incoherent actions. RAIS offices usually have between one and three members of staff, and regional authorities' average annual spending on investment promotion in 2004 equalled USD 185,000, or 16 cents per inhabitant. In fact, inadequate funding and staffing levels are the key impediments to the promotion process. They impact negatively on all stages of the promotional process, including research, planning and execution, and consequently on its coherence. As reviewed in Chaps. 4 and 5 the performed activities lack structure and long-term vision, and often are improvised and fragmented. The promotional activities are rarely underpinned by purposeful research as regional authorities tend to rely on general, publicly available information. Less than a third use consultancy firms or experts while planning and executing promotion. Moreover, other organisations engaged with promotion tend to operate on annual budgets, and do not make long-term plans.

Furthermore, it is often unclear which socio-economic circumstances play a dominant role in regional authorities' involvement in the promotion process. The wealth of the region or the existing state of the regional economy seems to have little influence. Examples of regional authorities of prosperous regions and those struggling with prolonged structural difficulties have been found to be both heavily involved with promotion, and do little to attract investors to their areas. For example Podlaskie voivodeship, where in the mid-2000s the average GDP per capita was less than 75% of Poland's average, spent less than USD 50,000 on promotion in 2004, yet Łódzkie voivodeship, with GDP per capita close to 95% of the county's average, spent close to USD 1 million. The most evident factor conditioning the level of involvement, as established in Chap. 5, seems to be associated with the broader arrangements and principles guiding the operations of public administration in the countries studied. Centralisation of powers and responsibilities within the National Investment Promotion Agency is the key issue determining the actions of regional authorities and other participants of the process.

The extent and severity of the circumstances discussed above vary between the three countries studied. Overall Polish regional authorities and other participants of the process tend to present more systematic approaches than their Slovak, and particularly Czech, counterparts.

The fourth research question has been predominantly addressed in Chap. 5, so at this point, it is important to revisit the key findings related to the different approaches to promotion and their influence on the governance, strategy and implementation level in the countries studied.

The variety of institutions involved with the promotion process offer much potential, which however is yet to be fully utilised. In mid-2000s the organisation and management of their promotion seemed only at an early stage. Numerous organisations claim to participate in the process; however, only a few are actively involved in it. A number of institutions comprise a core of the regional promotion framework in each of the studied countries, and those are complemented by several country-specific organisations. The majority of those are public, with private capital and civil society underrepresented in all three countries. The core comprises regional authorities and regional development agencies at the regional level, National Investment Promotion Agencies and regional capital city authorities at the national and local levels, respectively. Additionally, all of these, to some degree, operate in wider national networks expanding vertically, that is, crossing levels of the public administration hierarchy, and horizontally involving partners at an equal level. Some promotion actors also participate in international networks, the nature of which, however, is rarely exclusively promotion-oriented. The multi-agent, yet poorly coordinated and managed, nature of investment promotion in Central-Eastern European regions results in the emergence of disparities on a strategic and implementation level, leading to duplication of activities, inefficiencies and conceptual inconsistencies in promotion planning and implementation.

The influence which the individual organisations have on the process is conditioned by several factors, including legal prerogatives, their own interests and resources, but mainly, the authority of the National Investment Promotion Agency. In general, Polish regional and local institutions tend to be more involved and have more control and impact on the process. This extends to the degree of active lobbying and exerting pressure on the NIPA, as demonstrated by actions of some of the regional promoters of Wielkopolkie voivodeship. Conversely, their Slovak and Czech counterparts are progressively more dominated by the NIPAs.

Such decentralised and centralised frameworks in terms of incentive and authority, however, are not accurately reflected in the actual execution of promotion adopted by their individual, component agencies. While, as has been emphasised earlier, investment promotion in all three countries is unsystematic and often disjointed from wider development strategies and circumstances prevailing in the regions, levels of this vary. Decentralisation, characterising the Polish arrangements, does not automatically entail a higher degree of incoherence, but to the contrary stimulates bottom-up, more agreed and consistent approaches demonstrated in similarity of process participants' decisions on the key strategic issues of, for example, target groups and the definition of competitors. Equally, as evidenced particularly by the Czech case, a centralised framework does not guarantee superior quality, efficiency or increased coherence. Instead, it limits the engagement of the regional institutions with the centrally driven promotion process, and thus impedes coherence and fosters inefficiencies stemming from the improvised and unsynchronised actions of the regional actors.

Therefore, in general terms, the key consequence of the identified approaches is the chaotic nature of promotion, with varying levels of inconsistencies conditioned by the degree of decentralisation and involvement of regional actors. Potential developmental consequences comprise another set of outcomes related to the diverse approaches identified. An analysis of the changing stock of FDI in the studied regions in the period subsequent to the study offers some insights into these.

In the period between 2005 and 2009 little has changed in the FDI stock distribution in the studied countries. While it would be unreasonable to expect significant adjustments to take place from one year to the next, during the four-year period some evidence of change could be expected, provided the change is occurring. Instead, as evidenced by Table 6.1, the unequal distribution of foreign capital in the Czech Republic, Poland and Slovakia persists and only minimal annual fluctuations of regional share have been recorded.

Overall, the capital city regions maintain their dominant position within each of the countries, and equally the share of the national FDI stock in the regions studied remained mostly stable. Bratislavský kraj in Slovakia, as an exception, recorded a 5 percentage point drop (from 67.7 in 2007 to 62.7 in 2009) in its share, the majority to the advantage of the neighbouring Trnavský kraj, with other, more distant, regions benefiting little, if at all.

This confirms the observation made earlier. The inter-regional competition for FDI within each of the countries studied persists and is inadequately managed by the National Investment Promotion Agencies, who fail to direct flows into regions beyond the capital city. In a wider perspective of the promotional frameworks identified in the course of this study, these circumstances reiterate the need for more significant involvement of regional actors in investment promotion.

Furthermore, the persisting share of the FDI in the regions studied, and continuous foreign capital concentration in capital city regions, allows one to conclude that, based on the gathered evidence, it is not possible to categorically comment on the relative efficiency of the promotion frameworks identified. The differences in commitment and the

Table 6.1 Regional share of national FDI stock (%)

	2005	2006	2007	2008	2009
Czech Republic					
Praha & Středočeský kraj	64.4	64.2	63	64	64
Jihomoravský kraj	4	4.2	4.1	4.5	4.5
Poland					
Mazowieckie voivodeship	50.4	49.7	48.6	50.1	49.2
Wielkopolskie voivodeship	9.2	8.5	8.8	8	8.7
Slovakia					
Bratislavaský kraj	67.1	67	67.7	62.4	62.7
Košický kraj	8.5	7.9	8.8	8.9	8.7

Source: Own calculations based on CNB, CzechInvest, GUS and SARIO data

approaches, as discussed in Chap. 4 and particularly Chap. 5, overall are not significant enough to bring about diverse developmental consequences. Seemingly, what matters most is the inconsistent, chaotic and inefficient nature of the investment promotion process having little impact on the enduring regional disparities in FDI stock distribution within the countries studied.

Moreover, the persisting uneven distribution of FDI stock across the countries suggests the persevering nature of the identified frameworks and continuing limited regional focus of their operations. However further studies are needed to comment more on this issue.

6.3 Research Significance and Contributions to Theory and Practice

The book offered twofold contribution. Firstly, it further developed place marketing debate, by offering conceptual inputs in a number of areas directly linked to regional promotion aimed at investment attraction. Secondly, it provided quantitative and qualitative empirical evidence of promotion of regions in Central-Eastern European Countries.

To identify theoretical implications of the study, it is useful to consider how far the results of this research have confirmed the usefulness of the concepts reviewed in early parts of the book, and how they can be developed in the future. While it was not possible to explore all aspects of regional promotion aimed at investment attraction at equal depth, the chose focus led to a number of theoretical contributions.

The proposed broad understanding of place promotion proved to be appropriate for the analysis of investment attraction activities. The suggested conceptual framework of regional promotion aimed at investment attraction based on selected marketing concepts linked with FDI-focused concepts of exogenously oriented regional development theories, allowed to comprehensively analyse promotional reality in Central-Eastern European regions. The focus on promotion and its tools, juxtapositioned with investment-oriented regional policy measures, enabled going beyond the single-dimensional exploration of image-building activities, to include wider processes preceding core promotion actions (including, e.g., research, strategic targeting), and those which occur after the investment projects have been secured (e.g. post-investment services).

An important theoretical contribution offered by this study relates to the issue of scale, until now largely omitted by the literature. From the discussion in Chap. 4, and particularly Chap. 5, it can be concluded that scale matters, and promotion in the regional context differs from promotion of places both lower and higher in the administrative hierarchy, as described for example by Florek (2003), Wells and Wint (2000), Kulchina (2014) and others. The differences can be observed in a number of areas, particularly organisation of promotion and the level of coherence in its execution. On the regional level, the promotional effort is inherently more complex as compared to national and local levels. The key agents of promotion operate within complex networks extending both horizontally and vertically and include public authorities as well as private capital (albeit usually to a considerably lesser extent). Regional authorities alone declare promotion-focused cooperation with up to four other organisations in the Czech Republic, five in Slovakia and six in Poland. Within such networks an array of types of relationships develop between the partners, ranging from equal, to superior and inferior relations. However, regardless of their nature, the linkages are not necessarily reflected in reality and in strategic coordination of activities performed by individual partners within the networks. Instead, they often emulate contemporary political arrangements as exemplified by improvements in cooperation between Brno city and Jihomoravský kraj authorities attributed by both organisations to political alignment of the ruling elites, and limited cooperation between Košice city and regional authorities blamed by the former on differences between the ruling parties.

Another area of investment promotion affected by scale is competition. Predominantly scale affects the number of competitors an area has to beat in order to secure inward investment projects. For example, as indicated by Helinska-Hughes and Hughes (2003) the three countries studied during this research compete directly with one another for new investments, while on a local level Florek (2003) illustrates how communes compete against each other to secure investment projects within one region. Thus, scale also influences the qualitative aspects of competition.

A growing number of rivals increases their diversity and changes the nature of competition. As widely recognised by regional authorities and other promoters, on the regional-level regions compete for foreign investments with other regions abroad, but also inside their countries. The analysis in Chaps. 4 and 5 confirmed that neighbouring regions and countries within broader CEE are perceived to pose the most significant competition. Regional authorities in the Czech Republic, Poland and Slovakia are also convinced about competition existing between themselves and other regions within each of the countries and name deficiencies in infrastructure, inferior image and labour market conditions as their key competitive disadvantages. This is particularly relevant from the perspective of nationally pursued regional development policies seeking to eliminate income and wealth disparities between areas within a country, which ought to consider this type of intra-national competition. Equally, regional development strategies drafted and implemented by regional authorities should consider the rivalry amongst localities, which bears consequences for promotional activities pursued by any individual region.

The book also shed light on the relevance of promotion success factors identified by other writings (e.g. Almond, Ferner, & Tregasis, 2015; Florek, 2005a, 2005b; Lodge, 2002; Monaghan, Gunnigle, & Lavelle, 2014). As far as the organisational factors are concerned (see Table 3.1), arguably their mere existence is less important than their qualities. While a range of partnerships and cooperation links between a plethora of agents have been identified, the nature and characteristics of those relationships seem to be much more important in satisfying the 'implementation' factors, than their actual existence. Further, in case of promotion aimed at investment attraction, contrary to what has been observed elsewhere (e.g. Kotler & Gertner, 2002; Rainisto, 2003; Zimmerbauer, 2011), participation of a wide range of agents, rather than legitimising the efforts and improving their coherence, often contributes to inconsistencies and fragmentation, repetitions and at times conflicting actions—as observed particularly in the case of Jihomoravský kraj, but also Kosicky kraj and to a degree in Wielkopolskie voivodeship frameworks. Thus, it can be concluded that principally the 'organisational' success factors (Table 3.1), including partnership and organisation, wide participation, leadership and commitment, argued by the literature comprise an ideal set, but in reality often contradict each other. Individually, perhaps they could stand as a core feature of organisational models built around them, but collectively exclude each other. The 'implementation' success factors, including coherence with wider development goals, competitive positioning, targeting, image grounded in reality and others, seem to be present to a different degree in the activities of the various agents in the studied regions. To offer a more substantial discussion of their pertinence and theoretical significance further studies should focus on the effectiveness of promotion.

Finally, the research results, particularly those discussed in Chap. 5, confirmed some of the suggestions present in the literature (e.g. Loewendahl, 2001; Monaghan et al., 2014; Zanatta et al., 2006) concerning the influence of scale on the precision of promotional activities. As demonstrated by their familiarity with place offer and ability to identify image staples alongside shortcomings in the regional place product, regional authorities and other promoters seem to be equipped with intimate knowledge about the socio-economic situation in the region and the advantages it can offer to potential investors. Consequently, they (should) have the ability to accurately identify targeted sectors, and adopt adequate approaches in delivering relevant and bespoke promotional messages while performing tailored activities.

The analysis conducted also offers noteworthy perspectives on the dissonance between a conceptual, marketing-based approach to place product, and actual orientation presented by promoters. Place marketing literature proposes a demand-driven approach to place product and suggests place promoters need to develop understanding of the needs and wants of the target groups and design the place accordingly before promoting it (Kotler, Apslund, Rein, & Haider, 1999; Rainisto, 2003). As demonstrated in Chaps. 4 and 5, the evidence testifies to a contrary approach adopted by those involved with promotion. Their perception of place product, arguably a more realistic one, is predominantly driven by the level of influence and control the organisation has over it, that is, a product is what the organisation can supply (e.g. for NIPAs it is national business environment, for CTP office space and storage capacities, for Wielkopolskie voivodeship authorities it is the sites ready for investments), and naturally it will not satisfy the requirements of all target groups equally.

Further, such results confirm suggestions made by some scholars (Morgan, Pritchard, & Piggot, 2002; Florek, 2005b; Schotter & Beamish, 2013; Kulchina, 2014) indicating that one of the inherent features of place (mega) product is that it often remains beyond the control of those who promote it.

Policy implications extend beyond product development. Regional promotion aimed at investment attraction occurs alongside wider promotional activities and is linked to other developmental policies, hence presents organisational and governance challenges and poses questions about allocation of resources. The findings presented in the book point to a number of issues that could be addressed in order to achieve a more effective and efficient regional investment promotion of CEE regions. In relation to the research questions, two sets of interlinked measures are considered here: those concerned with organisation and those related to implementation of regional promotion.

In the context of organisation of promotion the key elements requiring attention and revision are linked to the powers and responsibilities of National Investment Promotion Agencies. A further decentralisation of authority is recommended, particularly in the Czech and Slovak cases. Additionally, a clear definition of duties and prerogatives is called for in the Polish case, while overall, not only a mere involvement of regional actors but rather their dominance in the process is advised. Such an approach would be in line with the EU-stipulated subsidiarity principle of regional governance, and allow for increased efficiency of the process by avoiding conflict and duplication of activities, and preventing divergence and contradictions in messages being promoted.

This could happen through the creation of a region-centred investment promotion system with a strong, dedicated regional body consulting, overseeing the actions of, and closely cooperating with other, diverse regional stakeholders. Such a 'promotion executive' agency could result from the partnership between the major decision-makers and pressure groups in the region, including regional and local authorities, private capital, citizens and their interest-group representatives. The effective internal organisation should enable knowledge and information flows to increase the coordination between the project officers and participating actors, and also to make effective use of the market intelligence in order to efficiently prioritise resources to support companies which will create the most benefits for the location (Cleave et al., 2016; Loewendahl, 2001; Monaghan et al., 2014). In such a scenario NIPAs would be responsible for coordination and the national coherence of the activities designed and implemented on the regional level, rather than imposing one-size-fits-all solutions. This in turn would allow for a clear division of functions and duties amongst those engaged with promotion, contributing to the development of the complete, effective and efficient promotional process. Additionally, operating within broad partnership would make the organisations eligible for structural funds support.

Efficiency and effectiveness are the key reasons behind the advocated process approach to implementation of promotion. In the policy perspective it allows the development of links with, and the anchoring of promotion in, a wider context of regional development strategy. As a result, it is suggested that the CEE regions move away from often naïve, ad-hoc generic activities such as abundant leaflets and promotional folders actions, and utilise resources on targeted activities focused on lead generation.

Another policy recommendation concerns investment incentives. Considering their ambiguous impact on the investors' location decision, perhaps the often-scarce public resources should be shifted away from generous incentive schemes to enable provision of comprehensive investors' services, foster research-informed approaches, and support development of other promotional activities by the relevant agencies.

6.4 Limitations and Future Research Directions

The study discussed in this book has been underpinned by methodological rigour, conceptual thoroughness and discipline, the key characteristics of academic research. However, it also shares another feature inherent in all academic work—imperfections.

The methodological limitations include weaknesses intrinsic to selected data gathering and analysis techniques. The conceptual limitations result from the restricted availability of literature within the field of regional promotion aimed at investment attraction, forcing this research to rely on general place marketing literature, much of which had been developed with little empirical testing. However, it is believed, that this shortcoming provided the project with an opportunity to propose an original set of ideas and test them in an empirical setting.

Another shortcoming of the book is associated with the selectiveness of issues it covers. Place promotion, including regional promotion aimed at investment attraction, offers vast research opportunities and choices, not all of which could have been explored during this study. The clarity of the chosen research focus guided by the research questions, however, permitted an in-depth exploration of selected issues, while the matters not addressed by the book present opportunities for future studies—and these are as follows.

First, in order to further develop the ideas presented in this book a longitudinal study of the investment promotion in Central-Eastern Europe would be welcome. Such research would allow observing the evolution of the governance frameworks and, considered within the context of evolving regional socio-economic circumstances, provide further insights into relationships between promotion and regional development.

This is particularly interesting when recent global political and economic developments are considered. The financial crisis has had a negative impact on inward investment flows and companies' strategies. Equally, it affected governmental spending and compelled public authorities to implement cuts in their budgets, undoubtedly including promotion budgets. The study of impacts of the crisis and subsequent recovery on the investment promotion could reveal durability and popularity of the process with the public authorities and offer further insights into its perceived and actual role in long-term regional development. Linked to that, such a study could provide an overview of the changes in practices imposed by the crisis and disclose whether the more competitive environment encourages relevant promotional bodies to utilise more efficient, targeted and sophisticated approaches or if it provides grounds for a general and broad promotional approach. Such a study could be equally generic and examine investment promotion of a place in its totality, or focus on individual aspects of promotion implementation, for example coherence with developmental goals, targeting, image staples or investors' services. Further insights could be drawn by considering recent geopolitical developments, and examination of the impact that introduction of protectionist trade policies had on investment promotion.

Secondly, considering the limited scope of existing empirical studies, and their pervasive focus on general promotion and image creation in the Western world, broader geographical and thematic research perspectives are needed. The necessity of further empirical evidence arises also from the fact that the current studies tend to be positive in nature, while only substantial empirical evidence can lead to the development of a more normative debate, and emergence of more precise models and frameworks.

One area which could particularly benefit from such developments is effectiveness measurements, of both the totality of promotional efforts, as well as its individual components. Other aspects should include investigating the lessons drawn from flagship investors' involvement in the promotional process, and use of good practice in different regions. Comparative studies, particularly involving places in emerging economies, can offer a considerable contribution to this issue. However, perhaps even more accurate assessment models can be developed based on studies of investors' behaviours and attitudes towards promotion, a third important research direction.

Finally, on the most general level it remains unclear how to accommodate various target groups within places' promotion efforts, or indeed, if such need exists at all. Perhaps promotion to generate developmental effects needs only to be addressed to selected groups, namely investors and tourists, while other targets can be treated as secondary and will appear as the effect of developmental processes and increasing prosperity of the promoted area. Alternatively, such questions can be posed from the opposite perspective—can promotion be used to solve any and every challenge places are facing, or is it only helpful for post-industrial and environmentally and culturally rich locales?

References

Almond, P., Ferner, A., & Tregasis, O. (2015). The changing context of regional governance of FDI in England. *European Urban and Regional Studies, 22*(1), 61–76.

Cleave, E., Godwin, A., Sadler, R., & Gilliland, J. (2016). The role of place branding in local and regional economic development: Bridging the gap between policy and practicality. *Regional Studies, Regional Science, 3*(1), 207–228.

Crescenzi, R., & Iammarino, S. (2017). Global investments and regional development trajectories: The missing links. *Regional Studies, 51*(1), 97–115.

Florek, M. (2003). Territorial marketing: Theoretical issues and empirical survey in wielkopolska communes. *Quaderno di ricerca, 2*, 1–28.

Florek, M. (2005a). The country brand as a new challenge for Poland. *Place Branding and Public Diplomacy, 1*(2), 205–214.

Florek, M. (2005b). Struktura i możliwości aplikacji instrumentów marketingu terytorialnego. In H. Szulce & M. Florek (Eds.), *Marketing terytorialny—możliwości aplikacji, kierunki rozwoju*. Poznań: AE Poznań.

Helinska-Hughes, E., & Hughes, M. (2003). Joining the competition: Central and eastern European challenge to established FDI destinations? In N. Phelps & P. Raines (Eds.), *The New Competition for Inward Investment*. Cheltenham: Edward Elgar.

Kotler, P., Apslund, C., Rein, I., & Haider, D. H. (1999). *Marketing places—Europe: How to attract investments, industries, residents and visitors to cities, communities, regions and nations in Europe*. London: Financial Times-Prentice Hall.

Kotler, P., & Gertner, D. (2002). Country as brand, product and beyond: A place marketing and brand management perspective. *Brand Management, 9*(4–5), 249–261.

Kulchina, E. (2014). Media coverage and location choice. *Strategic Management Journal, 35*(4), 596–605.

Lodge, C. (2002). Success and failure: The brand stories of two countries. *Brand Management, 9*(4–5), 372–384.

Loewendahl, H. (2001). A framework for FDI promotion. *Transnational Corporations, 10*(1), 1–42.

Monaghan, S., Gunnigle, P., & Lavelle, J. (2014). 'Courting the multinational': Subnational institutional capacity and foreign market insidership. *Journal of International Business Studies, 45*(2), 131–150.

Morgan, N., Pritchard, A., & Piggot, R. (2002). New Zealand, 100% pure. The creation of powerful niche destination brand. *Brand Management, 9*(4–5), 335–354.

OECD. (2003). *Checklist for foreign direct investment incentives policies*. Paris: OECD Publications.

Paddison, R. (1993). City marketing, image reconstruction and urban regeneration. *Urban Studies, 30*(2), 339–350.

Rainisto, S. K. (2003). *Success factors of place marketing: A study of place marketing practices in northern Europe and The United States*. Espoo: Helsinki.

Schotter, A., & Beamish, P. W. (2013). The hassle factor: An explanation for managerial location shunning. *Journal of International Business Studies, 44*(5), 521–544.

Ward, S. V. (1998). *Selling places, the marketing and promotion of towns and cities 1850–2000*. London: E&FN Spon.

Wells, T. L., Jr., & Wint, A. G. (2000). *Marketing a country—Promotion as a tool for attracting foreign direct investment*. FIAS Occasional Paper 13, IFC-MIGA, Washington.

Young, C., & Kaczmarek, S. (1999). Changing the perception of the post-socialistic city: Place promotion and imagery in Lodz, Poland. *The Geographical Journal, 165*(2), 183–189.

Zanatta, M., Costa, I., & Filippov, S. (2006). *Foreign direct investment: Key issues for promotion agencies*. UNU Policy Brief, No. 10, UNU-MERIT, Maastricht.

Zimmerbauer, K. (2011). From image to identity: Building regions by place promotion. *European Planning Studies, 19*(2), 243–260.

Index[1]

[1] Note: Page numbers followed by 'n' refer to notes.

P. Capik, *Foreign Investment Promotion*, https://doi.org/10.1007/978-3-030-13658-1

FSC
www.fsc.org
MIX
Papier | Fördert
gute Waldnutzung
FSC® C083411

Kolibri 360 GmbH
Ferdinand-Jühlke-Straße 7
99095 Erfurt, Deutschland
produktsicherheit@kolibri360.de